SEXY DRAGONS AND NAKED ANGELS

By Samuel Wheeler

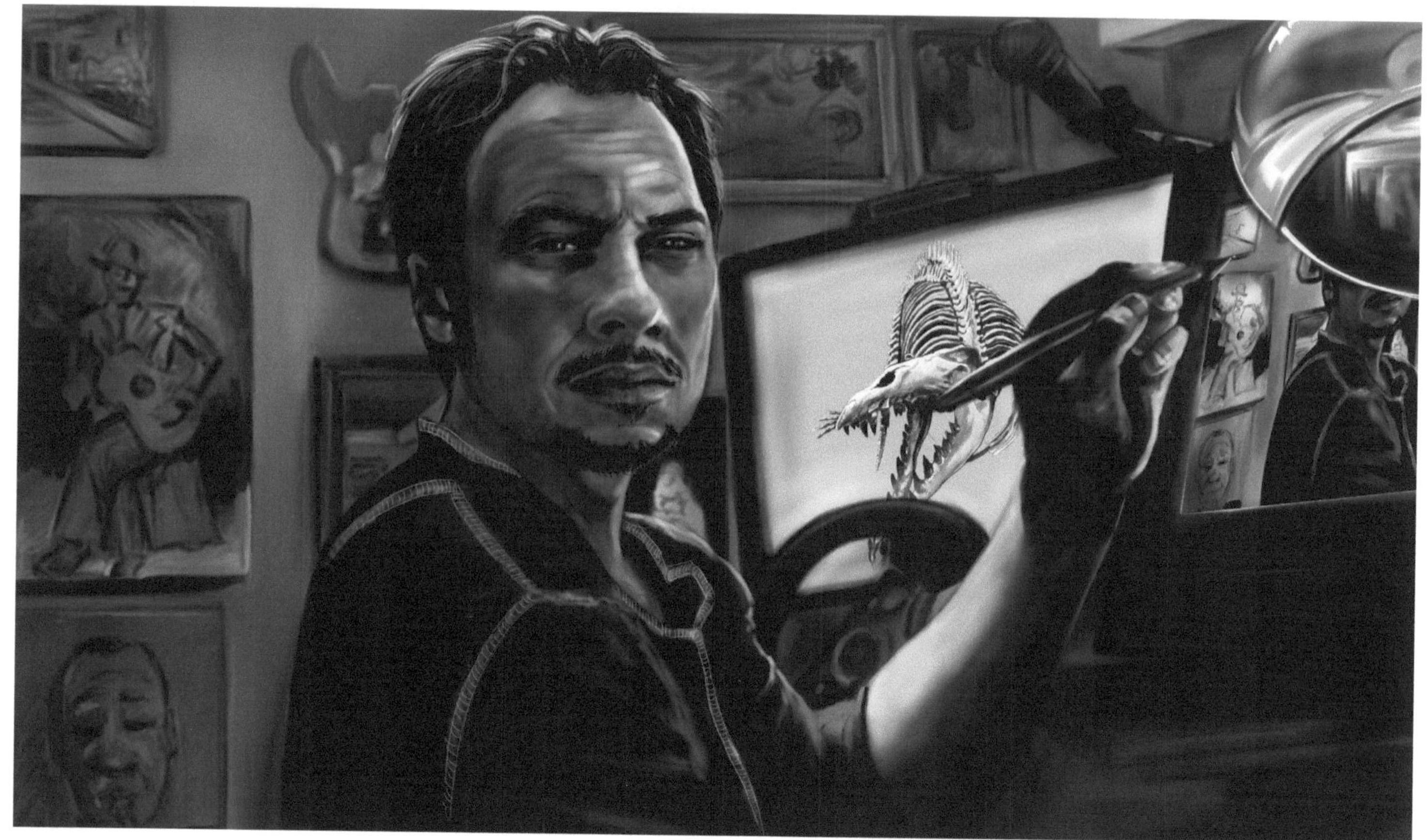

The Prophet Samuel and the Black Spiral Dancer (A Mythos)

King David quested for the lost prophet Samuel after his disappearance during a sabbatical of judgment in Israel. He searched the world with the help of his armies, but it was not in this world that he laid eyes on Samuel again.
One day King David found a portal deep within the Himalayan Mountains to another world. Through a star gate set there by an ancient evil, David forged forward with the Angel Michael guiding him. They came to a dark land called Nocturnia where the prophet Samuel lay shackled and cursed with the dreaded disease of lycanthropy.

The evil King Anu and his reptilian geneticists had twisted his spirit and corrupted him with a demon wolf essence.
The Black Spiral Dancer. His plan was to cast the Prophet so far into the darkness and primal rage that he would never find God's light again.

David rescued the Prophet with the Angel Michael. Protecting them from the Black Knights of the order of the Dragon. Carrying his beaten and starved body back through the star gate, King David returned the Prophet Samuel to his home in Ramah. Still cursed with his dreaded affliction, the Prophet Samuel was chained within his Altar every lunar cycle, when the Black Spiral Dancer took hold, it twisted his form into that of a great black wolf with eyes of burning fire, poisoned claws and teeth.

Samuel eventually learned to control his curse through prayer and devotion to God and the light. He continued to advise King David, judging over the cities of Israel. Except on the night of the full moon when he would pray at his Altar at Ramah. For the salvation of his soul, and for the holy spirits light to shine through his darkness.

King Anu was furious and despondent. His curse had only forced the Prophet to develop a closer connection with the light in order to control it. His plan had backfired. He had never accounted for the faith and the passion of the Prophet, or the courage of King David and strength of Michael's army of archangels.

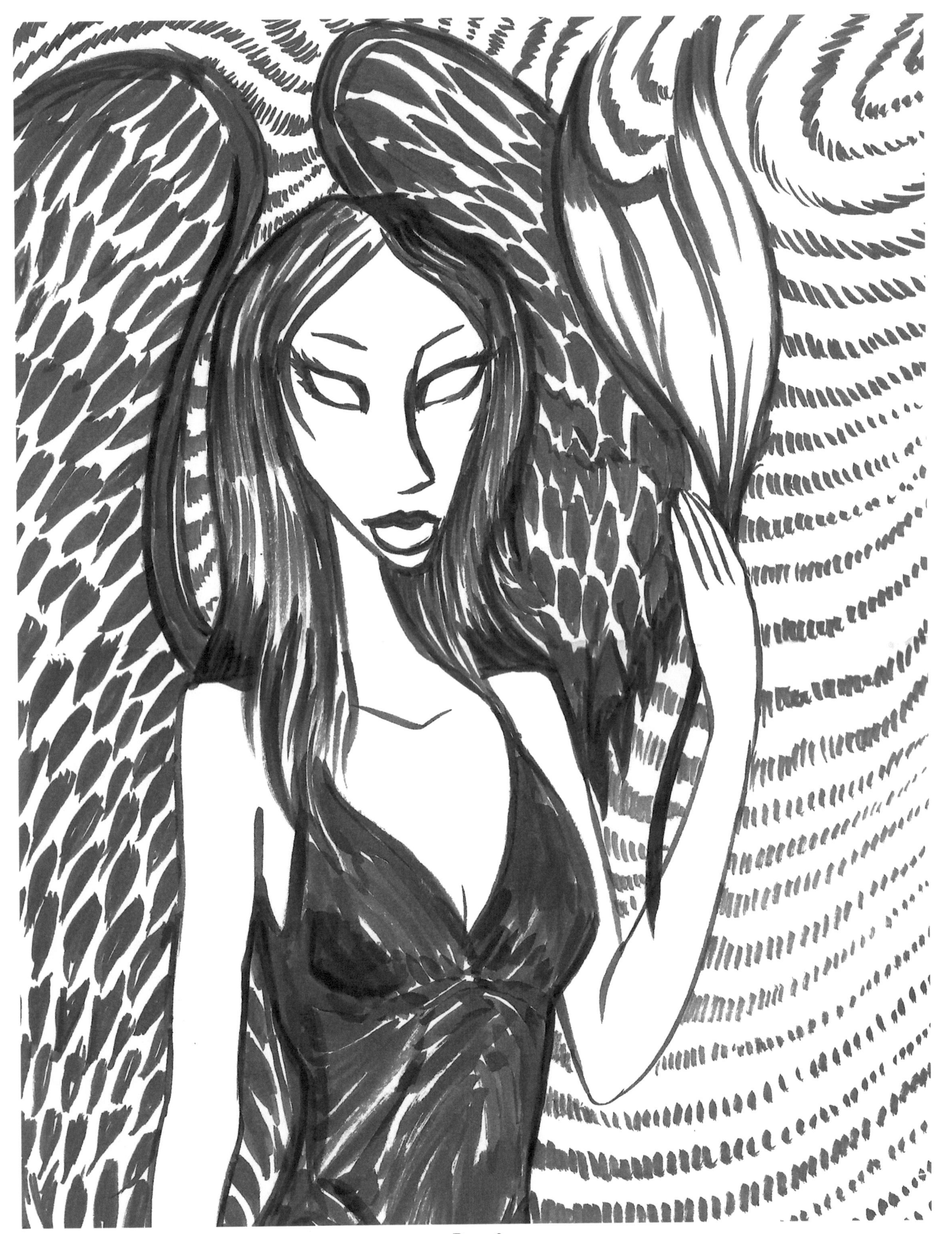

Once a long time ago mankind knew of dragons. All dragons were linked to the earth by love. Their love for humanity and the humans love for them.
The dragons would help mortals keep the crops going, and the mortals would always give the selection of the best crops back to the dragons in their places of worship.

Soon the humans tired of bringing the best of the crops for the dragons, until they only brought offerings every 10 years. Ten turned to twenty, twenty to forty and forty turned to a hundred years between offerings.
The dragons became angry at this neglect. They tore apart the crops they helped to build, the soil became hard and unyielding.
Soon the dragons demanded human sacrifices instead of corn and bread.

After a thousand years of tormenting the generations of those who had forgotten them.
The dragons flew away, and a low wail came up from the blackened lands.

All magic in the lands of man died that day, for all magic's source was the dragons.
The mortals wailed. Even though the torment they had endured was over they realized what they had lost.

From that day forth no mortal ever again saw a sight as magical or beautiful as a dragon in flight.
The last dragon circled. A great golden dragon with a mane of flame.

She spoke to the wailing humans.
"Now you weep. This love is dead. You let it die. No longer is this world blessed with dragon magic."

The great golden dragon wept tears of liquid rock that hardened as they hit the ground. Then she howled as she hurtled away from the dull planet she left behind.

One day many years hence a small girl was born who loved the stories of the dragons. She couldn't stay away from the tears of stone.
She made them a place of stillness for her soul and sang songs to them.

She spent time there learning the music of the stillness around the stone.
Her songs were so beautiful that the birds sat around her and listened.

All the insects and animals listened to the dragons songs of love and sadness. One day the magic of the music was heard by the masses of quiet listeners.

They wept with the beauty of the dragon songs. She didn't see the strange movement in the stone, or the smile in the eyes of the dragon softly flying past.

Past the world of pain, the world of mistakes, through the magic that still remains,
as always and forever.

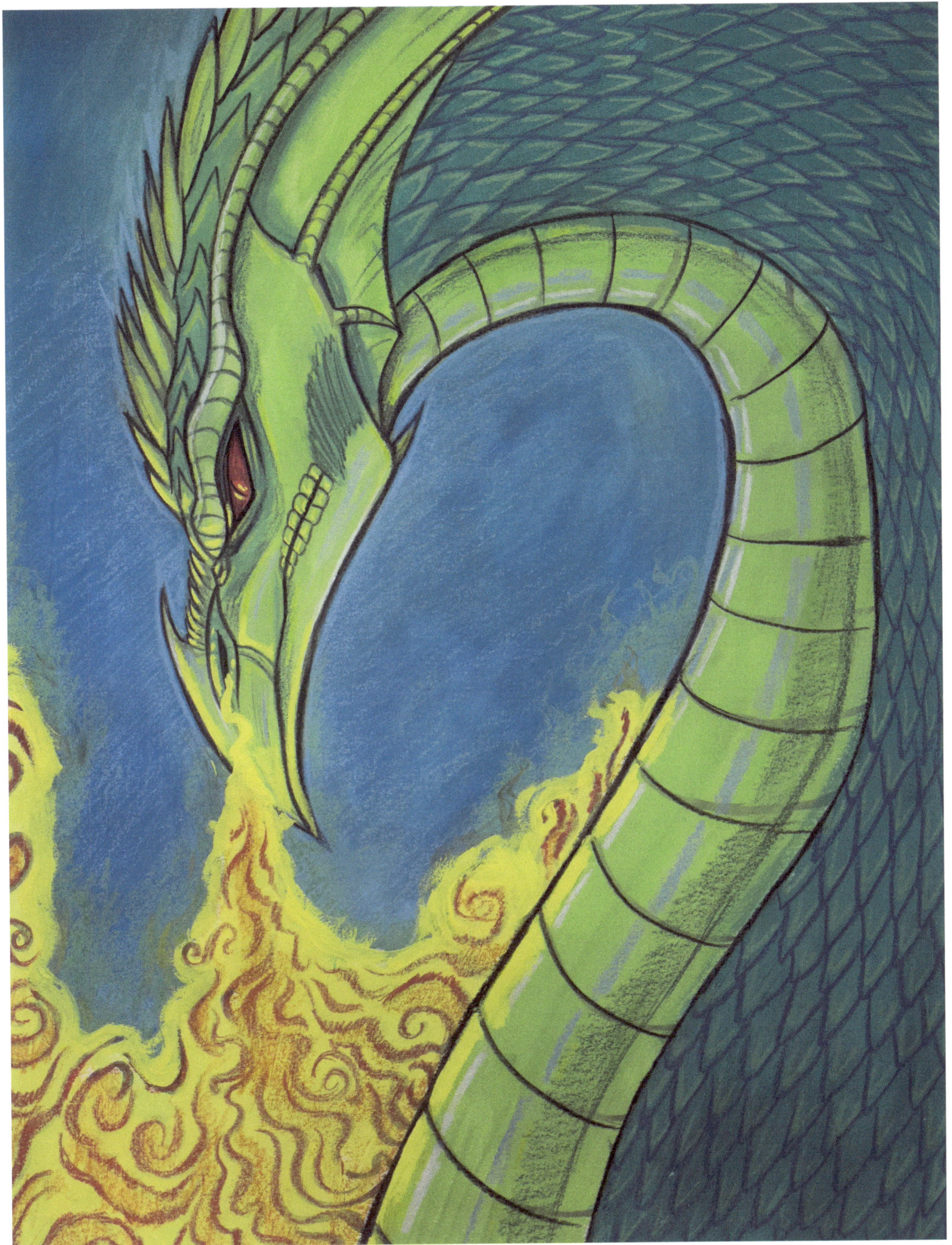

Naked Angels

Mine is the Divine Empire.
The place where the glowing cups provide warmth.
Finding the greatest trials begun,
Can no longer deflect from the simple dream.
That the sea shall support our steps,
The clouds shall cushion our minds and spirits,
And shall prosper under the giving sun.

Wings are folded beneath our bellies,
As we dive into the shimmering surface of our unconscious minds.
In the darkest depths,
The Material World dissolves,
And the self is found where there was nothing.

In this emptiness we all carry within,
Where the spark of the individual identity lives.

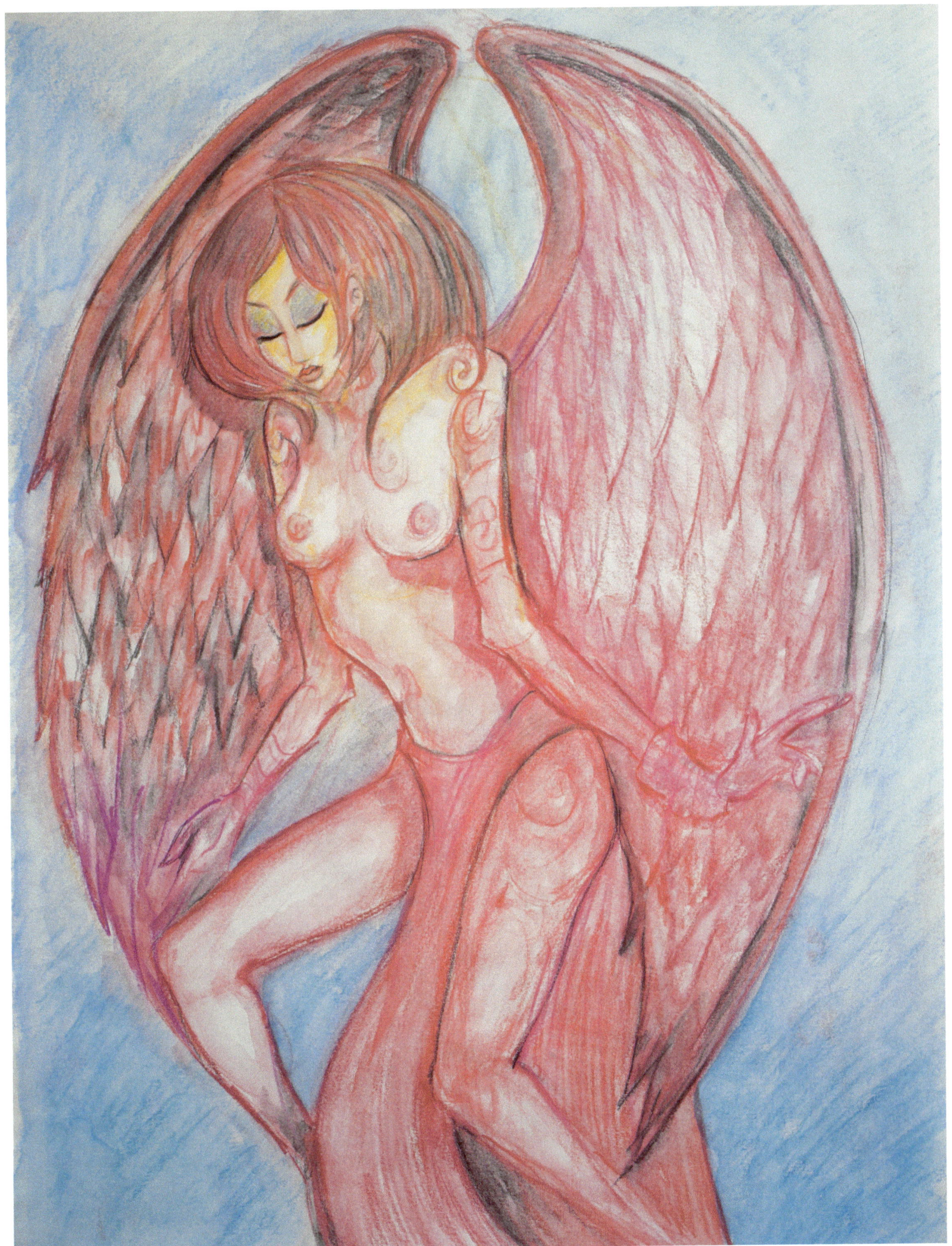

Solace

Always on the outside
Looking in.
Always take the wrong road into sin.

I cried me a river,
I put it down in words.
I'm lost in the space between places,
All I've got is this song.

I'm always broken hearted,
I can't win.

I can't make that connection,
I can't begin.

I think what's going on here,
What's going on in my head?
Still don't know if I care,
Still don't know if I'm alive or dead.

I don't own it,
I don't own this life.
Its borrowed time.

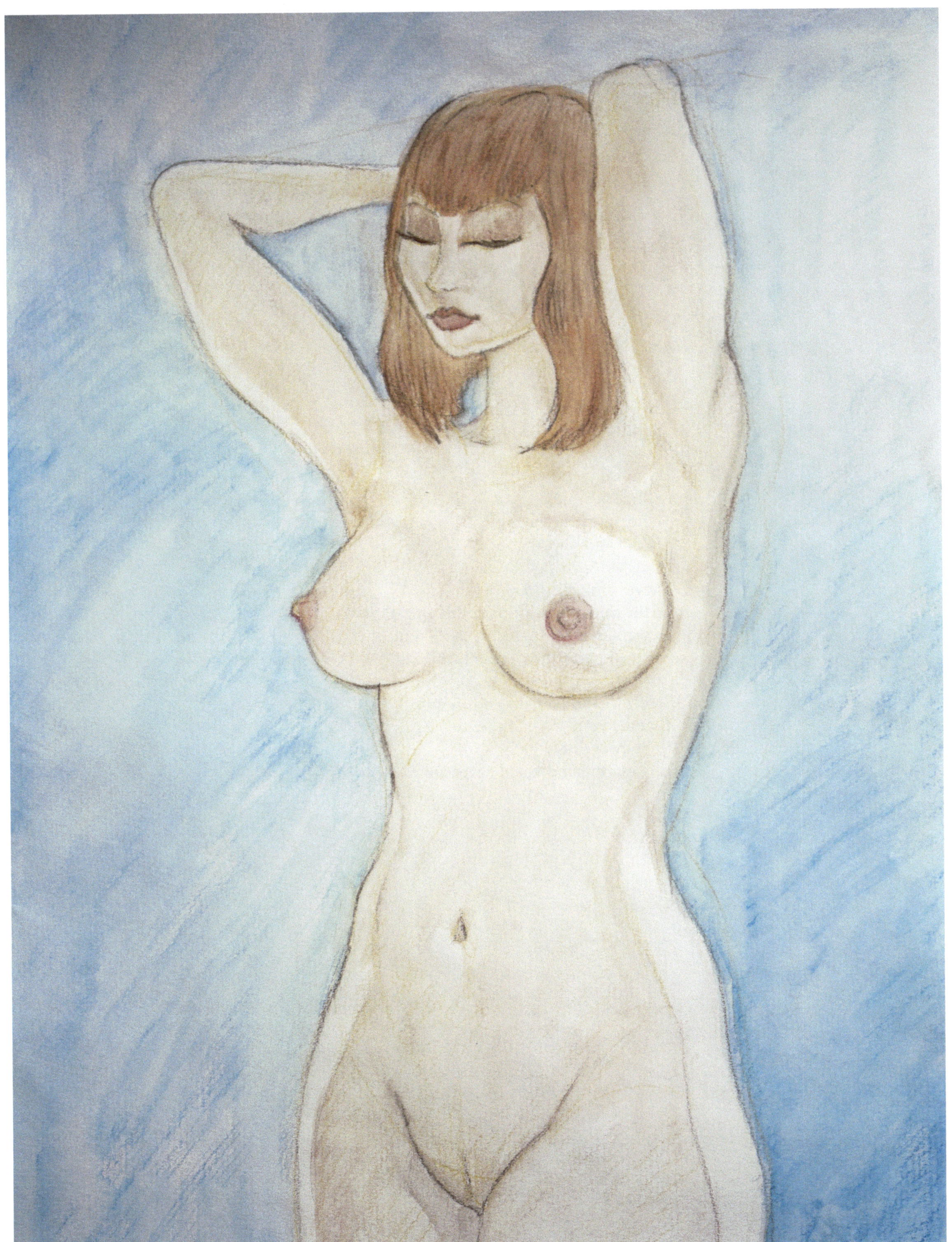

Meeting in dreams

Just when I thought I figured out this life,
Then I go and blow my world apart.
Just when the pieces can't fit back again,
You help me make a brand new start.

My worlds receding,
My tide is peaking.
These times are fleeting,
I fold it and start time again.

I never took much notice
To the changing seasons in this world.
I always thought there'd be more time,
But then my friends began to fall.

Surely we should have known this,
That the years would begin to pass us by.
Nobody ever told us,
That our dreams would never die.

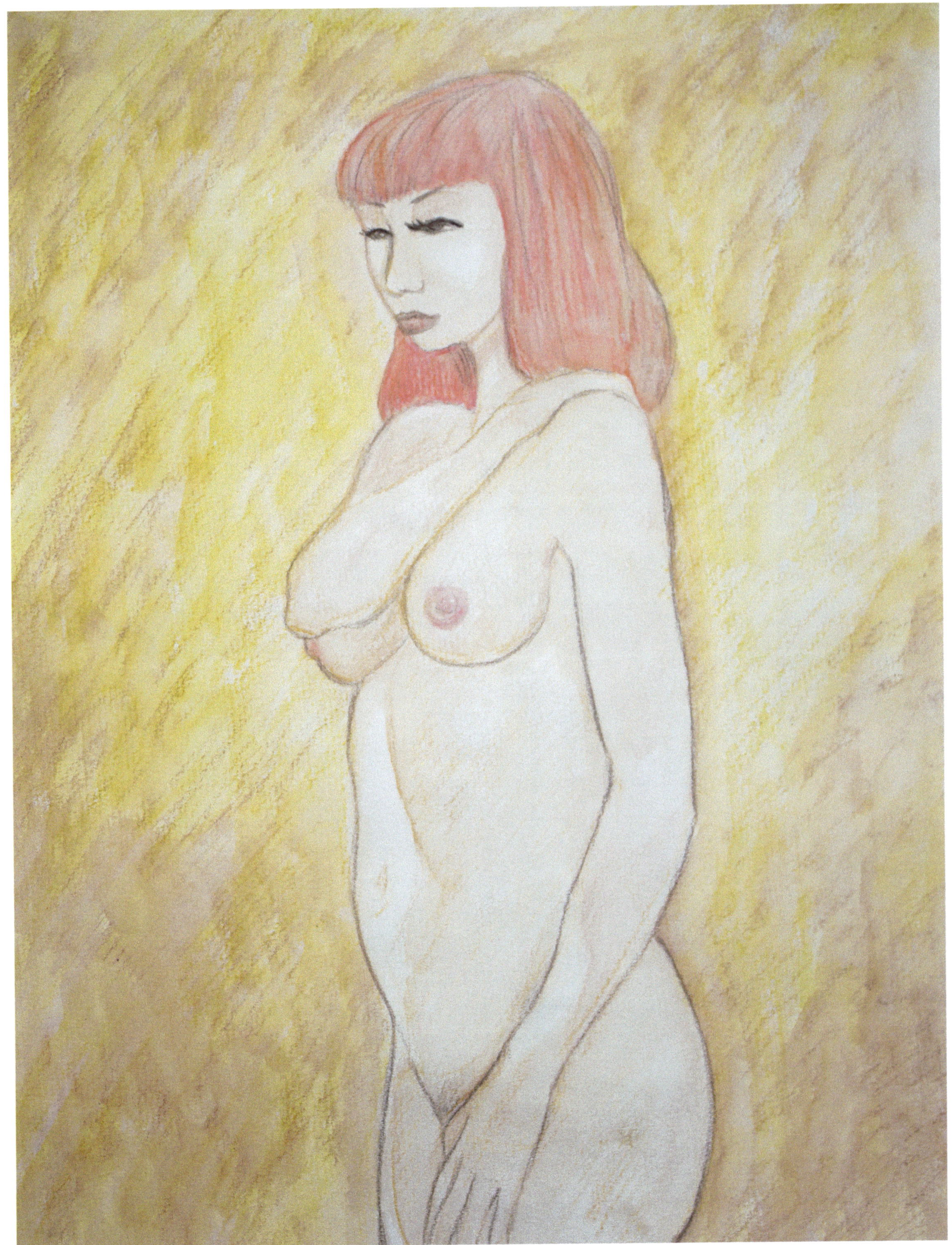

Smooth

Sit down and tell me a story,
Of how it's going to be.
How our loves going to change things,
And set your people free.

But I ain't your savior,
I ain't your knight on a steed.
I'm just a Hairy Maclary,
Smoking a bowl of weed.

...And it's smooth without you.

I had me a bad headache,
And baby it was you.
So I found a solution,
To all my endless blues.

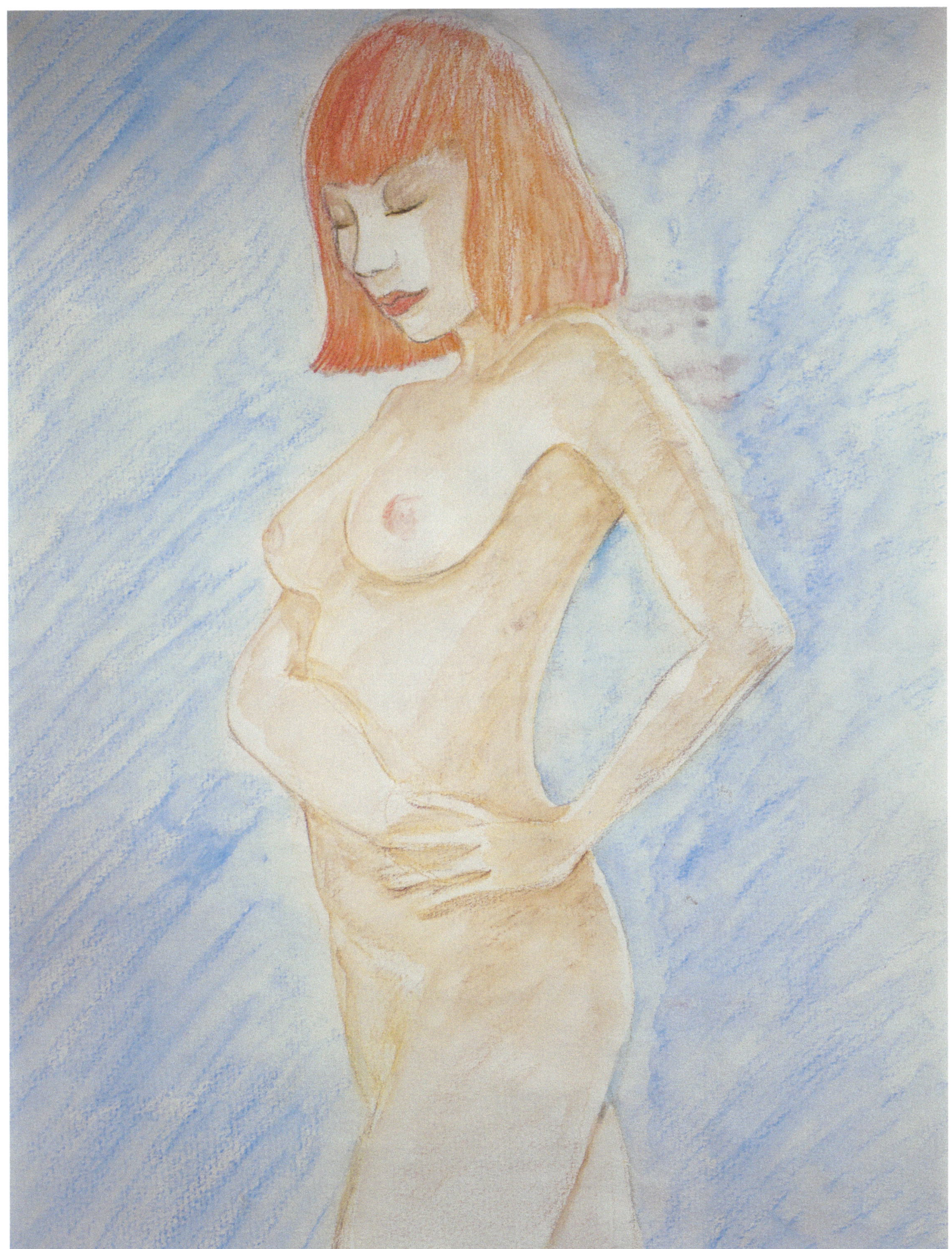

I took her away from the crowds,
And led her to the beach.
She took my hand.
We walked between the chaos,
Till we reached a secluded spot in the rocks.

Then I kissed her.
The night was clear and the crowds were faint,
Intruding only a little,
As I touched her where she asked to be touched.

Then I began to shake again.
Like I did when I first truly kissed a girl.
My head was clear,
There were fireworks and shooting stars.
We ignored them all.

We missed the turning of the year.
I could smell her,
Taste her.
I could feel her energy in me,
And I let it go.
I let it pass into her,
A little part of my soul.

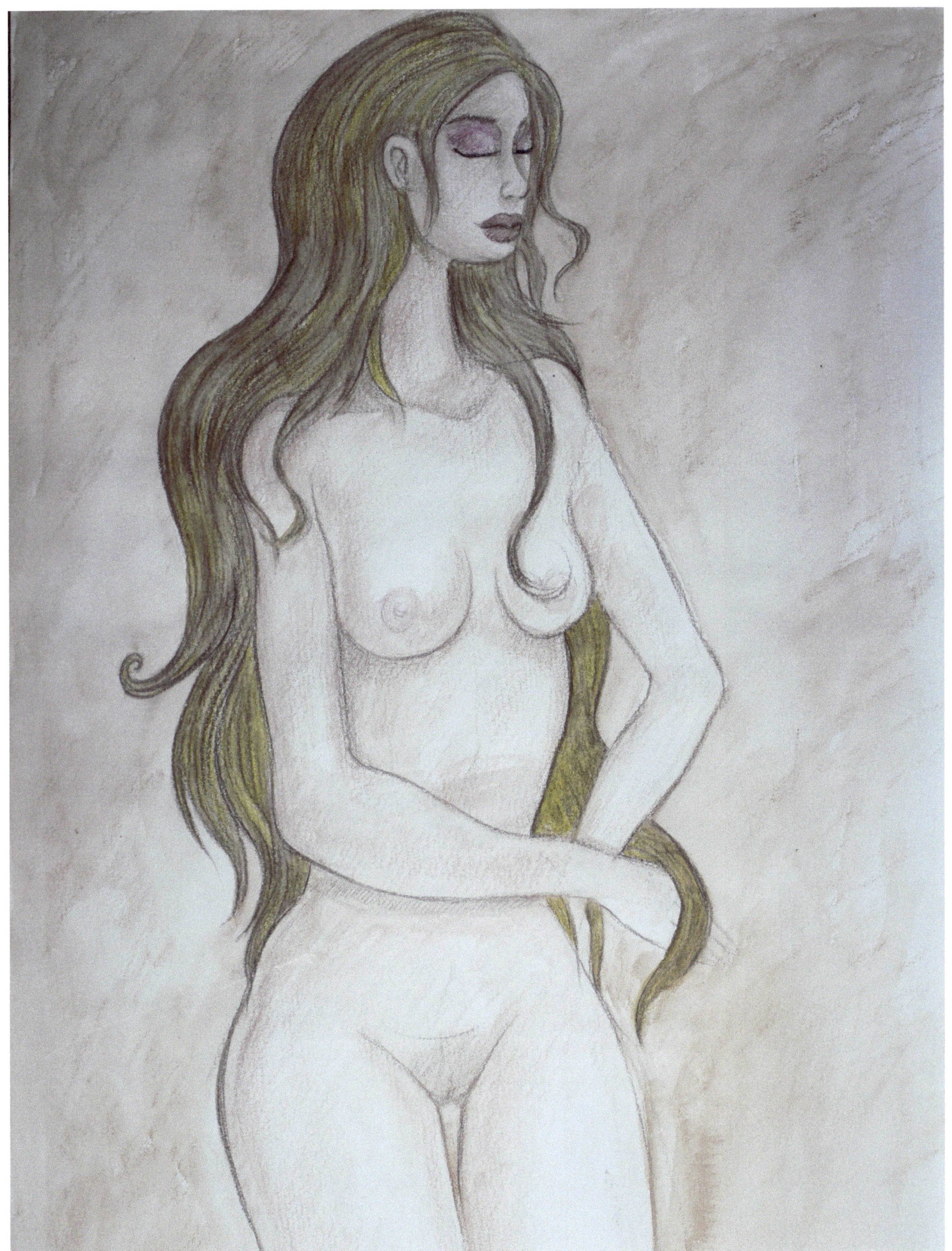

Evershade

Where did you father go to then?
He sounded kind of ominous,
When he went down the that road.

Then we waited by the open door,
But he wasn't coming home no more,
Like waiting for the rain.

Now we sit here swapping compliments,
But what's really on our minds,
Is what happened to the time.

So when this world brings on the consequence,
Means nothing more to me,
Than this cold reality.

Hold me up to the sun today,
And break apart the evershade,
That's curled around my heart.

As we are mourning all our passing friends,
See another fall away again,
You take a little piece of me.

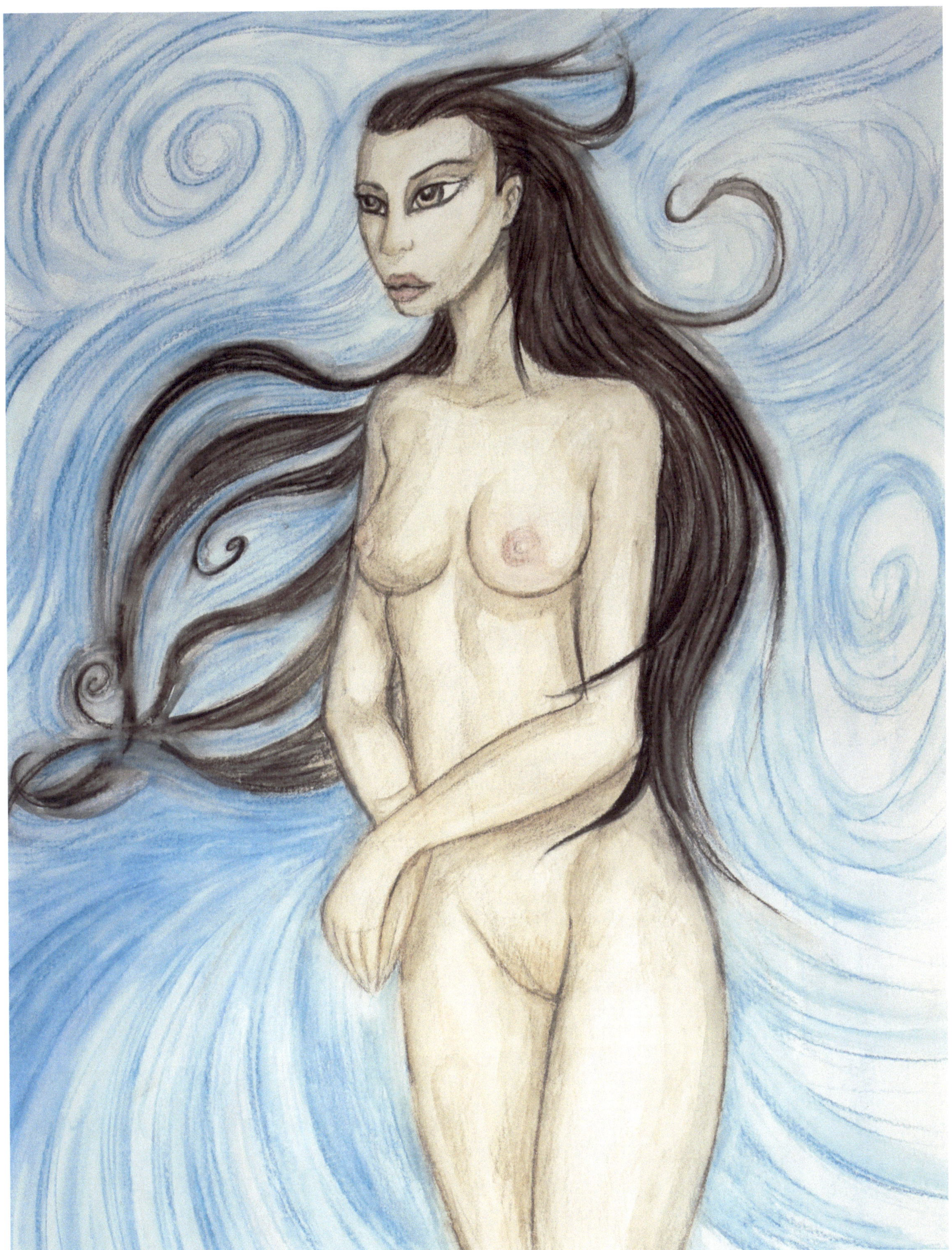

Your Final Call

Your final call,
Taking you under.
Your eternal soul,
Can't wait much longer.

...And paths beyond,
This Islands thunder.
Will take you up,
To all that you wonder.

You'll find it,
Your final call.
Here that's where you'll find it,
Your final call.

Your body rolls,
Mind's no longer.
Your breath belongs,
In lungs of others.

All pains denied,
All feelings squandered.
You'll never long,
For ever after.

You'll Find it,
Your final call,
Here that's where you'll find it,
Your final call.
Can't deny it,
Your final call.
Only comes once,
The final call.

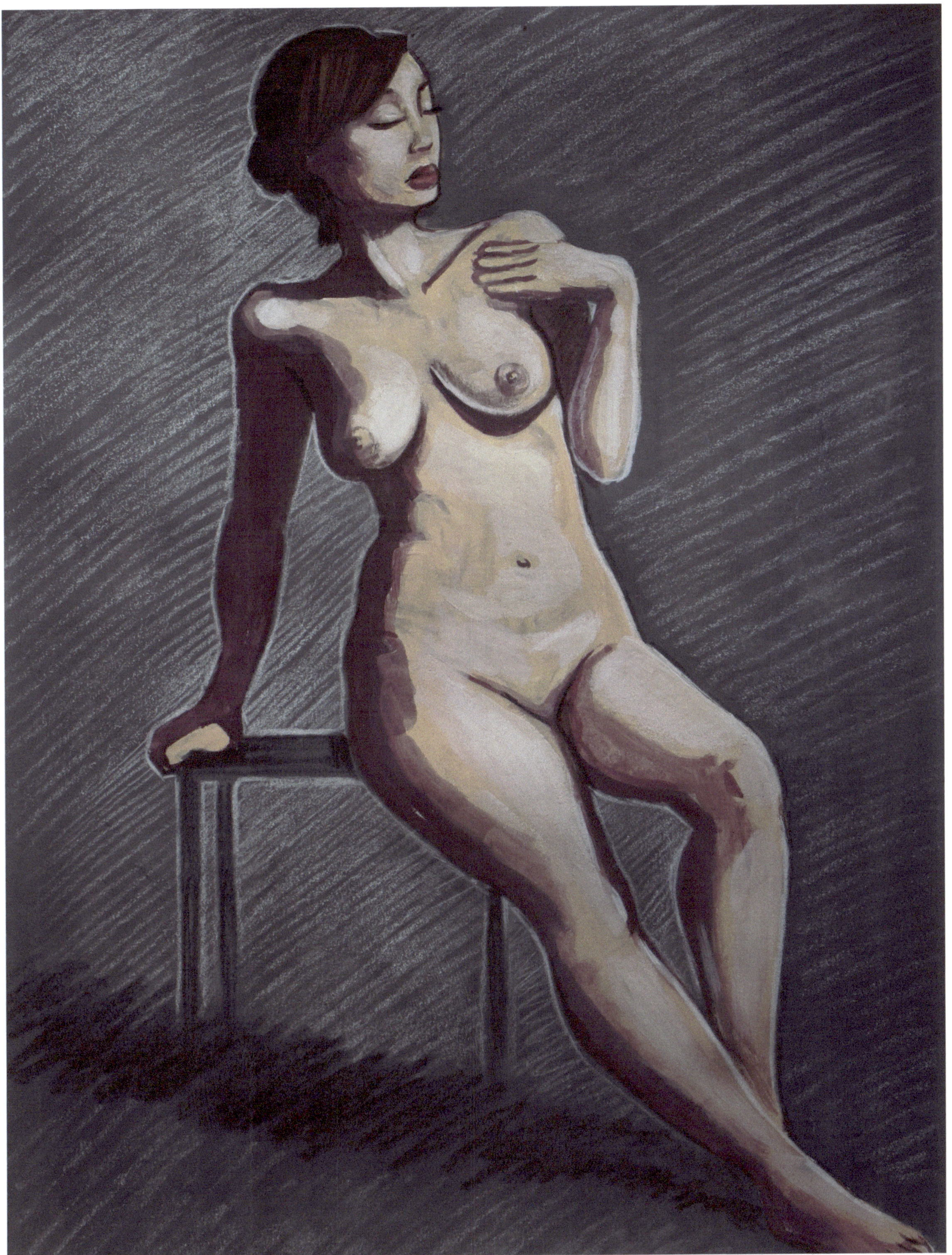

Deathhead

I will overcome.
They can't bring me down,
And I see your faltered step.
Don't fall and catch your death.

Said you're feeling Thirsty,
Well go ahead and take a drink.
Said you're feeling hungry.
So I better sit you down.
I'll take this knife and,
I'll feed you from my flesh.

Blind to your pain,
Just can't feel the same.
And here do I burn,
Until this day has turned.
I'll sin again,
I'll break the skin.
You'd be my only one.

Said you're feeling dirty,
So I'm tearing off your dress.
Said you're feeling hungry.
So I better sit you down.
I'll take this knife and
I'll feed you from my flesh.

Don't you know I'm dark?
I'll tear your heart apart.
Don't be my slave,
Can't be all you crave.
I'll take this gun,
And we'll have some fun.

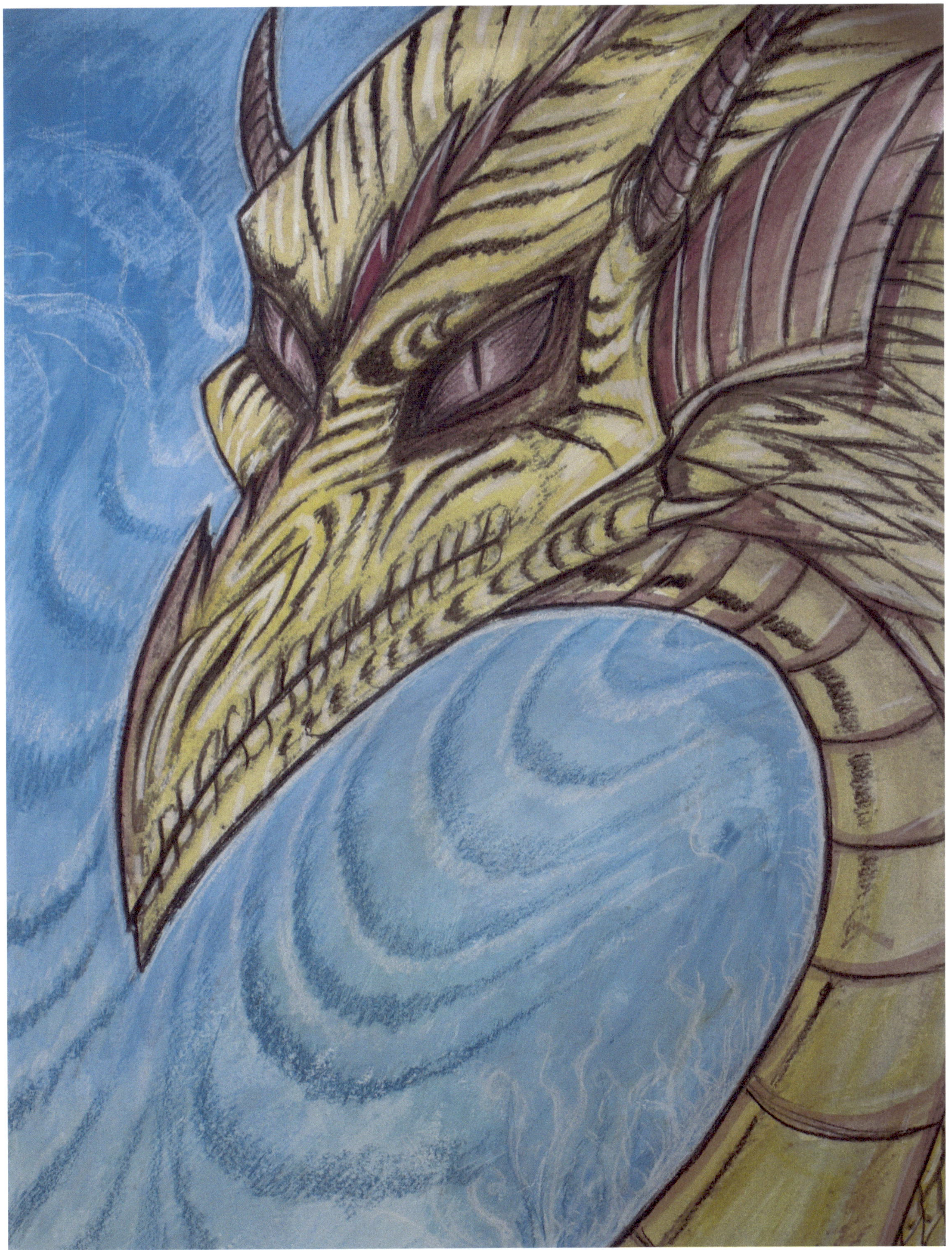

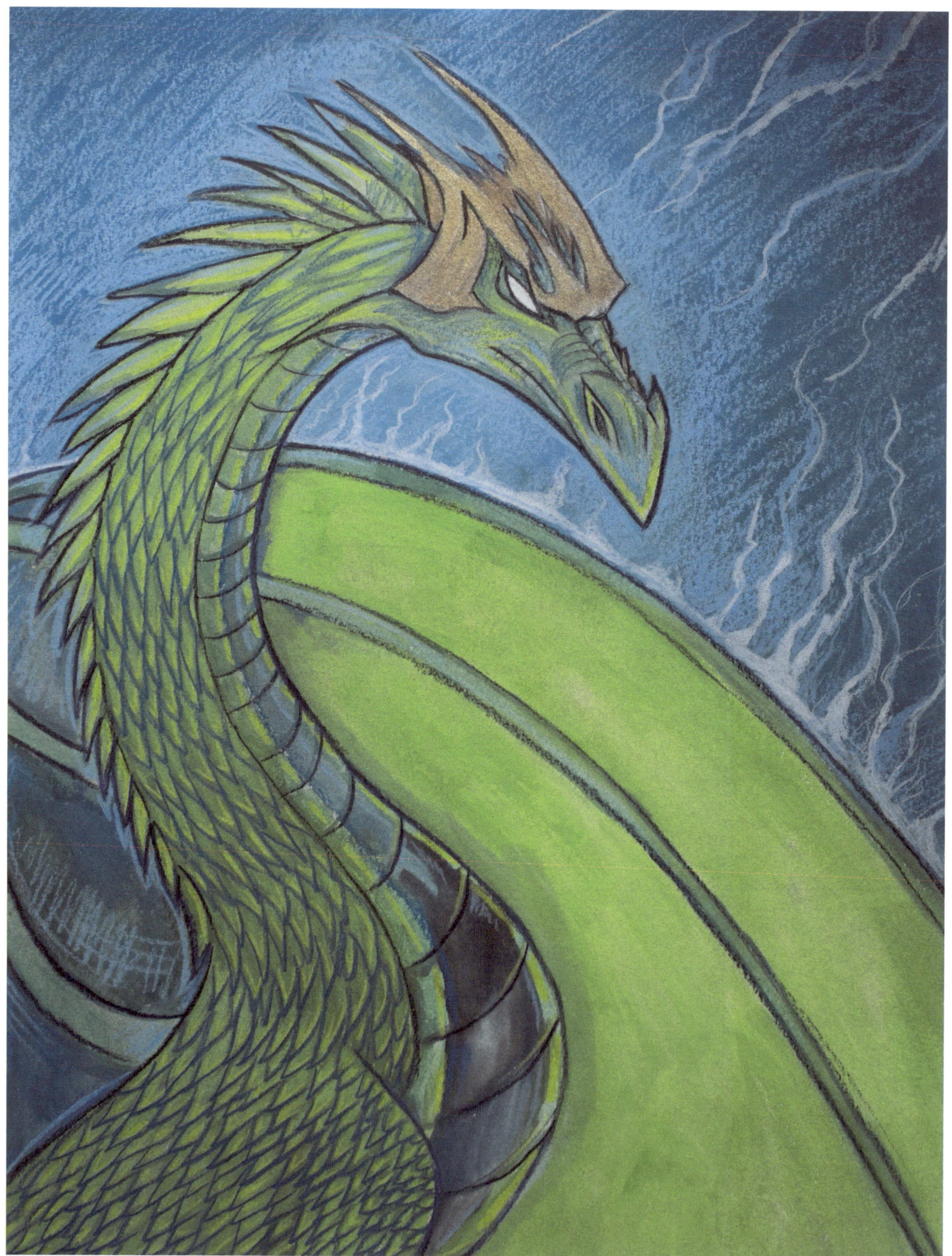

Harmless, harmful, what have, when have.
Momentums peace in sheep's fleece.
Slashed and gutted and hung out for the dogs,
While the wolves gather in me.

Perpetual night behind my eyes.
Thank wickedness for all the fools.
Blackened hearts that cry and sting,
With a wild and clumsy state of mind.

Through the essence of it all I flow, I fall.
I skin my head,
To let you see the overblown thoughts in my mind.
My eyes bleed to see the light,
But I love the dark,
I love the high.
Then I tie myself to this blade again.

That pain won't consume all that you are,
But it is part of what, who, where I am.
Sweet vice.
A sadist with you,
My beaten dog that knows nothing else.
Oh the music of the universe in your screams.

Carcass

Wouldn't make a difference,
If I said all the right things?
It's just a matter of moments,
Before I fuck it up again.

I been wrong for a long time,
Screwed up for a long time.
You think you can change this,
But you can't change who I am.

I live in the darkness,
Feeding of dead things,.
Trying to end my pain,
Trying to break these chains.

I long for the living,
Warm flesh against my skin,
Been cold for so long now,
Black flames they burn from within.

Oh why deny the mind,
Talking all the time.
Then how high you'll fly,
Show your other side.

It's alive I cried,
In darkness we will hide,
Taking all my time,
Into your life I slide.

Tempt this children's game,
Wrapped up in your shame.
Refuse to be the same,
Become the point of change.

My will won't be denied,
This soul is truly fried.
Until I face your lies,
It's time for you to die.

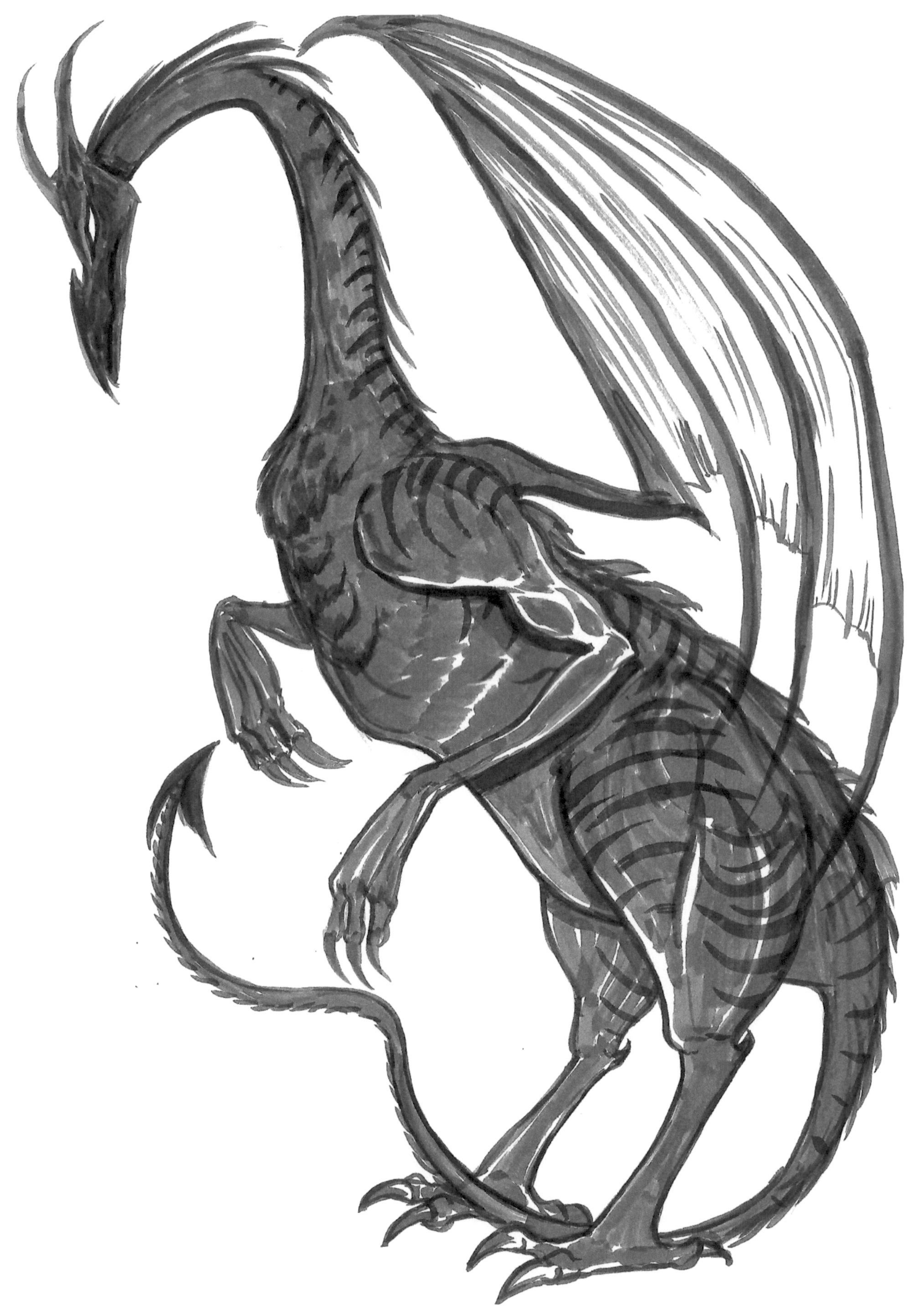

Creeper

We saw a lizard on the road,
We ran it over.
Locked in it's death-rows it's writhing on the ground,
Because it's over.
Like that Lizard you don't have chance,
I ran you over.
My loves like a runaway train,
It scares you sober.

Sitting in the dead sea,
But it's drying up Just like me.
I walk but I can't find, This peace, This peace of mind.

Soldier on like soldier ants,
We fight to the bitter end.
Same battles, same wars.
Same expression that you wore before.
I ain't saying that I can't change,
But I got bad wiring in my brain.
I know that you feel the same,
So why do we hide our darkness in shame.

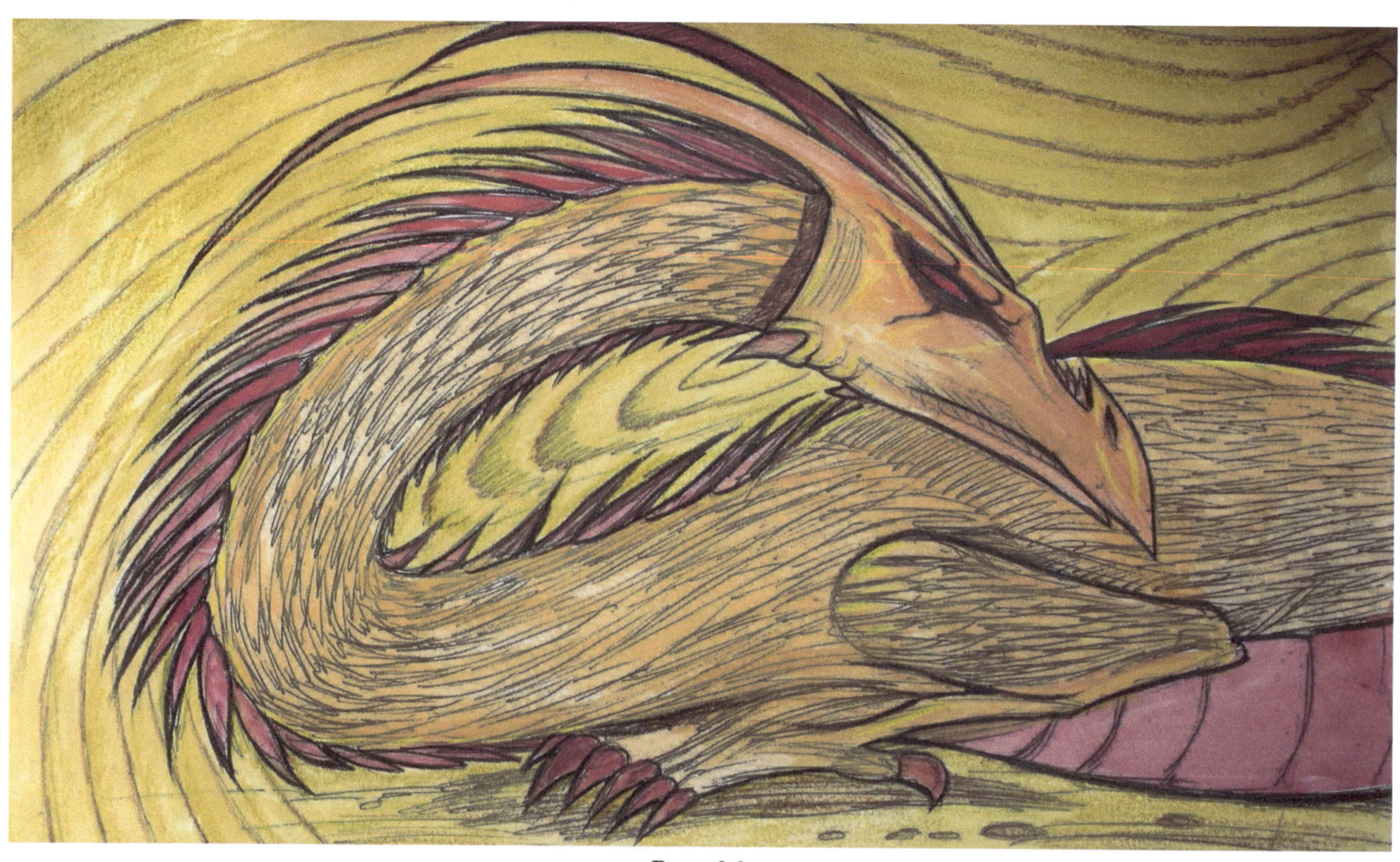

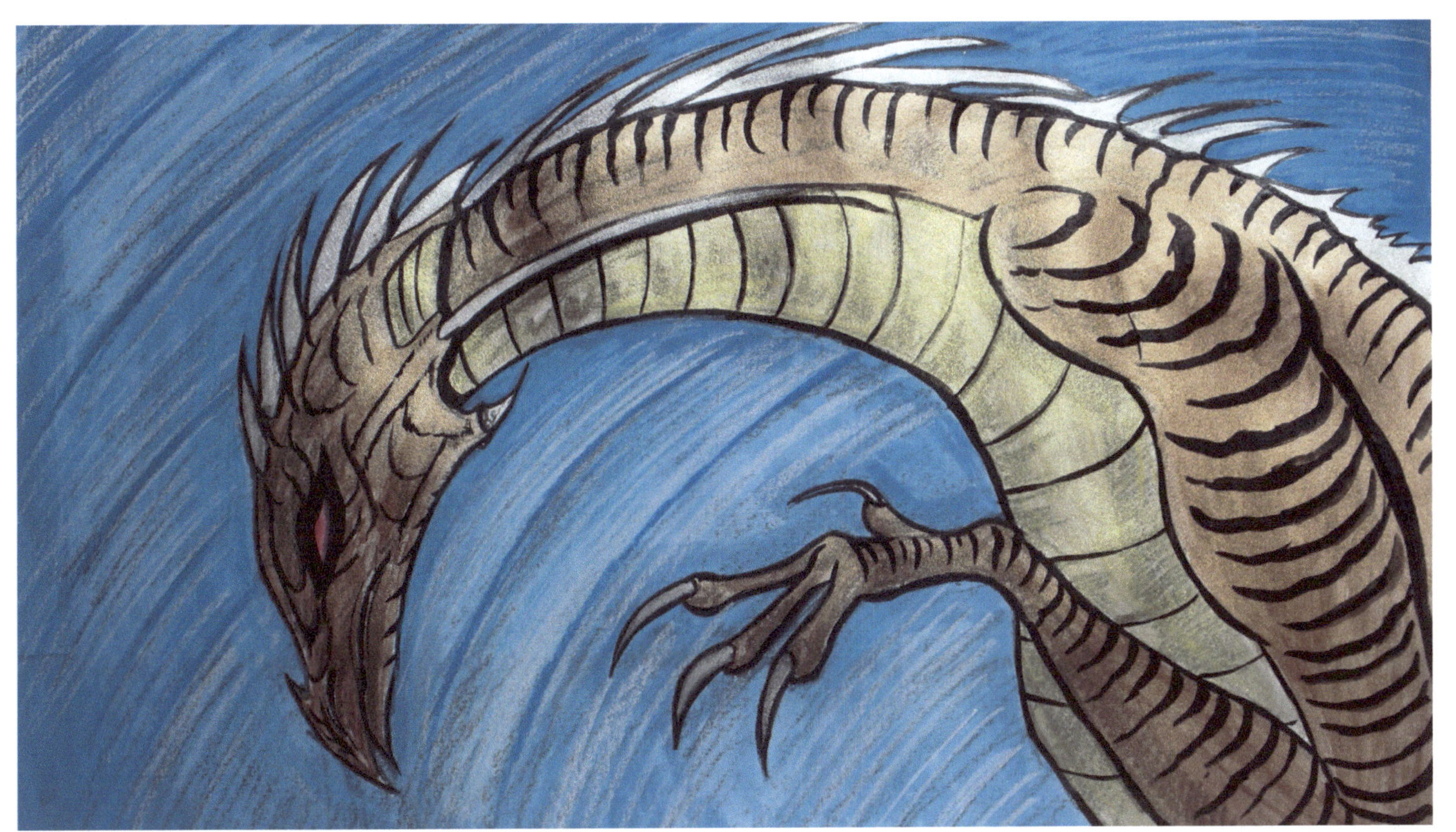

I am Monster

The curtains come up,
The theatre is open for surgery.

Once was human,
Once was alive.
Once knew love,
Once knew life.
But now I'm Monster.

With swift scalpels and a lightening needles
You made me,
From the bodies of your fallen lovers.
Made in your image,
And I am Monster.

As I lie here in the dark the sweet things dance around.
Things of light, creatures of life.
Celebrating love, breath and a life that stretches out before them.
While I watch on with a mortuary perspective.
What's left of my sutured heart leaps in an echo of joy.
A momentary glimpse of another world I can never reach.

For I am Monster.

Digging up old Bones

Finding you behind the gravestone,
You're a LIAR you're a LIAR!
You screamed loud enough just to wake the dead.
And I fire! And I fire!
Tearing up all the gravestones,
Looking for a place to rest.
I'm on fire! I'm on fire!

Tearing up all the pictures,
Breaking all the mirrors',
And I'm running with scissors,
Taking all the wrong tinctures,
Putting digits in fixtures,
While I'm sinking in quicksand.

Feasting on roasted brains like chestnuts,
And you're incapable of grief.
Turns out you're just the same as you've been,
And you've always been numb.

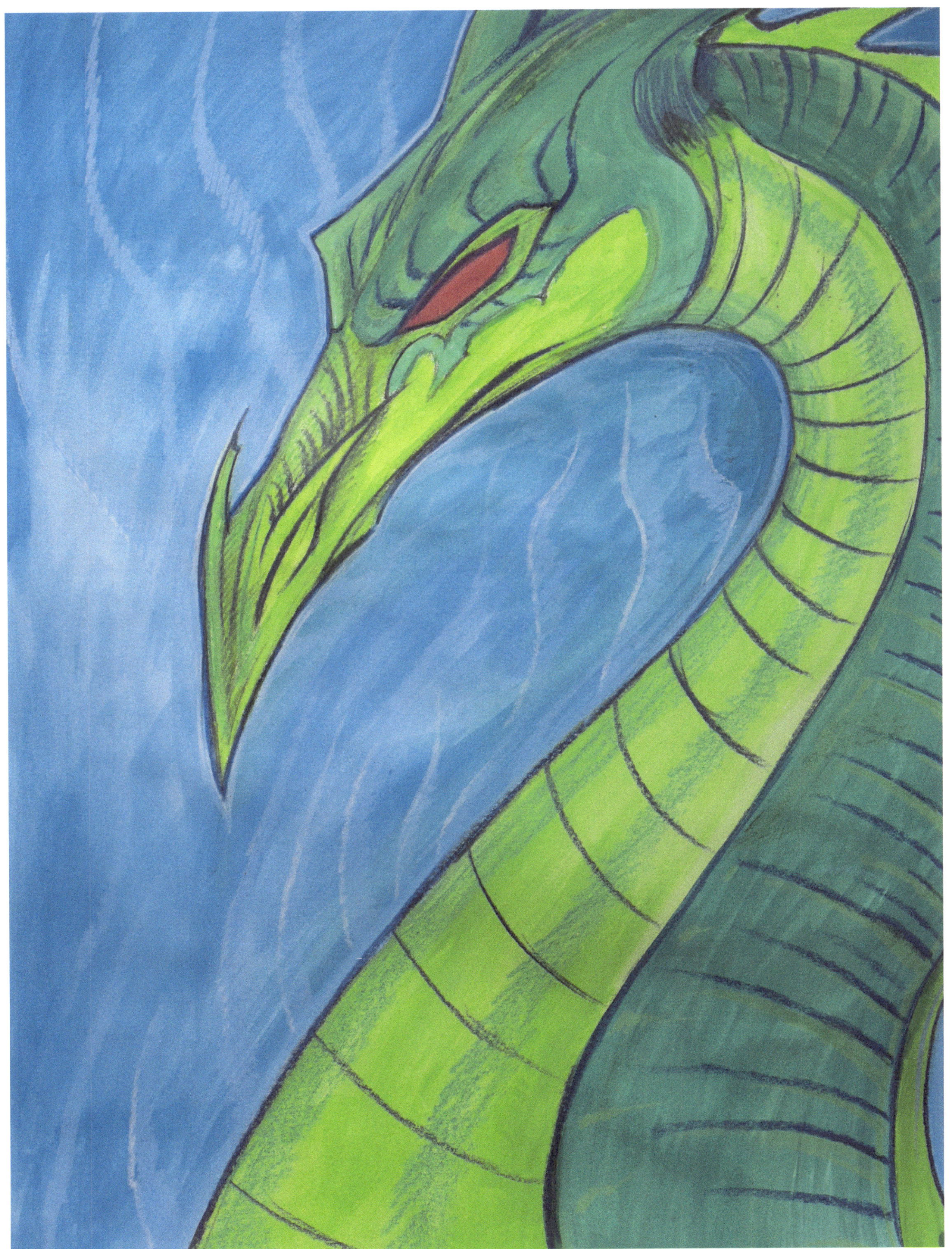

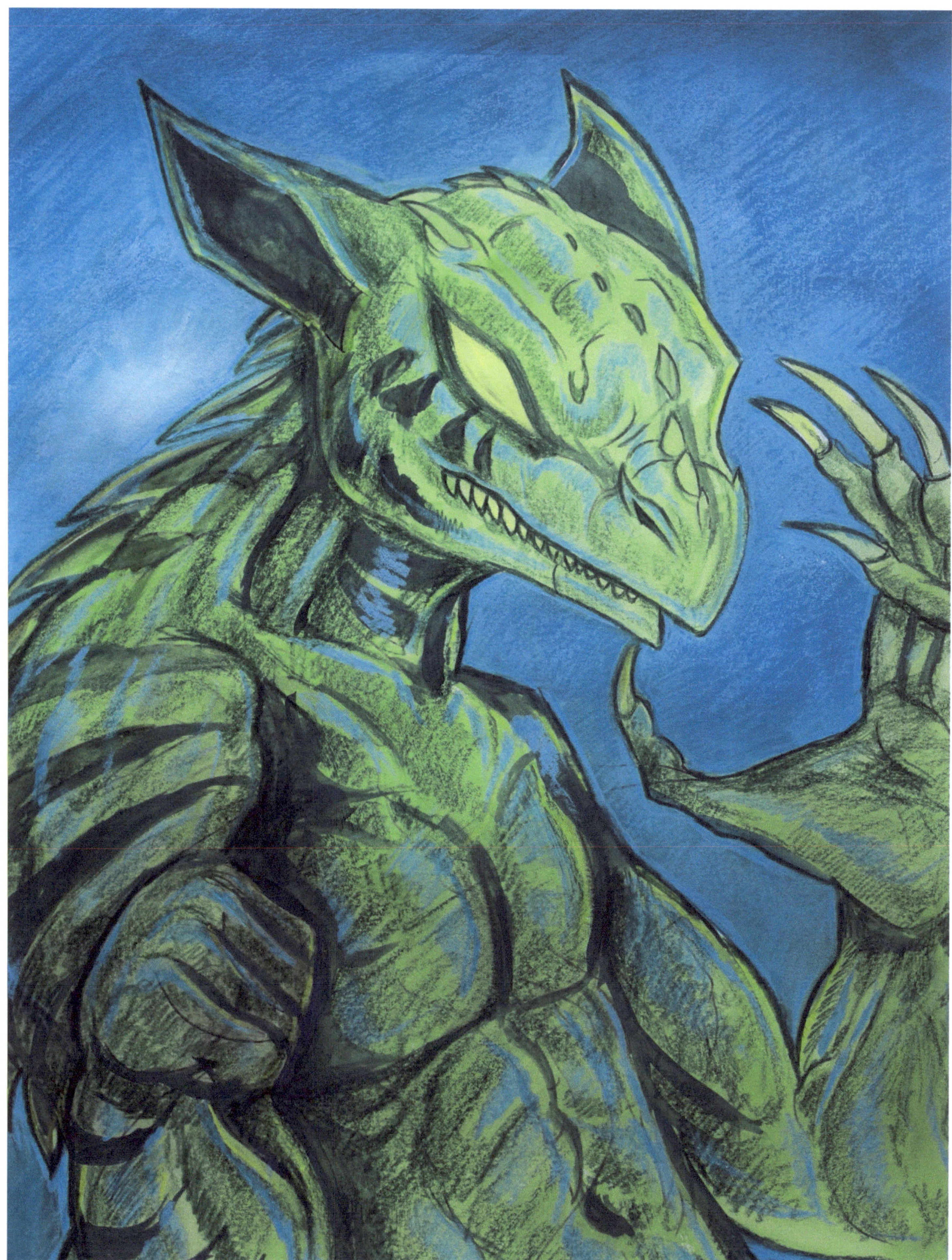

Floater

It should be so clear to me,
But inner poison drips within.
There should be no fear in me,
But caution pauses for the storm.

Forlorn waves flow,
Unknown direction.
Where we are born to go,
But where's conviction?

This next step could throw the boat,
But I drowned long ago.
With these fishes feeding on me,
Where the corpse comes to float.

Here this poison goes,
Unclear connection.
With nothing to show,

But future fictions.

Goddess of the Moon

Woke with your sun in my eyes.
Rise with your name in my Heart.
You move on and on,
Leaving me behind
In the dark.

You will see this sun with me.
You're my light,
While I'm the night.

I stall when I'm talking to you,
This fear of rejection is driving me crazy.
Cause you are the moon to me.

The sun brings no warmth to my soul just lately,
It's all I can do to move on.
Cause you mean the world to me.

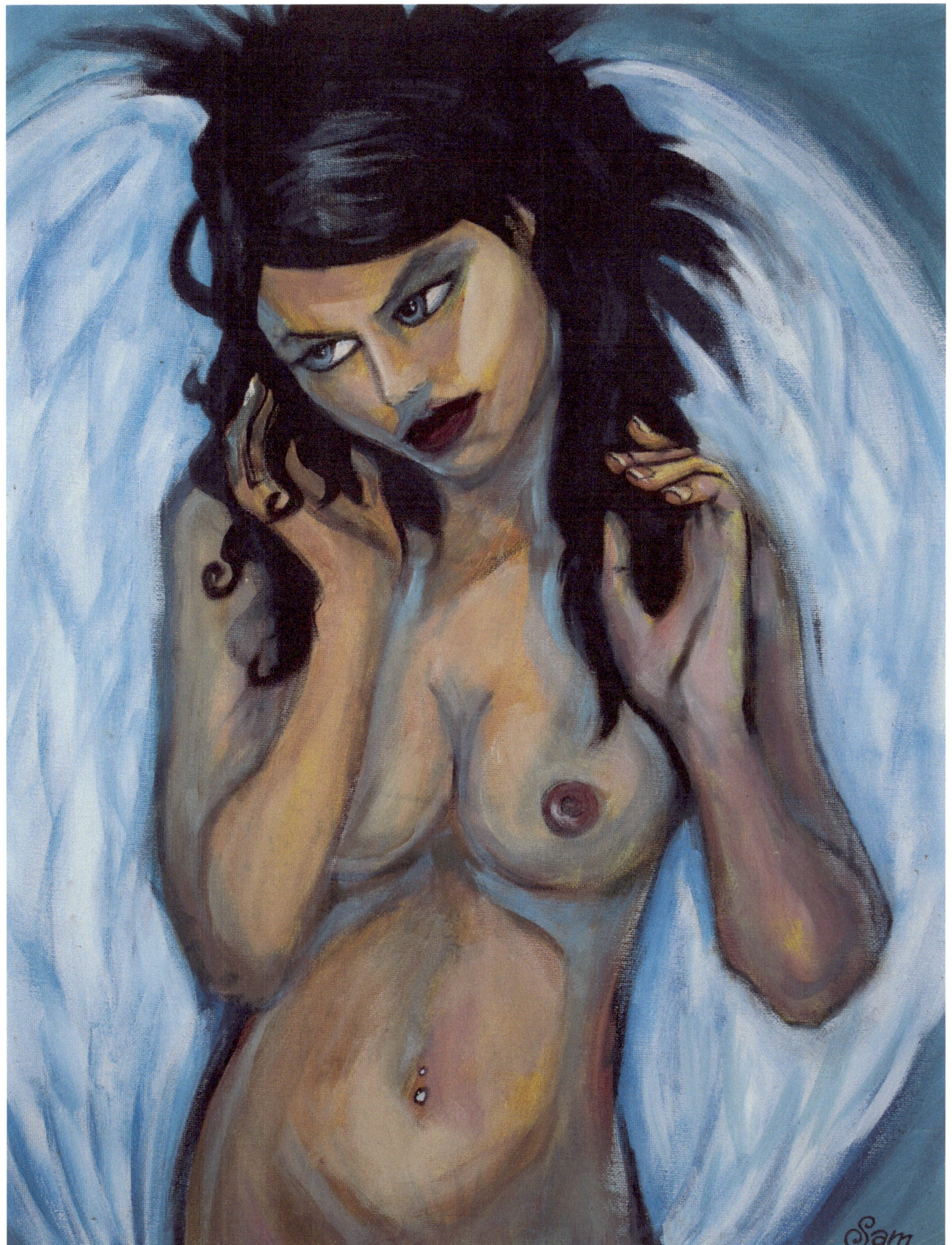
Sam

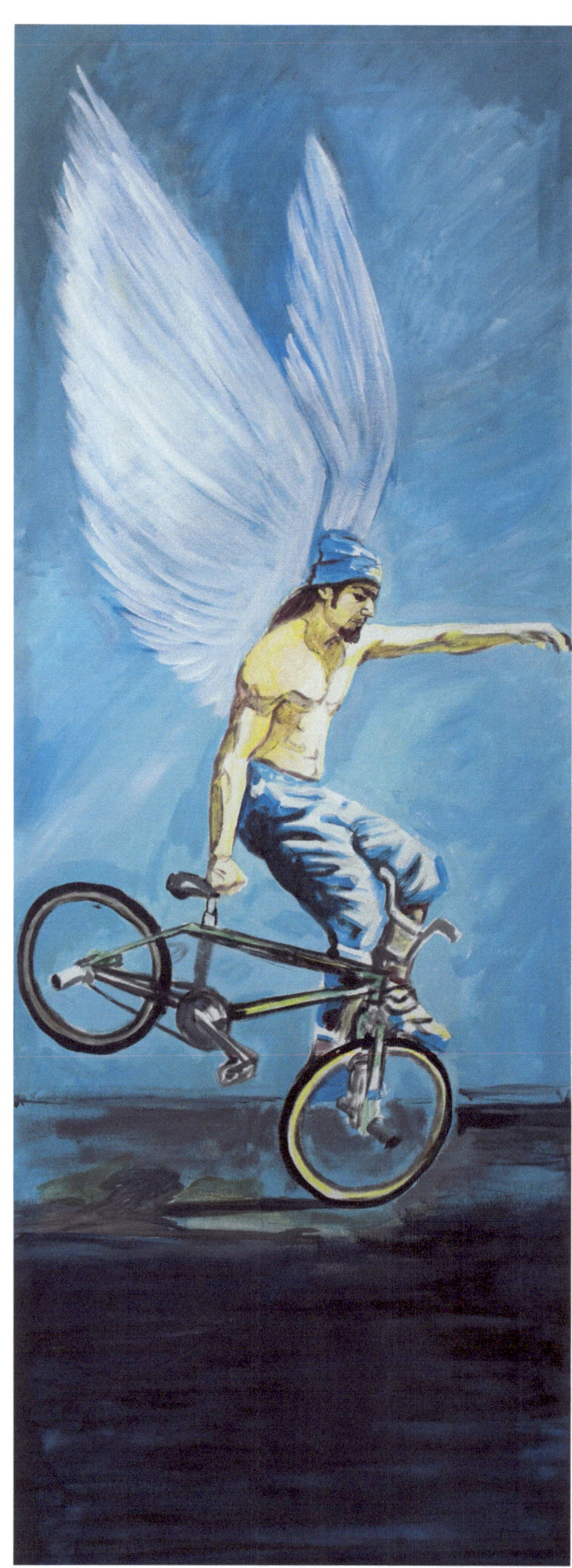

Portrait of Dion Geaney
R.I.P.
11th, October 1973 ~ 24th April 2011

Halloween

It's lonely on the outside,
I'm just a creature looking in.
So I'm paled to my life compared,
And my souls been wearing thin.

Been looking on the bright side,
Been working in the dark.
Tonight I'll dance in moonlight,
Tonight my life will start.

Halloween,
I'm gonna see my friend,
He's gonna walk again.

Halloween,
Just another drink or two,
What's the worst it could do?

Halloween,
It's the day of the dead.
Maybe I'll see my friend,
Once again.

Gonna wait till the witching hour,
Gonna use supernatural power,
Gonna talk to the dead,
Cause I miss my friend.
Gonna hide from the light,
Gonna make this my night,
And play with a ghostly symphony,
Till they bring him back to me.

Sweetest returns

Before we became friends,
Always felt so alone.
All the words from their lips,
But I never belonged.

But now I will never grow cold.
And now I will never cry for the dawn.
And with you in my heart,
And your love right their from the start,
I am free.

The greatest gift in this world,
Is the one you gave to me.
When you opened these eye's,
And taught this boy to see.

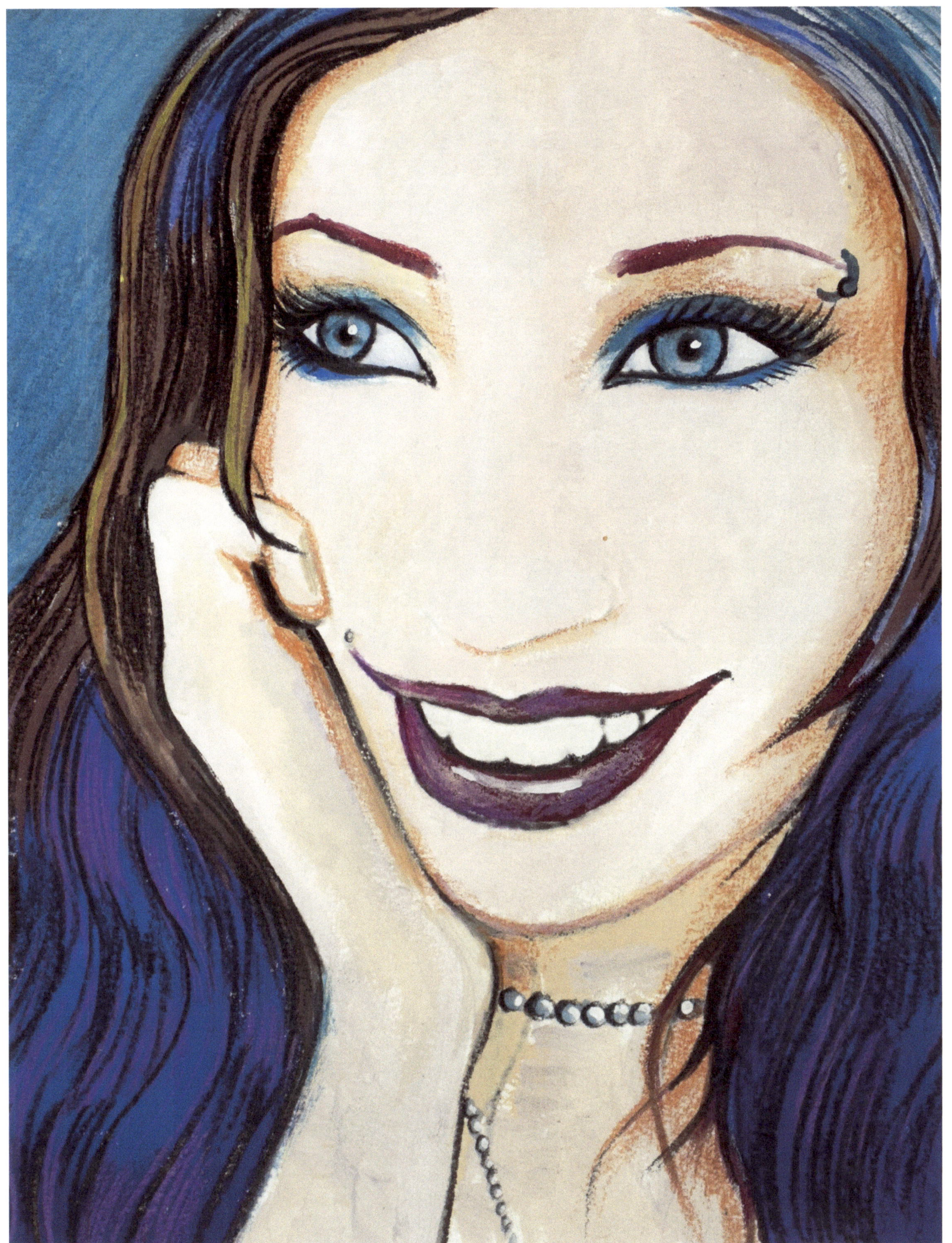

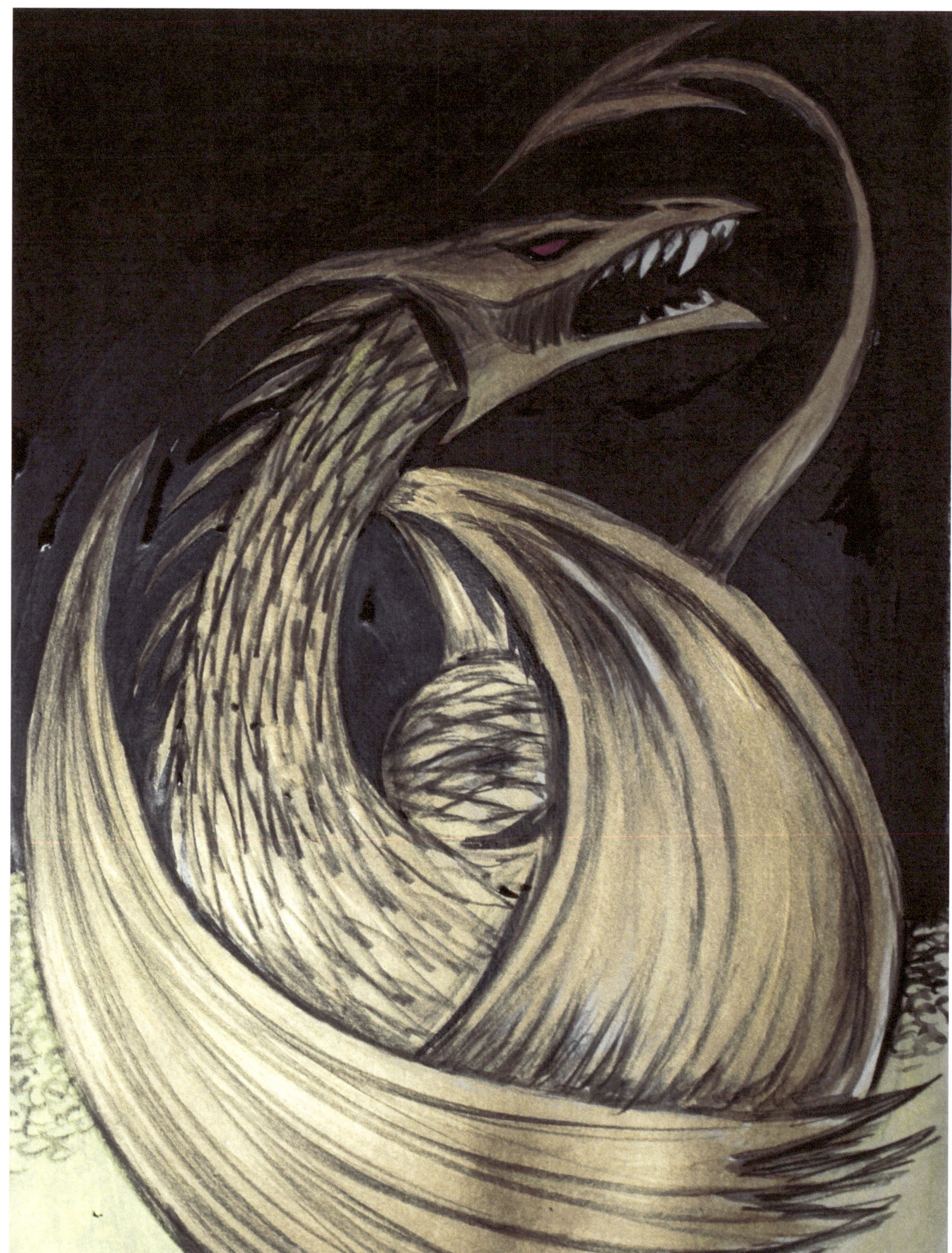

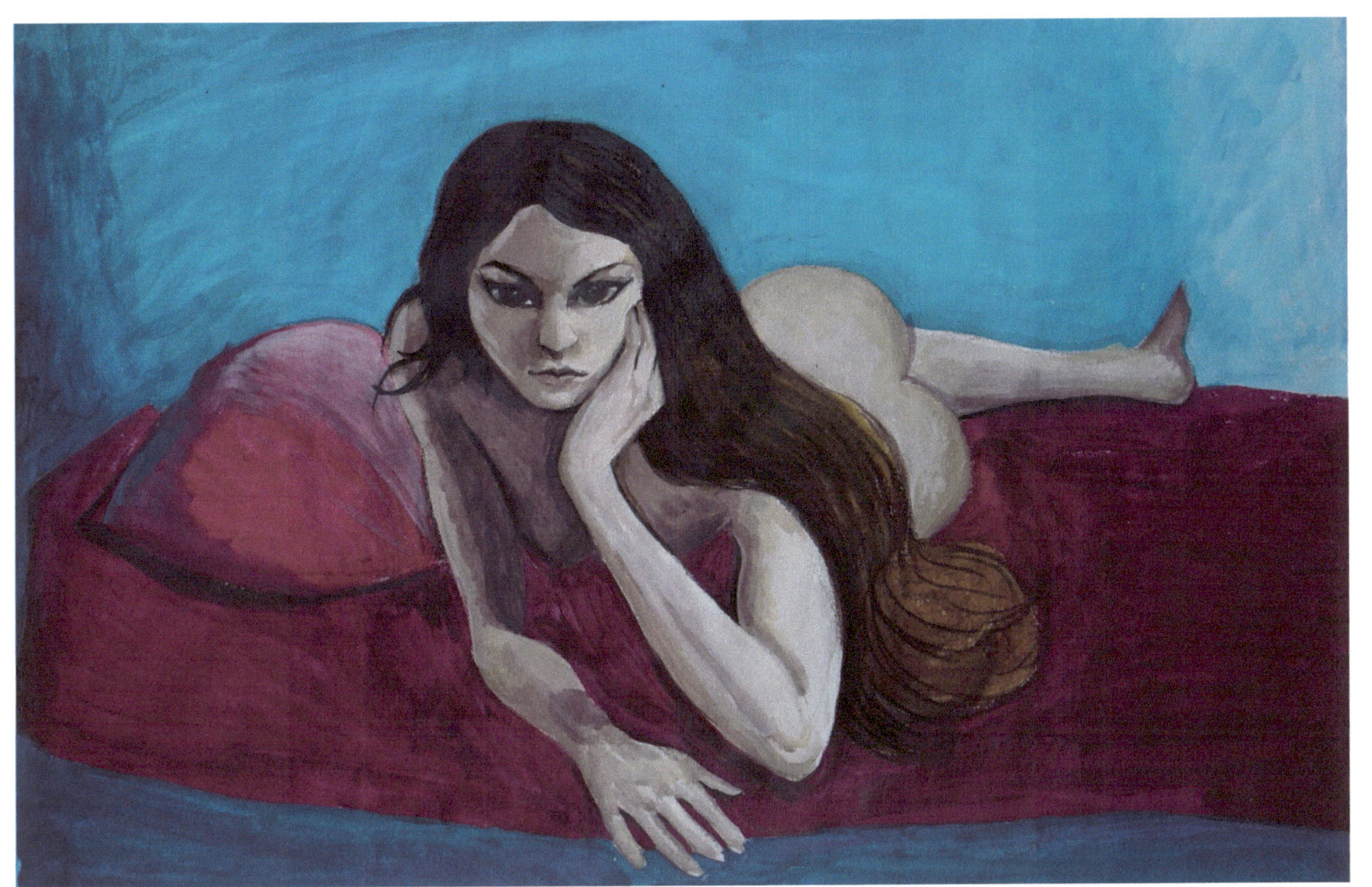

Cauliflower Ears

Release the pressure building inside of you.
Take the hornet for a joy ride.
All you're facing, all your drawn quarters,
Don't even know what you're fighting for.

Revolution don't mean shit to you,
Think it's the rising of the cows.
Just wait till they close your gate,
Trapped inside will all you hippies make it through?

Zen Bullshit,
Balance bullshit,
I am human ain't gotta clue.

Soaking in the Jazzcuzzi

I swear,
You mean everything.
Even though I know it doesn't seem,
But if you fade at all,
I'll fall.

I care,
Till it hurts too much.
That won't bring you back at all.
I just keep on walking through the woods.

These stories seem to never end.
The passing of our precious friends.
But we can have each other for a while,
So smile.

Who ever had it all?
Not you,
Not me,
Not we.

Who hasn't had a fall?
Not you,
Not me,
Not we.

So when,
We find your mind again,
I'll wait for your return my friend.
Still I'll keep on walking in these woods.

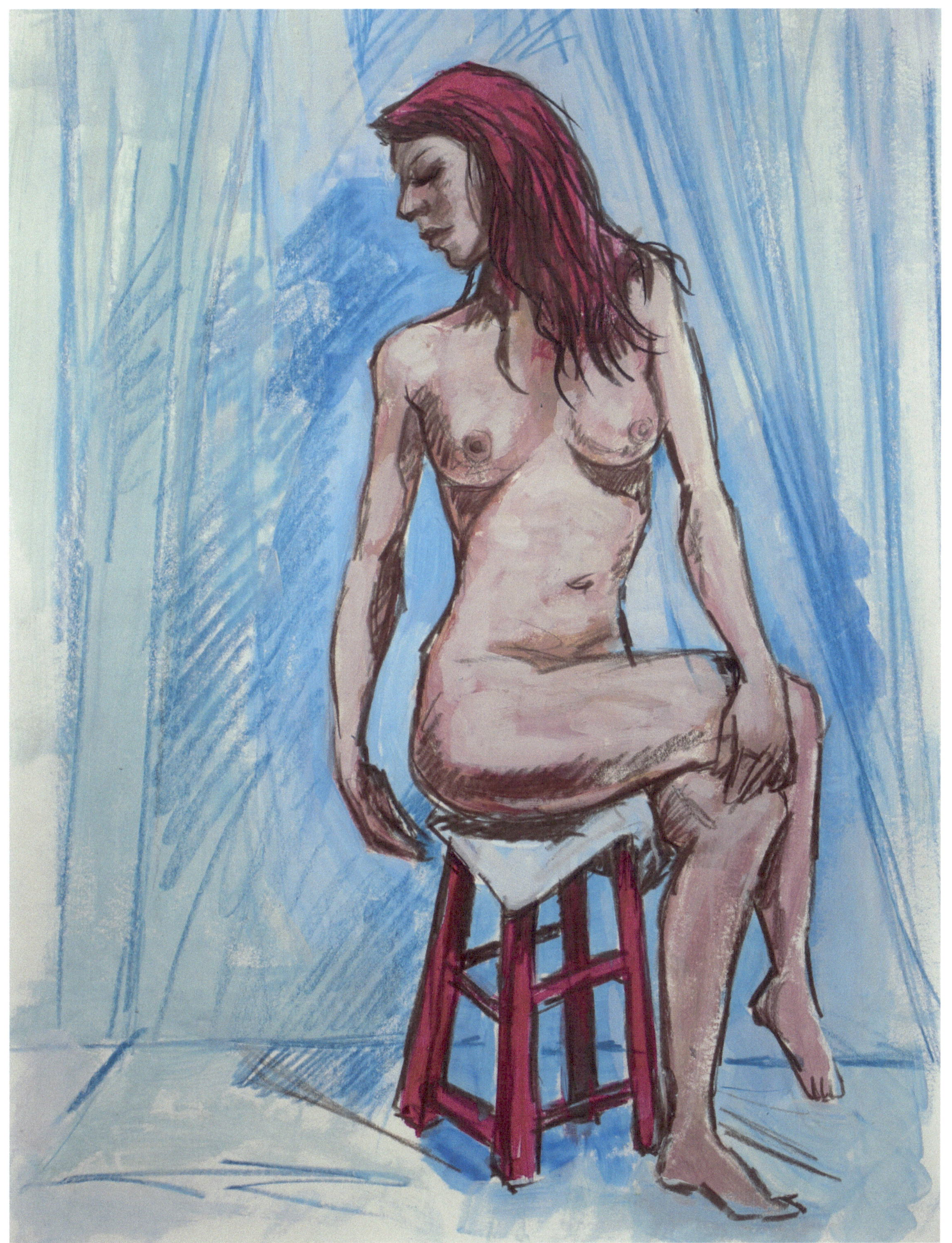

Splashed

Yellowed by the sun the papers turn.
I can taste you again.
Taste so sweet it drives me mad.
Gotta Deal with insanity again.

And I thought,
Things would change somehow.
And I thought,
I'd grow stronger today.
And I thought,
Of you three times today.
The lover,
The mother,
And the old maid.

You linger in the aftertaste,
While Shannon brings the house down.
And he's looking down and laughing' at me,
And the lies I try so hard to believe.

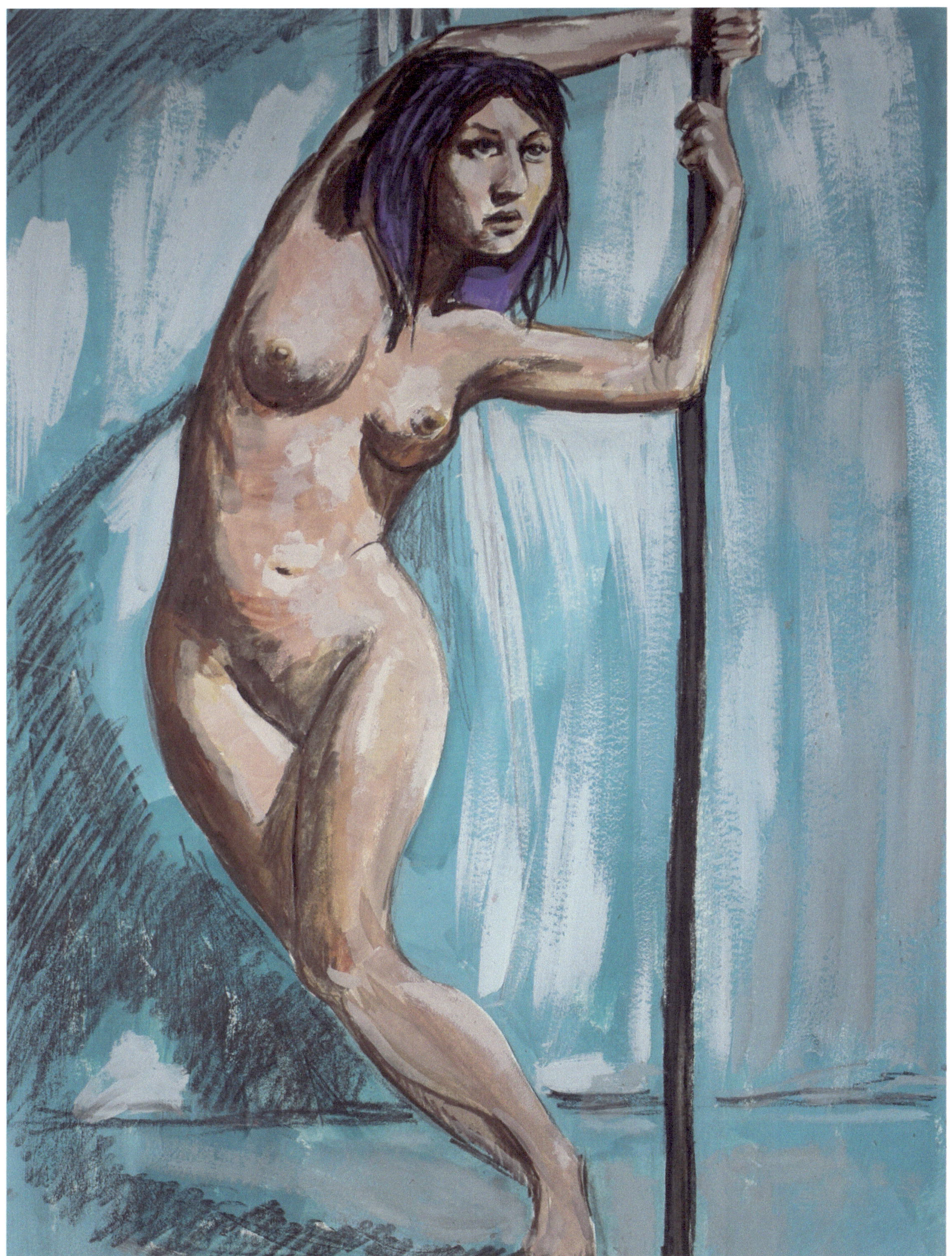

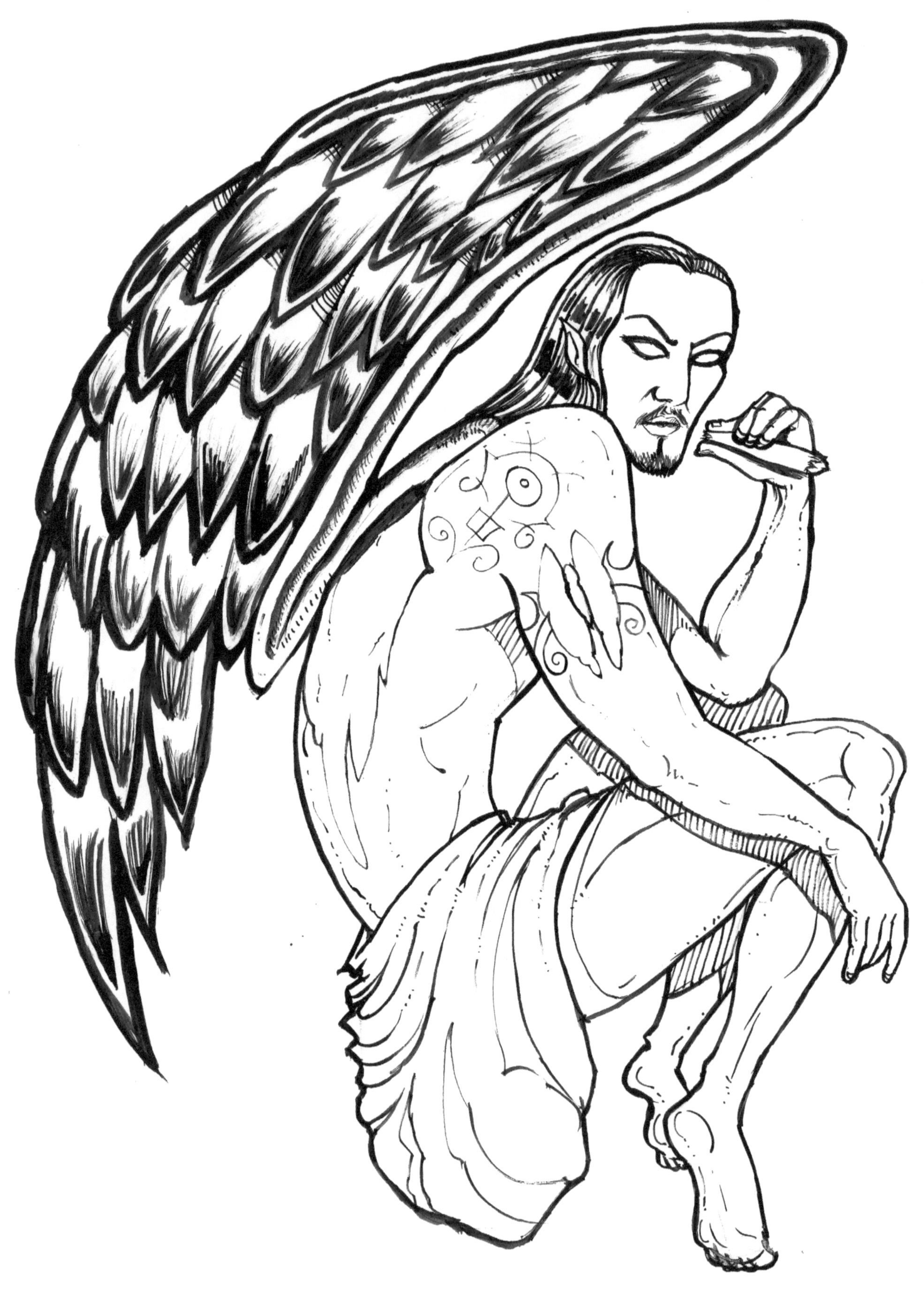

Chief Dancing Bear

Strange that the sun sets longer,
When there's no warm days.
Still we roll down the road,
Bound for oblivion.

Wrong in the way I viewed it,
But they all look the same.
I just can't choose between realities.

Hung up on Quantum physics,
But nothing physical,
I took a break from feeling so miserable.

Time runs between my fingers.
It means nothing at all,
Cause there's no more now or then indivisible.

Molding into the armchair,
Every thing's standing still.
I slip on down into oblivion.

Back and forth between the planes melding.
Can't keep my spirit still,
And there's a call from some unfamiliar.

Still waters always changing,
Reflecting turns in the wind.
Can't keep them hanging from every word you make.

Sunflower Queen

You're halfway,
Between dreams
And reality.
I can't Say,
Where all these paths will lead.

Dancing all around my head,
The leaves are filling up the air.
The winter has settled in me,
So I'll see you again in the spring.

She plays a fairy,
But she's lady.
The sunflower queen
Of everything.

Dancing all around our hearts.
I just don't know where to start.
The melodies are filling my head,
And the words are somewhere in there.

Some want pluck you and take you away.
I just want all of this beauty to stay.
When you can finally open to me,
Then all this world you will finally see.

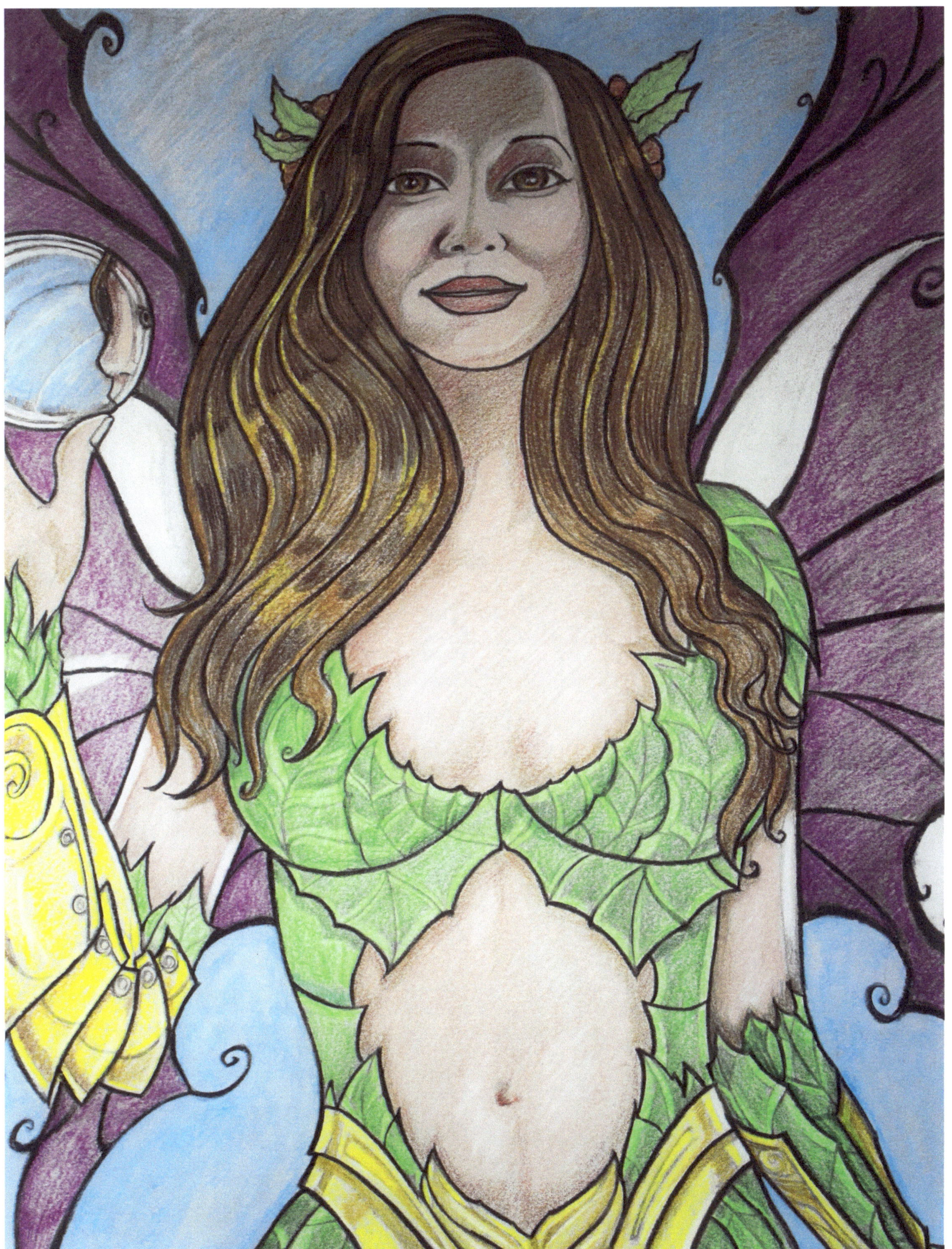

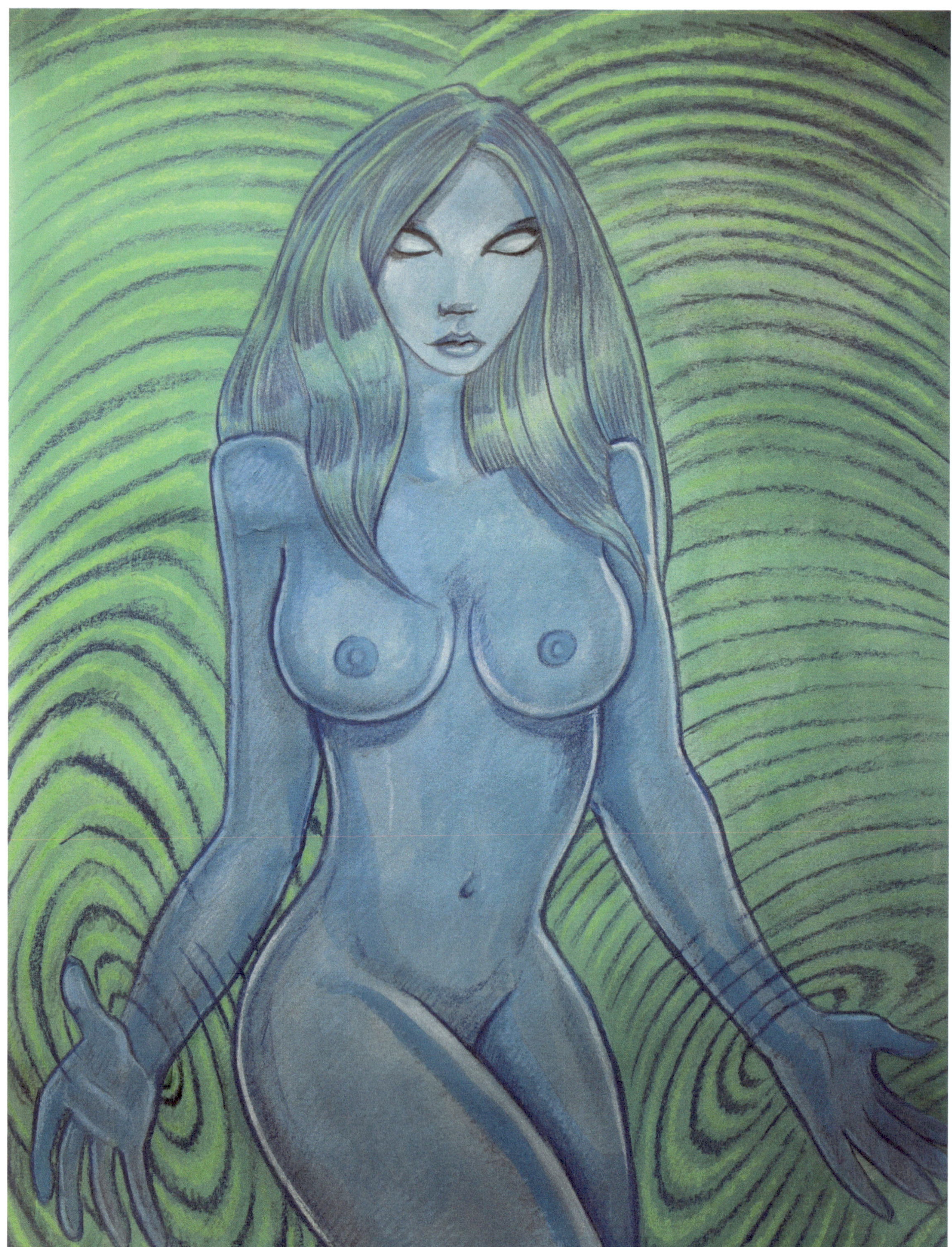

The rain soaks my skin, falling on my lips and eyelids.
Making it so hard to see my way.

I danced with you last night,
And in all the joy my sweat felt like tears dripping off my cheeks.
Salty and bitter.

But I kept on dancing. Dancing in rage.
Dancing like a demon,
Or dancing away all my demons.

It's dug deep into my back, fingers pulling at my spine,
Making me move like a marionette.

From the dark shores of the inner world arms spread like a condors wings.
Diving in a pool of molten lava,
Boiling in my belly.

Consumed by passion from the inside out.
The fire in my veins flowing through to muscle.
Eyes the burning coals of fire within.

I have always known you.
Within I see the black feathers slide through your veins.

At the tip of each feather a single drop of blood.
An aimless wound.

My father's eyes.
My swollen fist from battering the wall.
No pain, no more.

Curl those fingers to the sun.
Dig your feet deep into the earth.
Plant yourself.
Cling to the ground and hold on.

This life is gonna roller-coaster us into the unknown again.
How many lashes can you take?
Getting harder every day, a thicker skin every day.
Getting more bitter every day.

Want to make a new book.
Bind it, nurture it,
Make it into a beautiful thing.

To make a heart feel the warmth of the earth, and to taste the sweetness of life.
Time now to step again,
Forward into the blue healing light.

But these black barbs on the chains lashed to my skin.
Black nails through my feet to keep me from that first step.
So I gotta take a deep breath,

And try and loosen these chains.

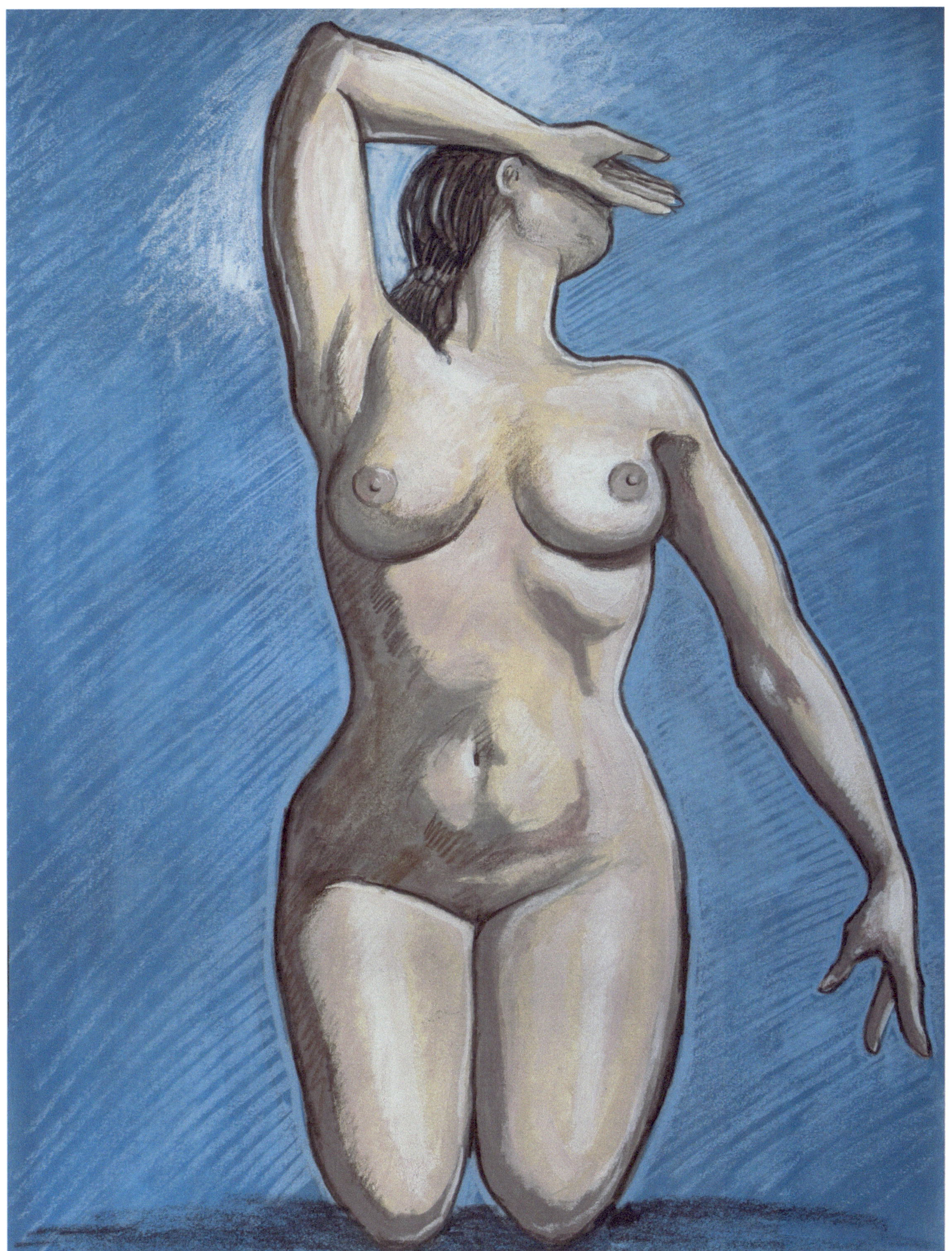

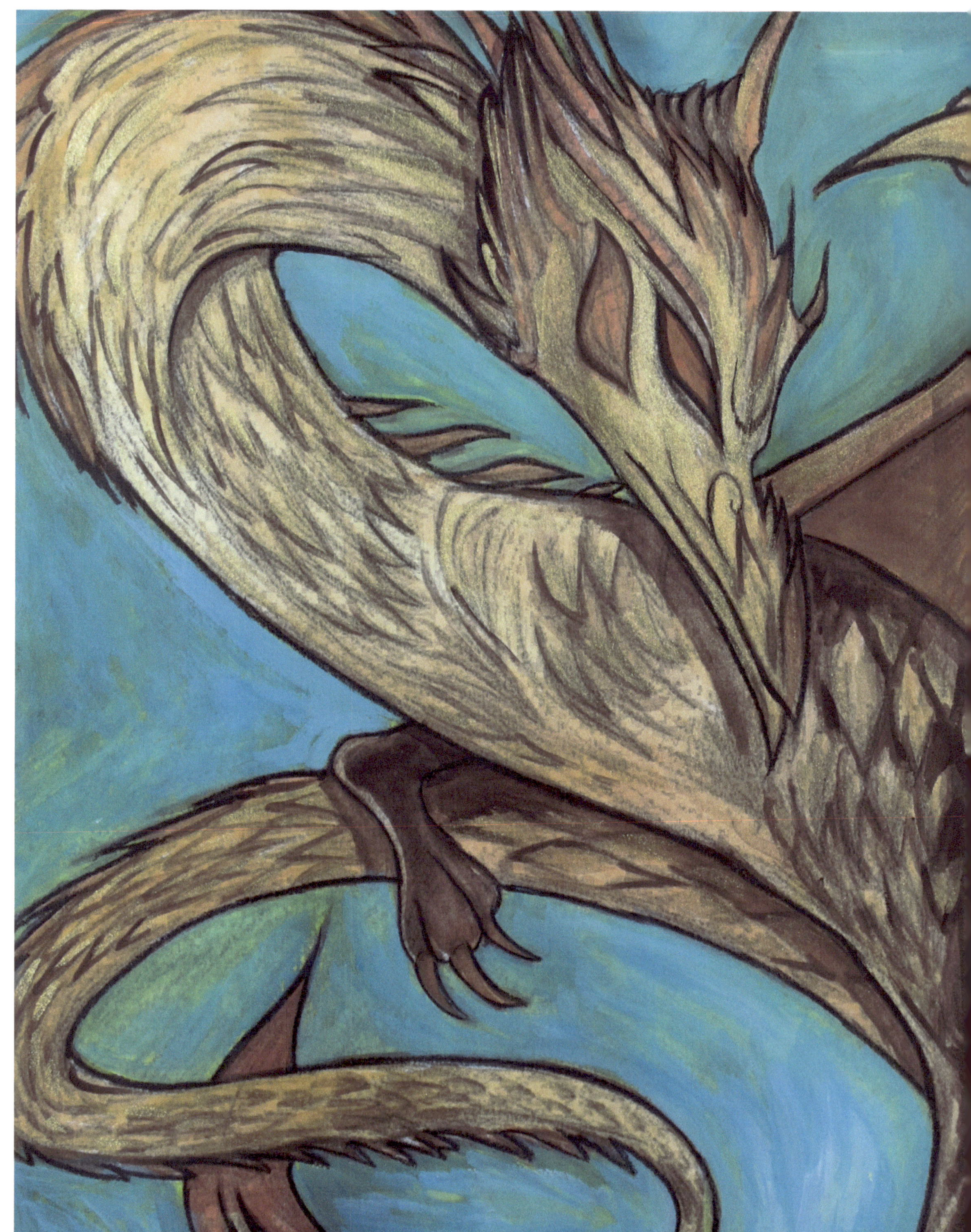

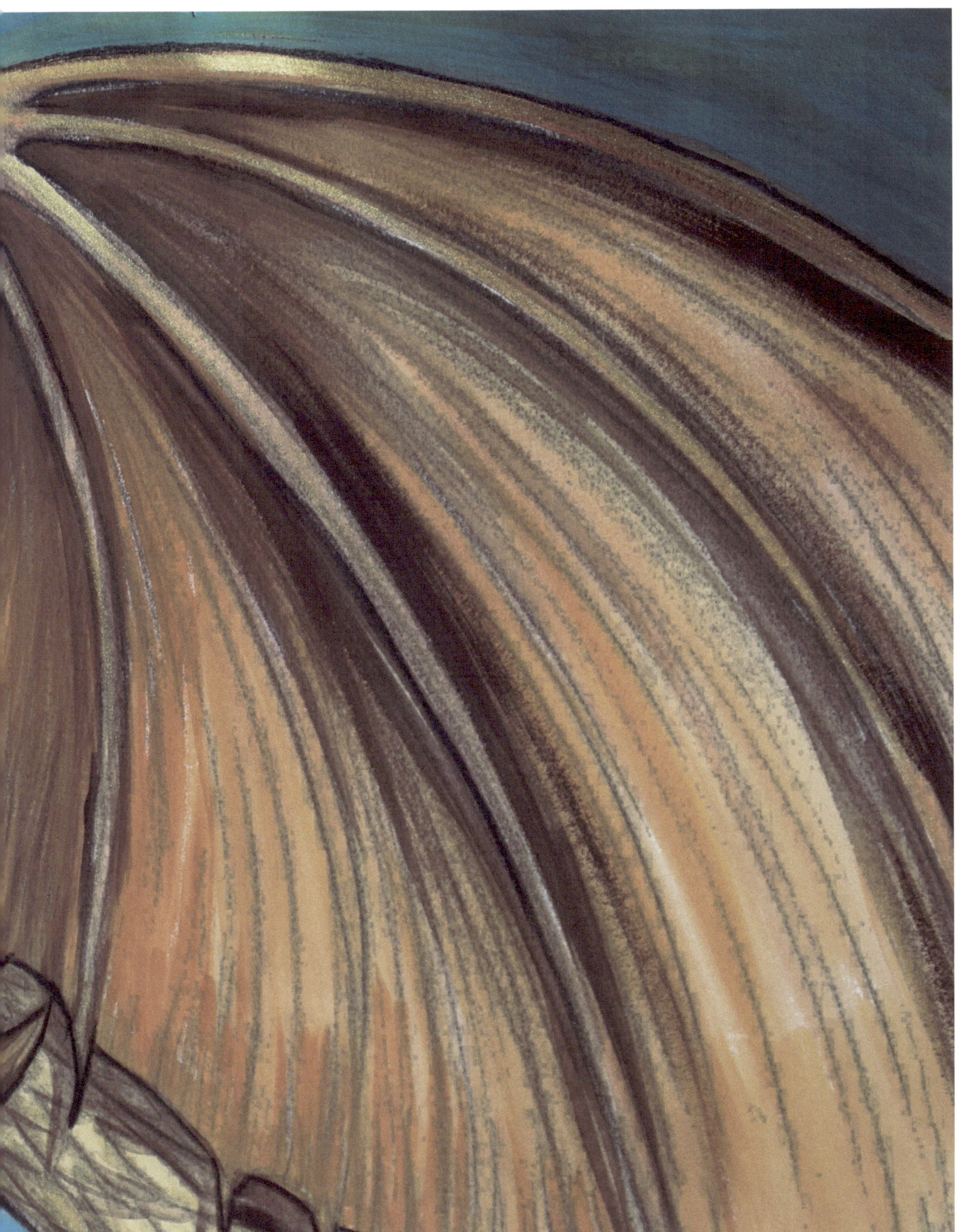

Clouds in your head

I feel I lost you
To the clouds in your head.
Pieces of the puzzle missing,
Or tumbling around.

All the stories turning,
Of what your heart is yearning.
It doesn't really matter to me.
You can be whatever you'll be.

We're trying to tell you
About reality.
But surrounded by the fantasy
It's to hard to see.

I hope you come back
From the land of the la.
But I'll be there wherever you are.

The soul is always learning
What the mind has forgot.
The ticking of the grand clock,
Is all the time that we got.

The years are calling,
We're all slowly falling,
But we still got a lot,

'Cause the beat don't ever stop.

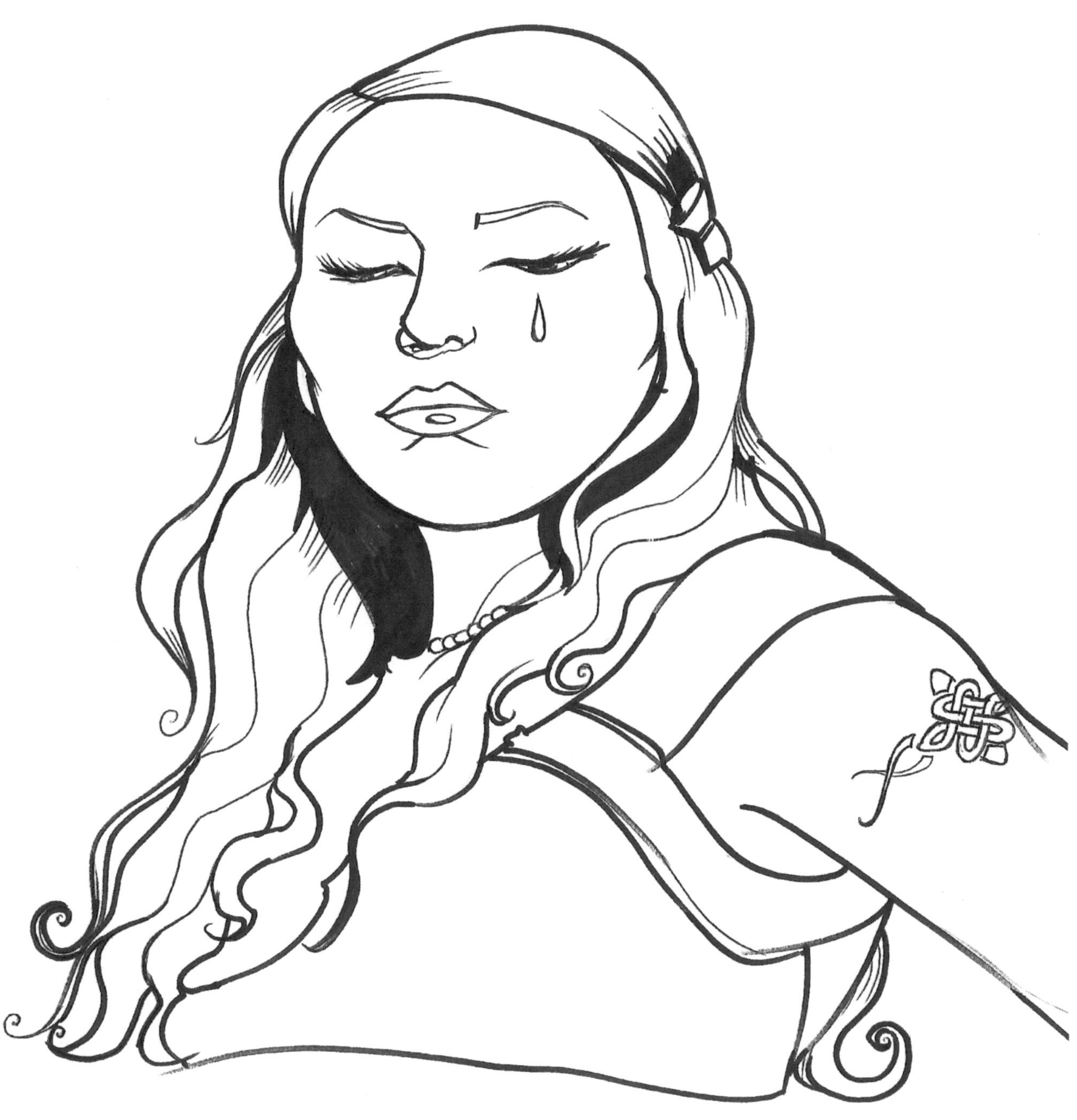

When I think of you this pain means nothing. You taught me to look to the beauty and light in this universe for my inspiration,
Rather than to pain.

I channel that, Create from it.
Mirror that beauty back to the universe.

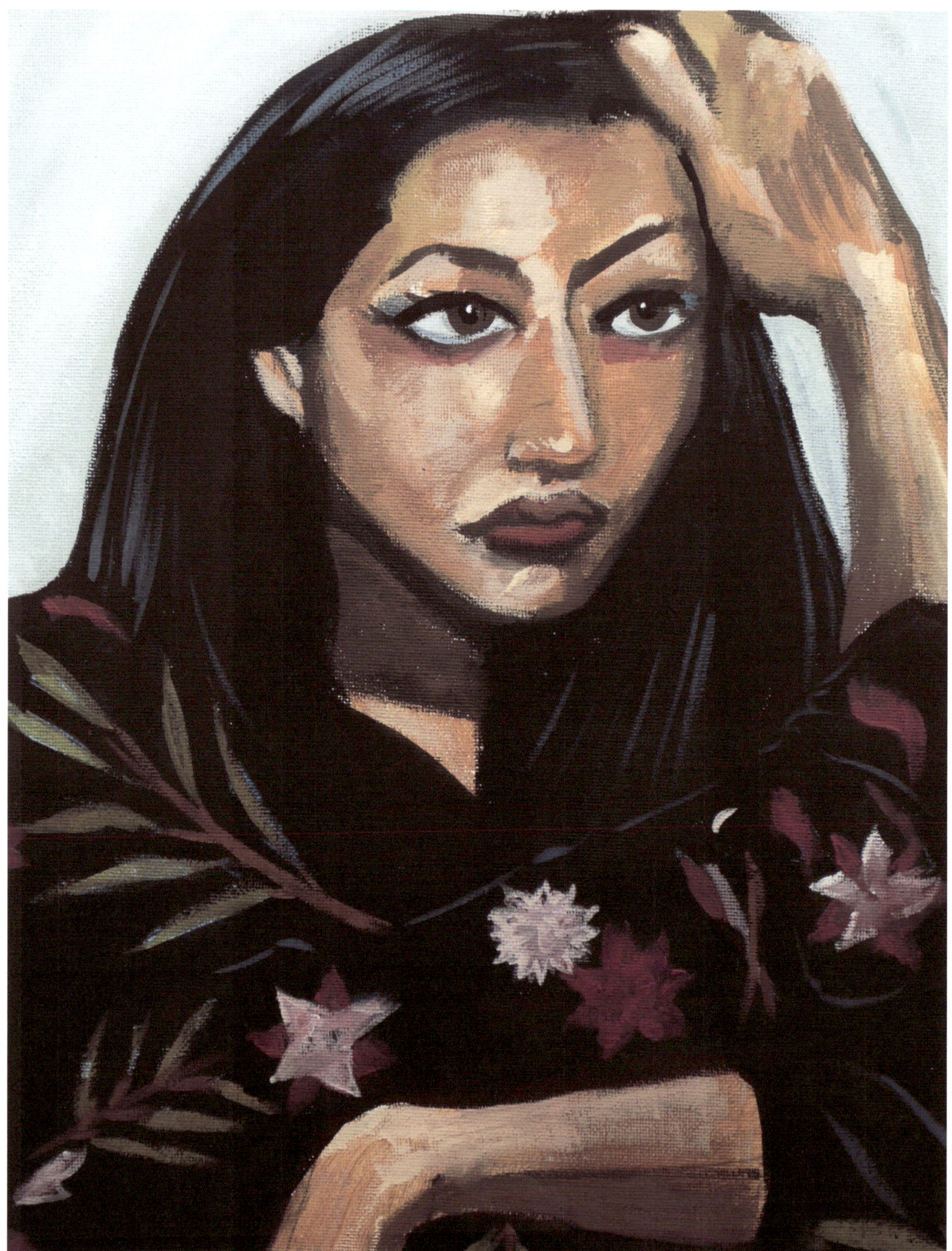

Find your voice

We were there when you found your voice,
You're a superstar.
No matter where you are.
It's all there when you make the choice.
You can rise so far,
No matter where you are.

Such a beauty
And you're leaving.
Will we see you again?

Your name in lights,
Tearing up the night.
You gonna turn some heads,
You're gonna make it!

Just when you think it ain't happening,
Somethings gonna change.
Just when you're feeling low,
You're gonna rise again.
It will never end.

The Laws of Attraction

Drawn together
See the future open up to me,
Wouldn't believe how far I've come
Until these visions seen.
I float through the shadows,
Searching for a place to be.
Down I spiral,
Drawn to your gravity.

Your Heart,
Your Mind.
You're All,
I desire.

All that I prayed for
Is coming up roses today,
Cause I've learned from you
Not to care what other people say.
Every night.
All I ask for is to find the right way to be.
Piece by piece,
The answers start coming to me.

I'm Yours,
You're Mine.
Our Souls,
Intertwined.

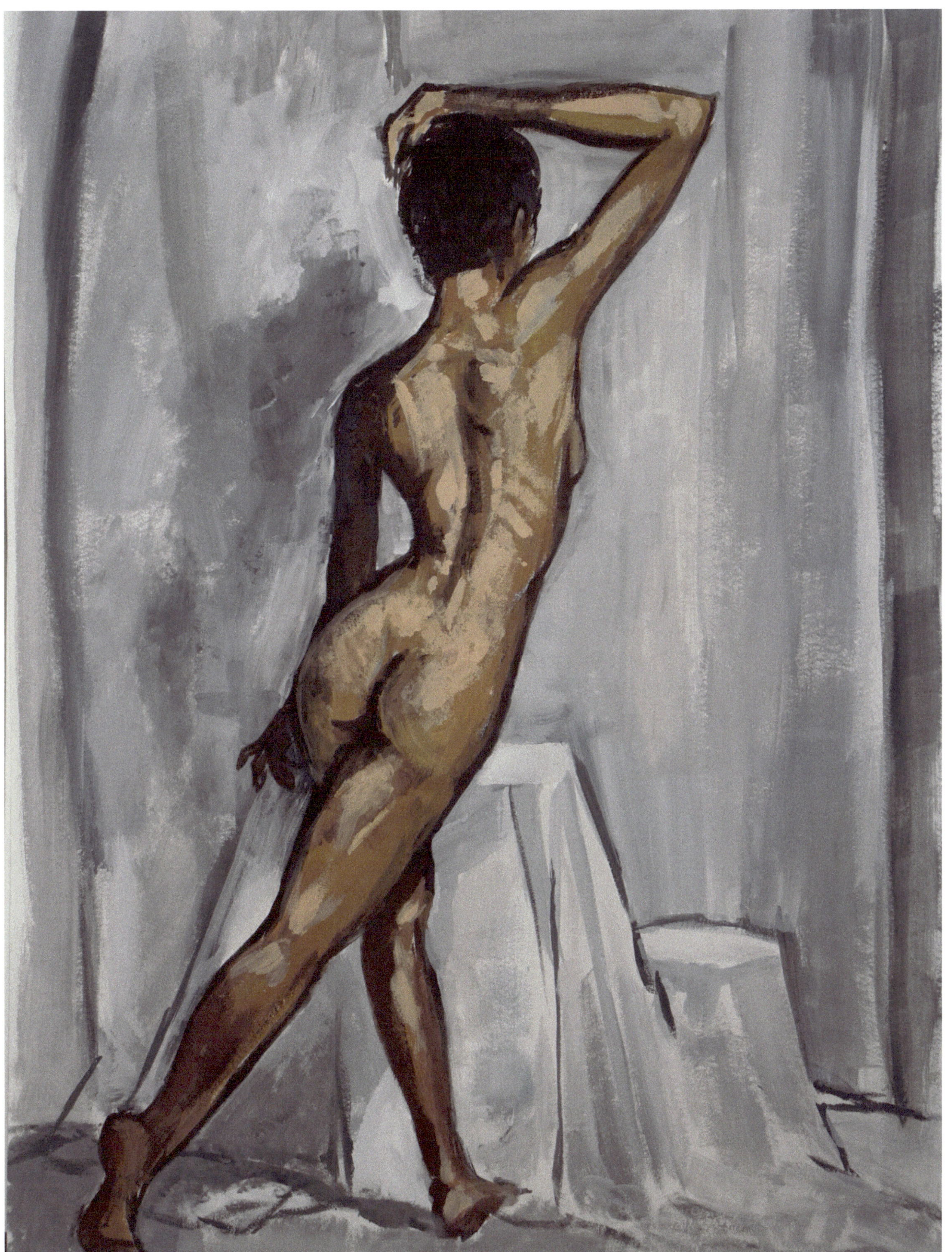

The Muse

She's my muse,
And I am the brush.
She's my sun,
And I am the moon.

And I don't wanna see you crying,
I don't wanna see you dying inside.
I wanna take your pain,
Cause I feel the same.
I wanna fight for you,
And keep you safe.

She's my friend,
Until my end.
With those green eyes,
My eyes see the same.

And I don't wanna wreck your heart,
So here I'll stay.
Don't let the shadows win,
Cause you are the light.

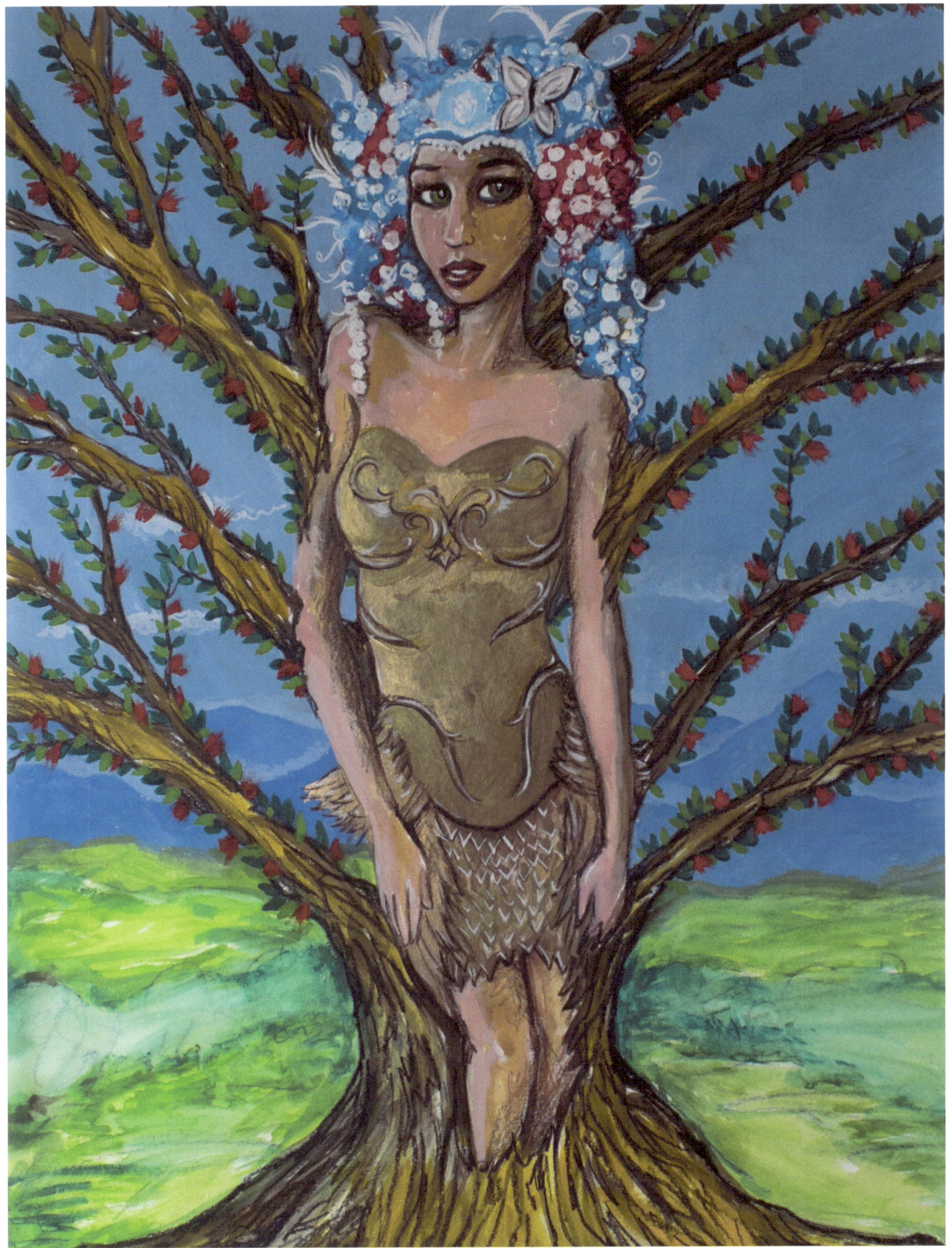

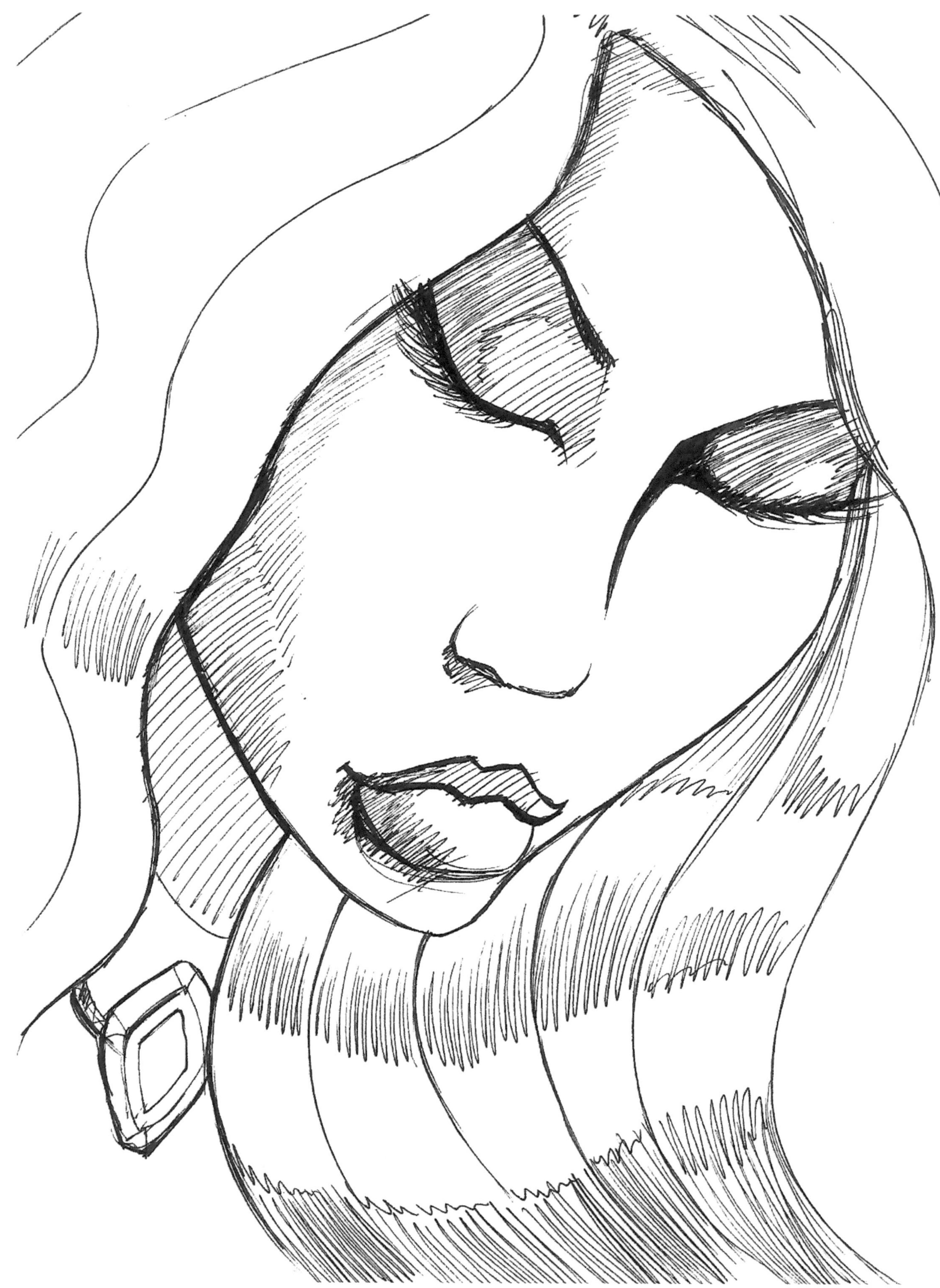

Weirdness

Animal crackers in my head.
Feeling cold,
My bones all turn to lead.
Unreal,
Unbelievable.
How concealed,
Not quite feeling low.

Spinal fluid is flowing through my veins,
I'm melting while I slay.
Unreal,
Intangible,
Reconstitution,
Now you're really low.

Animal farms surround the earth.
Swelling up and praising their real girth.
Unreal,
Unbelievable.
Why do people do it?
FINE, I don't need to know.

I can see it,
Still cant believe it.
Eating our children,
And swimming against the flow.

The Spin

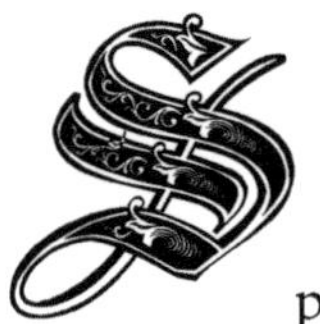
pin.
We'll be running around,
Bouncing off the walls in this one shot town.
With shoes that are falling apart,
And a dream that got stopped at the start.
In a spin.

This room just won't stay still,
My visions getting blurry and I'm feeling ill.
Thinking "...is this really the price?
This high just might take my life".

My lungs begin to drown in themselves,
I'm filling up with poison and destroying my health.
Just trying to run away,
From the darkness in every day.

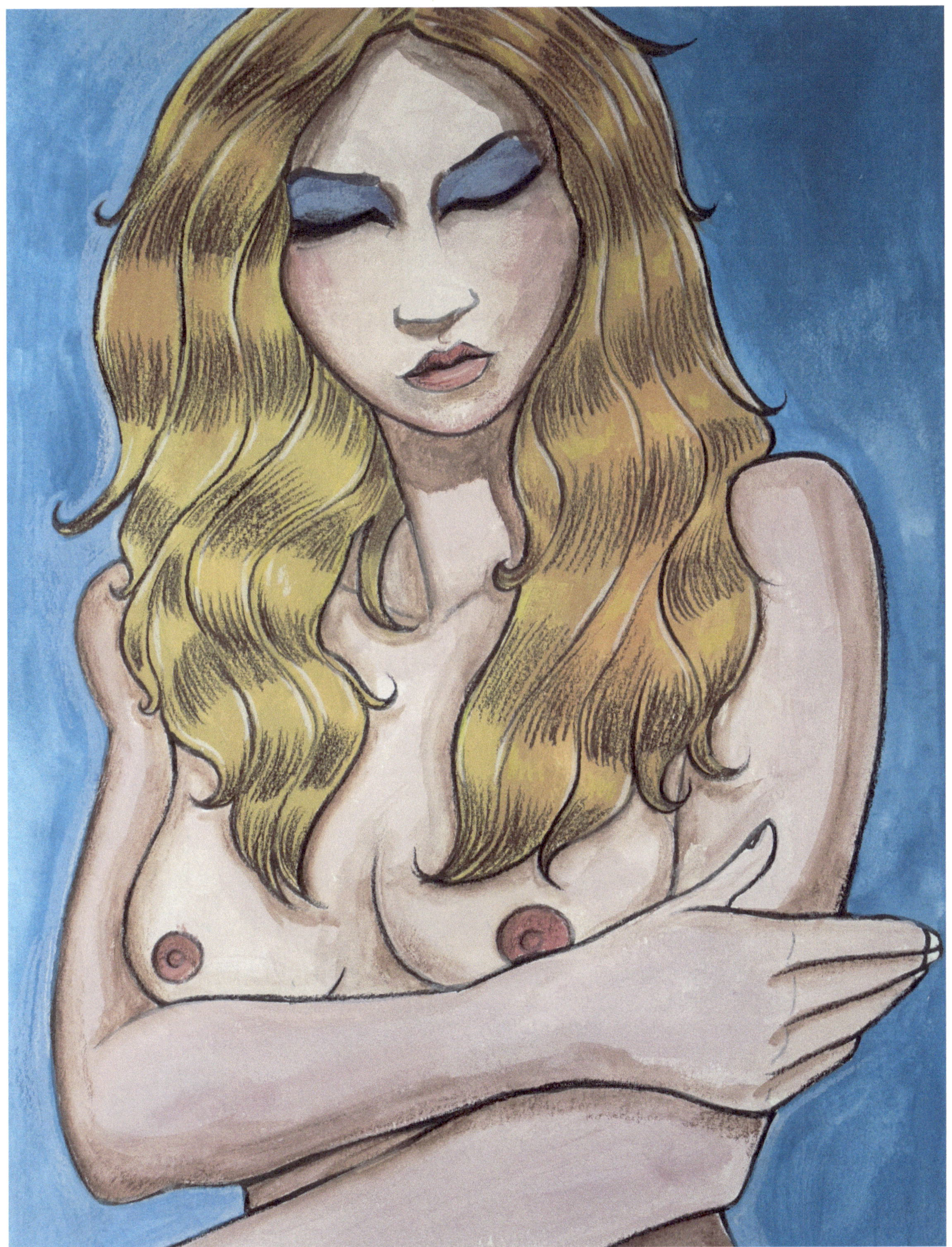

I thought of her three times today,
Each time it moved me.
Firstly came a vision of the young girl in a limpid pool of blue.

Every man's dream and a creature of infinite loveliness.
The lover.

Secondly an older woman.
Youth passed by but still powerful wit the strength of a glorious mind and spirit,
A boundless energy that only comes from a pure heart.
The mother.

Lastly as an old woman,
Her age was shown mostly by the touch of her hands.
Her skin whispers as it brushes my face and murmurs comforts of safe places,
Where the dark things can't reach me,
And sings songs of cultures long forgotten.
The elder.

The three aspects of fate personified.
The lover would collect the essence of creation,
The mother weaves it into the patterns of destiny,
And the elder cuts the threads of peoples lives,
And joins them as things come to pass.

All of these women carried themselves with an air of quiet dignity and infinite patience.
All showed the quality that told me they were you.
That was grace,
In your infinite grace and quiet patience we will revel.

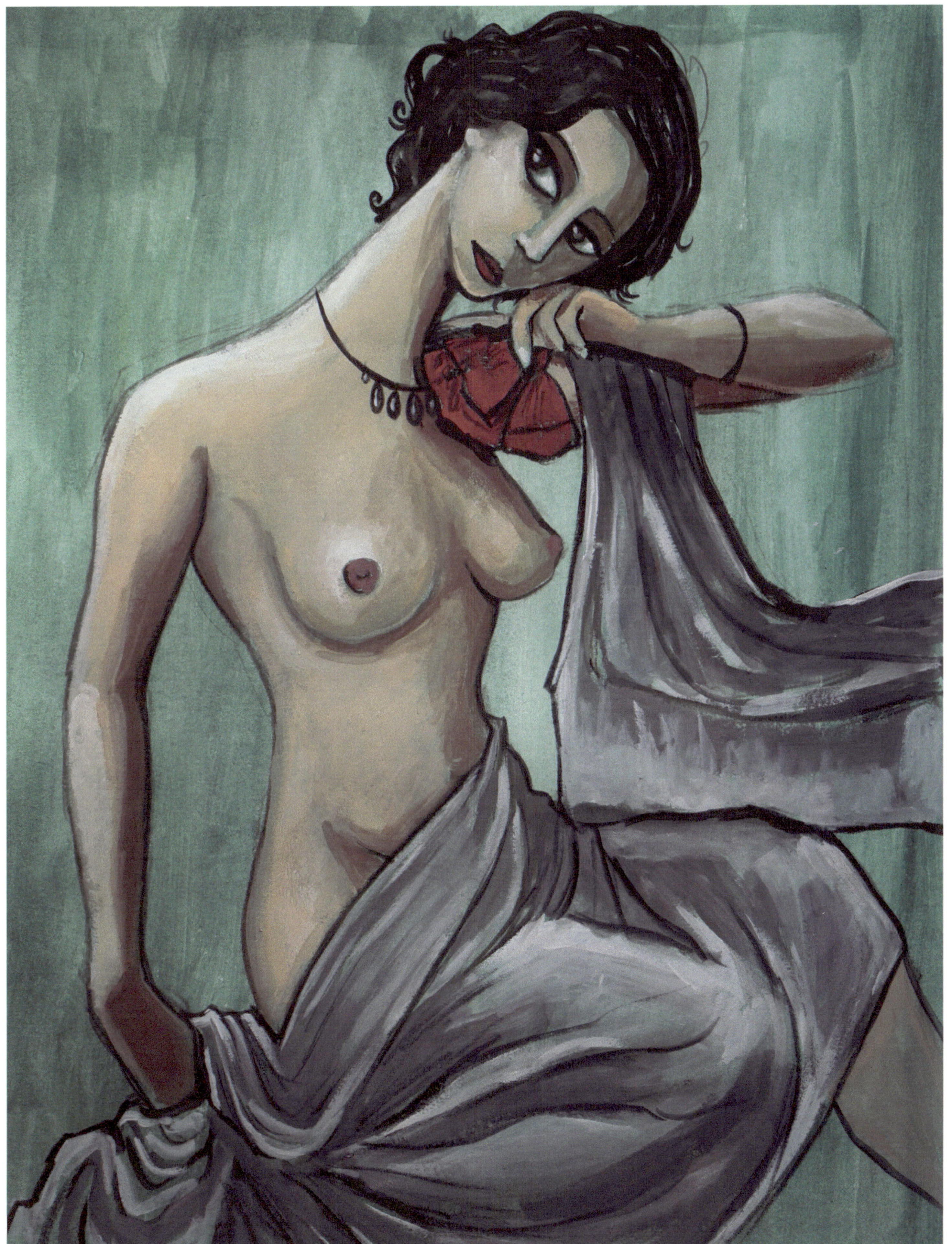

Trans-humanist Overlords

Oh, seemed a little bit odd to me,
How they seem to plan out our destiny.
Trans-humanist overlords,
Shaking off the trappings of an immortal god.

In time,
Will we all be machines?
In time,
Will computers start to breathe?

We find all these wanna be gods.
But they don't really know what they want.

01001100 01101001 01100110 01100101

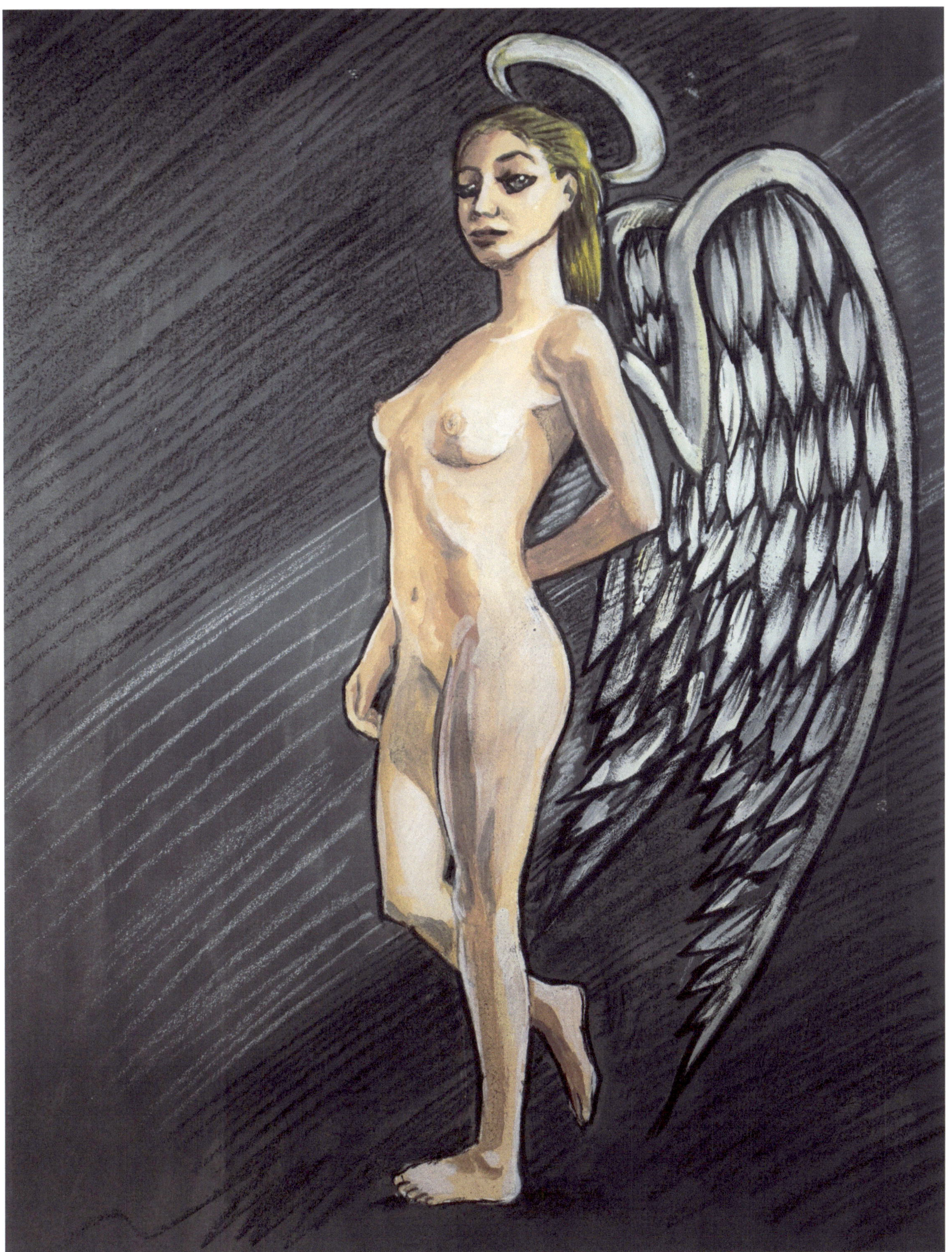

Webs

For a thousand years still been sitting here,
With you in my minds eye.
Only to find you gone.

For a thousand more I'll be waiting here,
As I watch your shadow fade away.

Still this house is your home,
But you're gone.

Never thought that I would be sitting here,
Watching time slip away.

Still fire keeps burning on,
But you're gone.

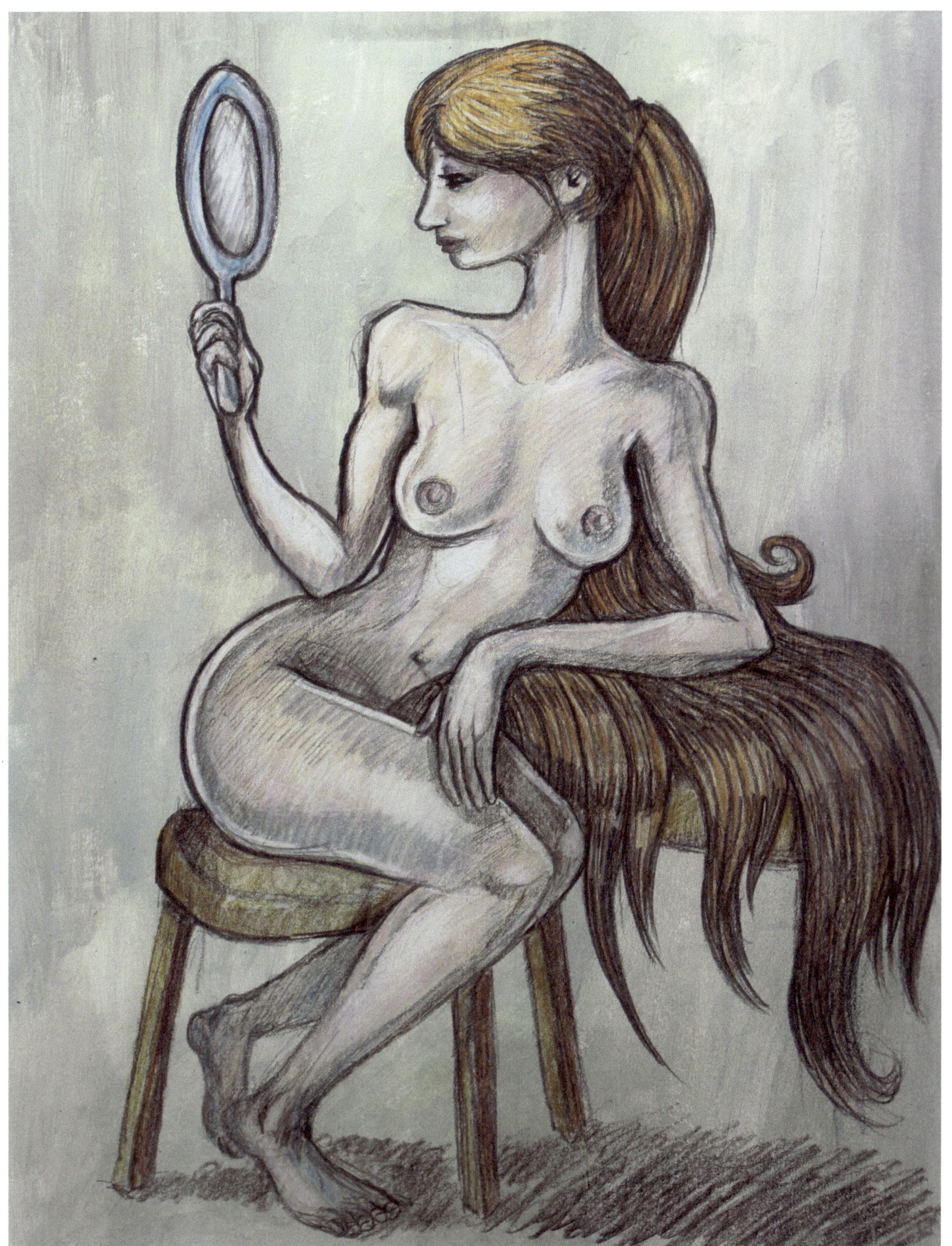

Blackness

Woke to find the blackness in my eyes,
...And killing on my mind.

Never thought this drug would take me this high.

I found out all your stories are getting old,
And the endless lies are losing hold.
So as we break the blackness we'll see some light,
And end the long dark reach of this endless night.

Oh let me near your light,
Give me divine sight.
Stop taking up that fight,

Won't you let me near your light.

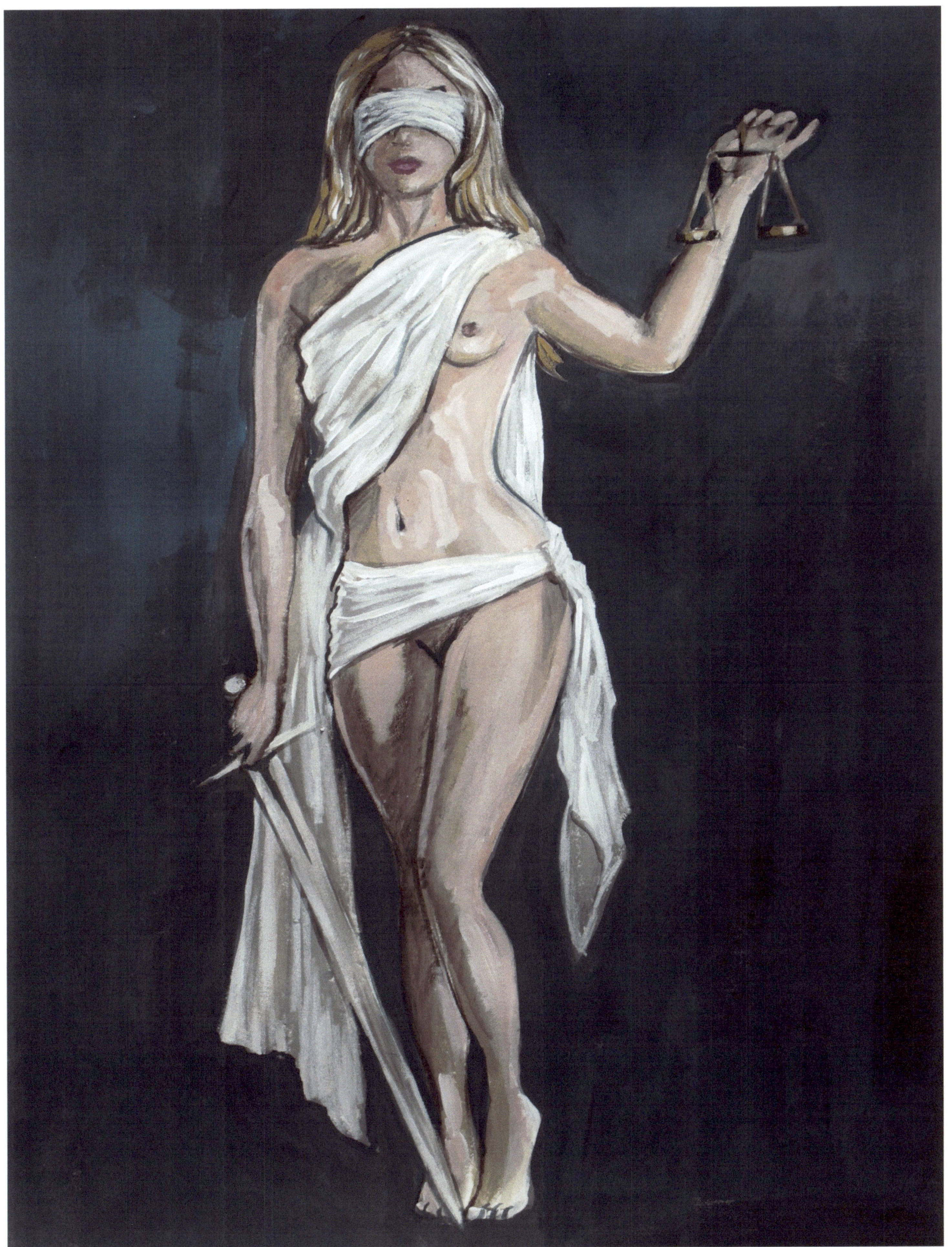

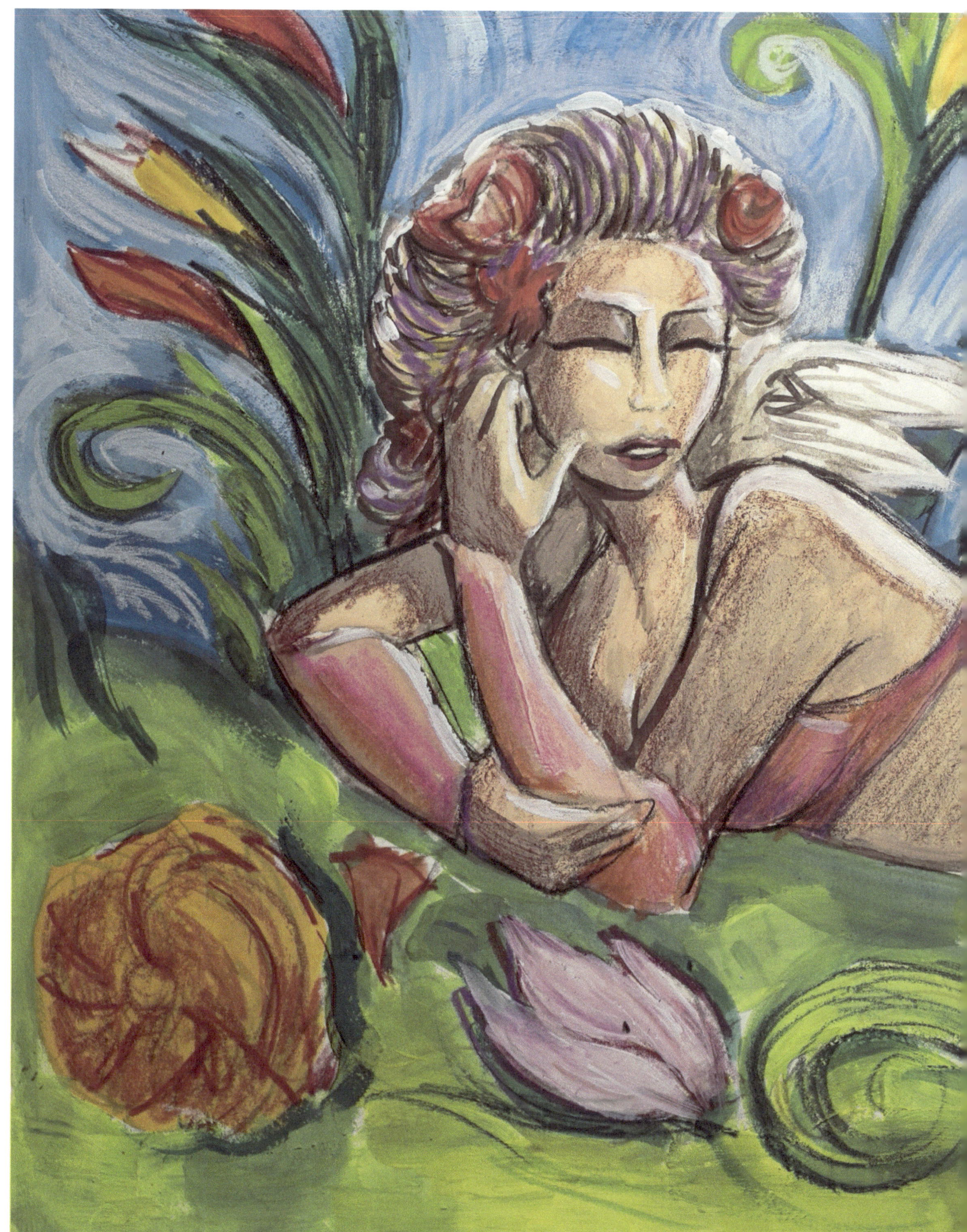

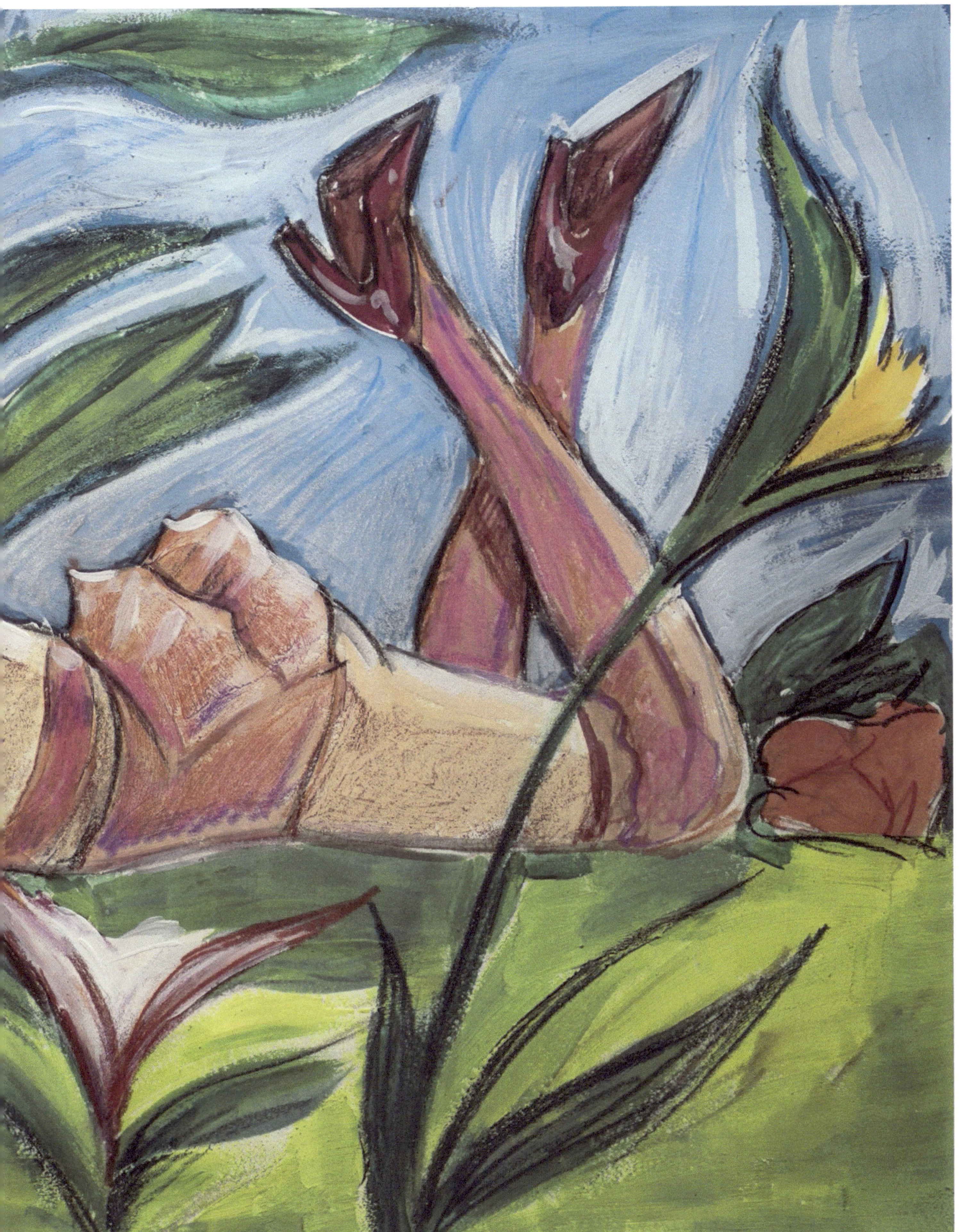

The Stepping

I stepped through the door,
To find the man that I was before,
But there's no turning back,
And no reason to relive the past.

The future holds more,
So pick your ragged bones from the door.
What makes you think your worlds so black,
When it's only fear you lack.

So when you cry out, as they hammer in the nails,
And it feels like the first time you fell.

Far reaching fool,
Try to keep your cool.

And there's no one,
To pick you up and brush you off.
You don't need it,
You can grow up on your own.

So take a good look at all the things you've got,
Count your blessings cause they really mean a lot.
And just tell them that you're a simple boy,
That takes pleasure from the things that mean the
most.

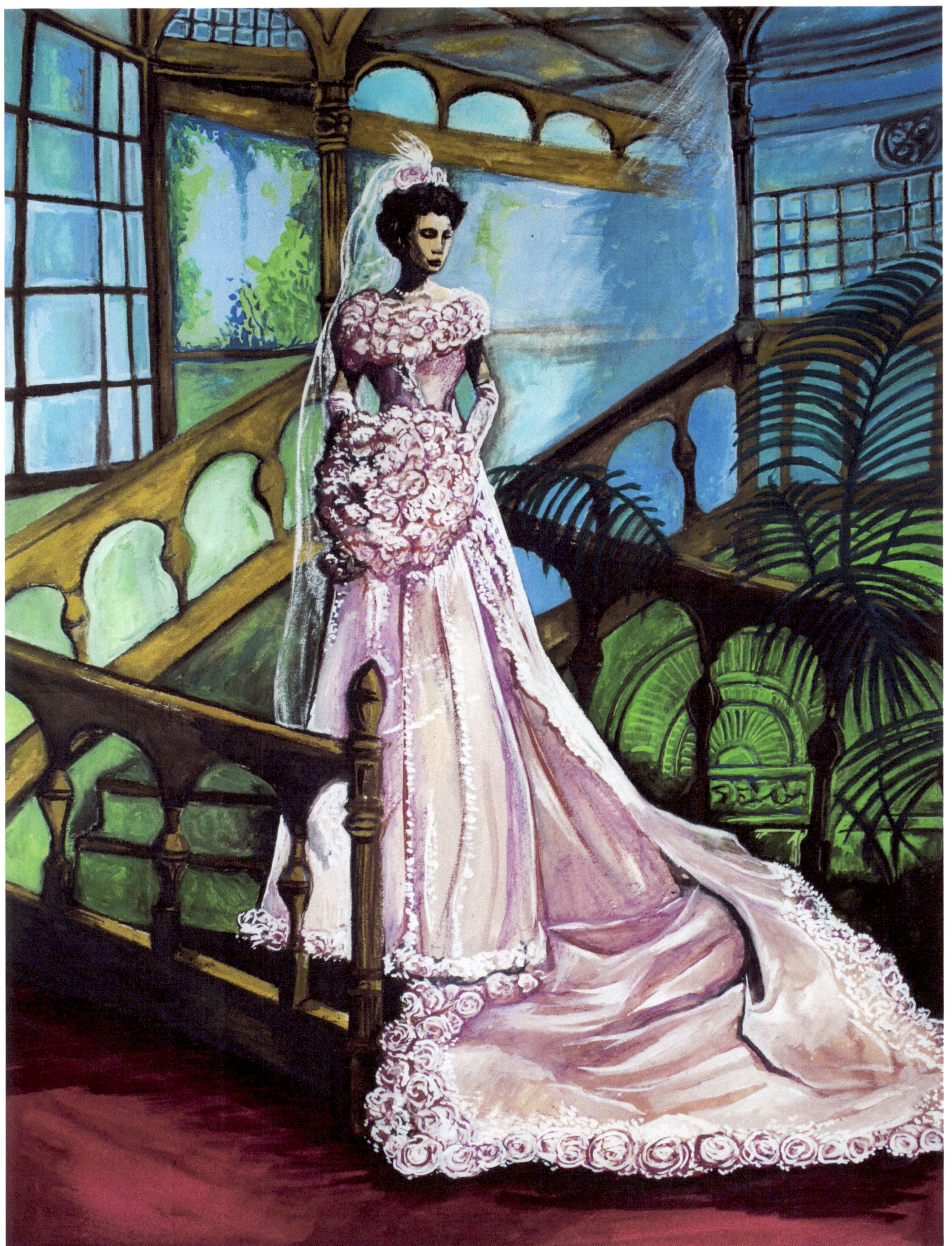

Drug Dazed

What you sitting on baby?
And what grave did you steal it from?

Metaphor it all,
The symbols dance before my eyes,
Drug dazed.

Wile fools us all and he just lay on his back.
Doctor donut couldn't see
The sugar that they lack.

Shanon Hoon's a hero,
So why does no one know his name?
Something about the outset,
And the cruel elusive fame.

Wile fools us all,
And he just lay on his back.
Doctor donut could see
The sugar that they lack.

...Or do they lack?

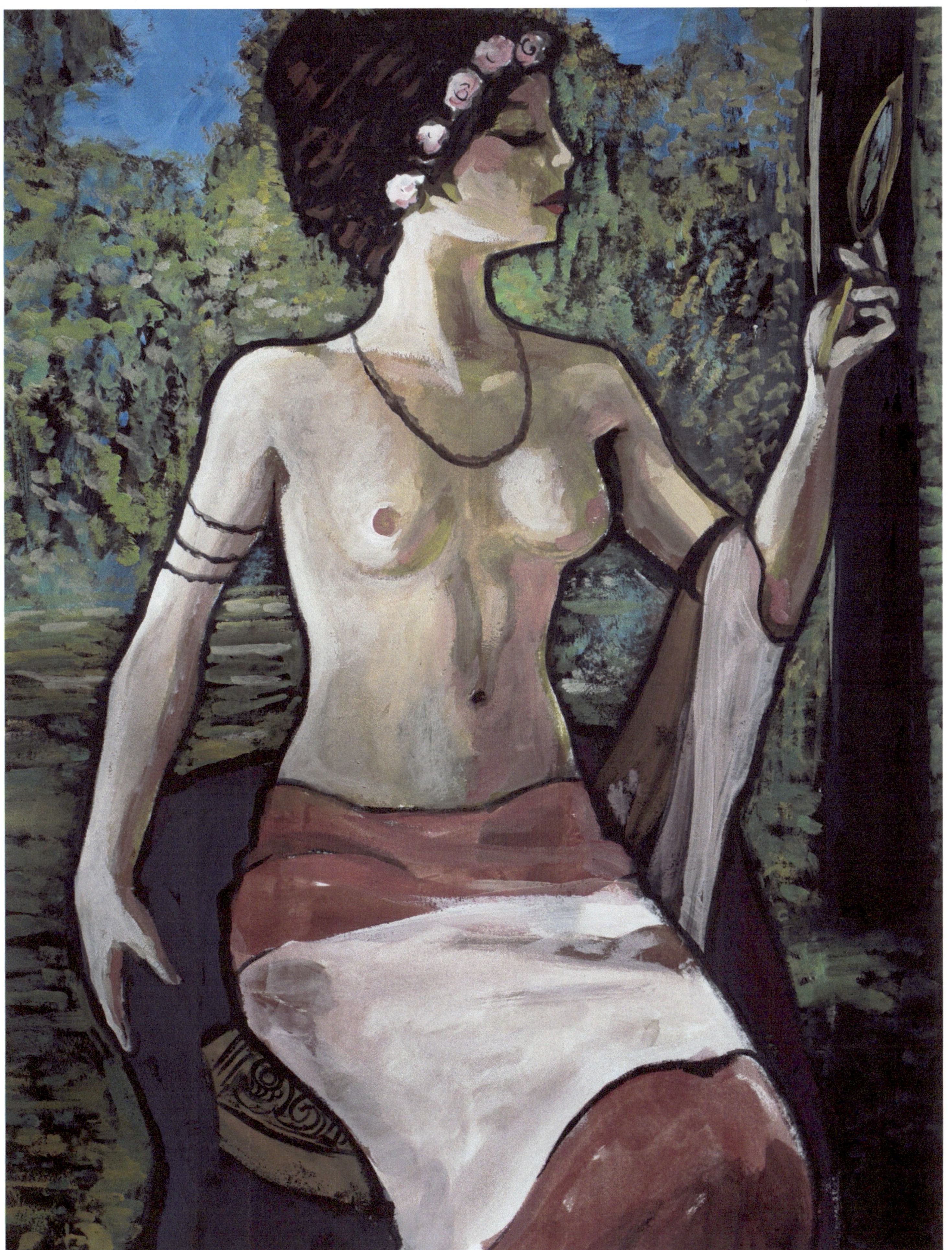

Shadow Proclamation

So your illness has begun,
Creeping past the sun.
This endless love sickness.

When you can only think of her,
And the life you had before.
These shadows blocked your vision.

Can you feel this freedom without her?
Without her memory?

With these chains at your feet,
Can't break free of her memory.

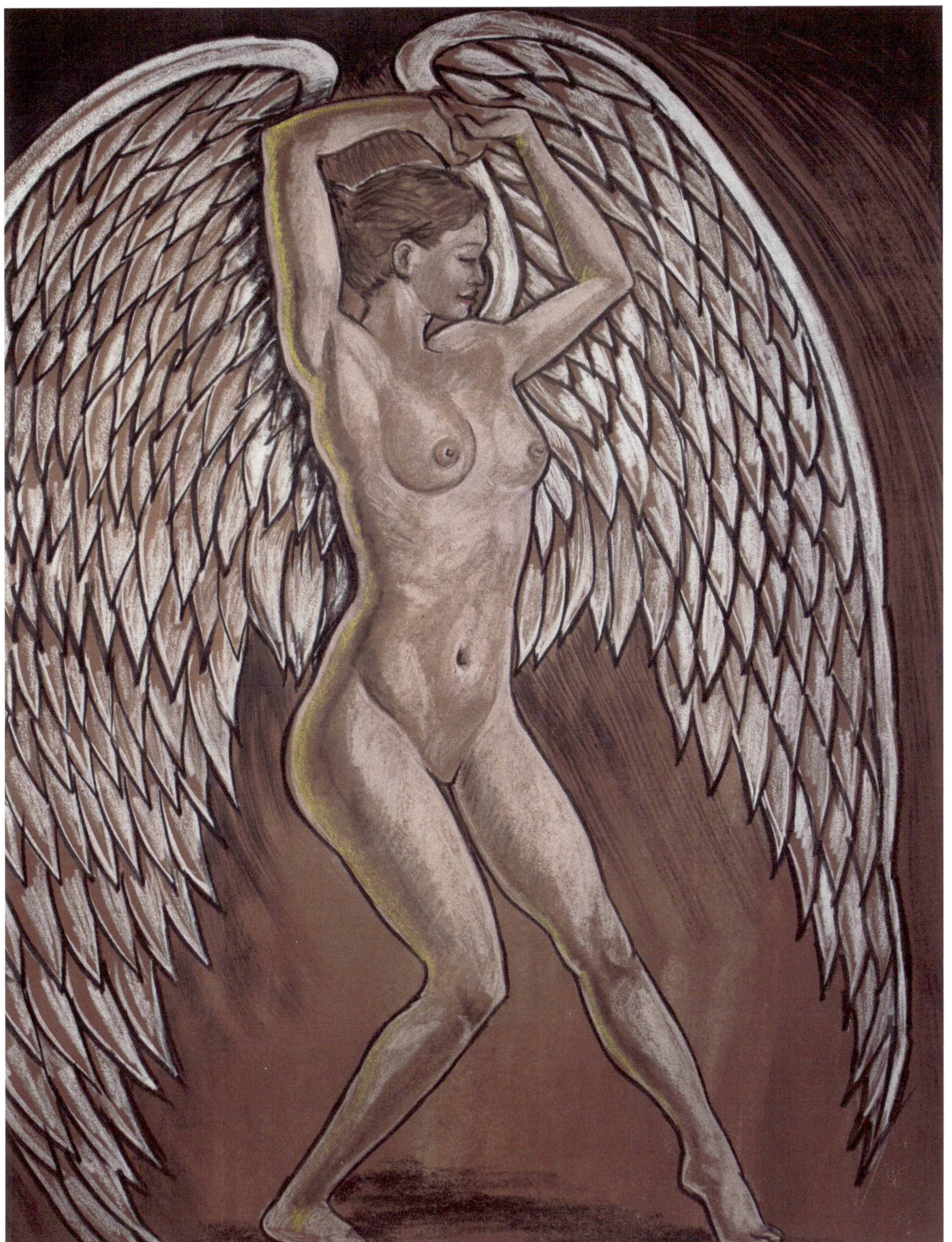

Tiamat's Death

Came down into the ocean,
All alone in a dusty world.
With no sun and no order,
And no god for her to turn.

Gotta live every day,
That was all she could say.
With all the fiends she could play.
As long as God was there to pay.

Marduk came upon her,
With a plan for laying her down.
Took blade then he split her,
She succumbed without a sound.

She is the sea,
Queen of calamity.

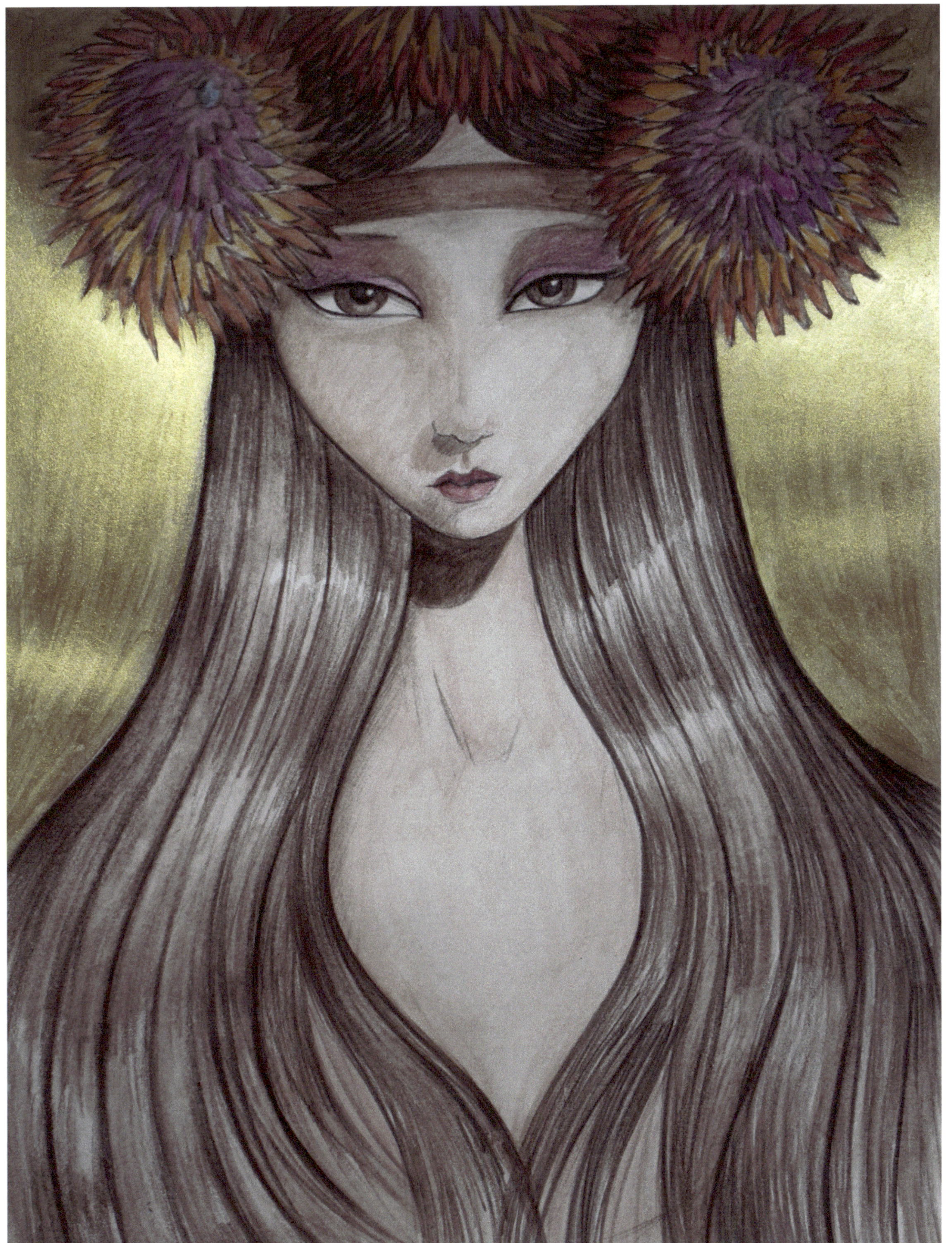

Mobius Strip

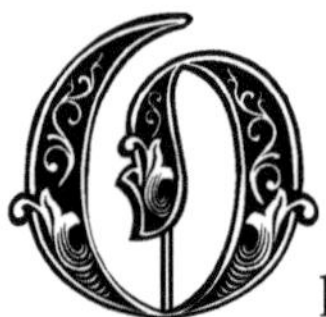h, I want one like her I said.
But no,
If truth be told,
I want to be like her instead.

Help me alone my thoughts scorned.
Help me alone to where I go.

My mysteries awakened from their gaze.
I dropped it all from staggering in this rage.

Can't hold this rose,
Mobius strip unfolds.

Time never called my hands home,
Just picked my bones and scattered them on the floor.
Misery has been a nice place to hide,
But now I heal and now I'm alive.

I gathered that I reached a port at shore,
But my feet won't land just rise above the floor.
I bend my head to listen to their veins,
Their blood can flow,
I try to do the same.

Spent hope for love,
Now I've had enough.

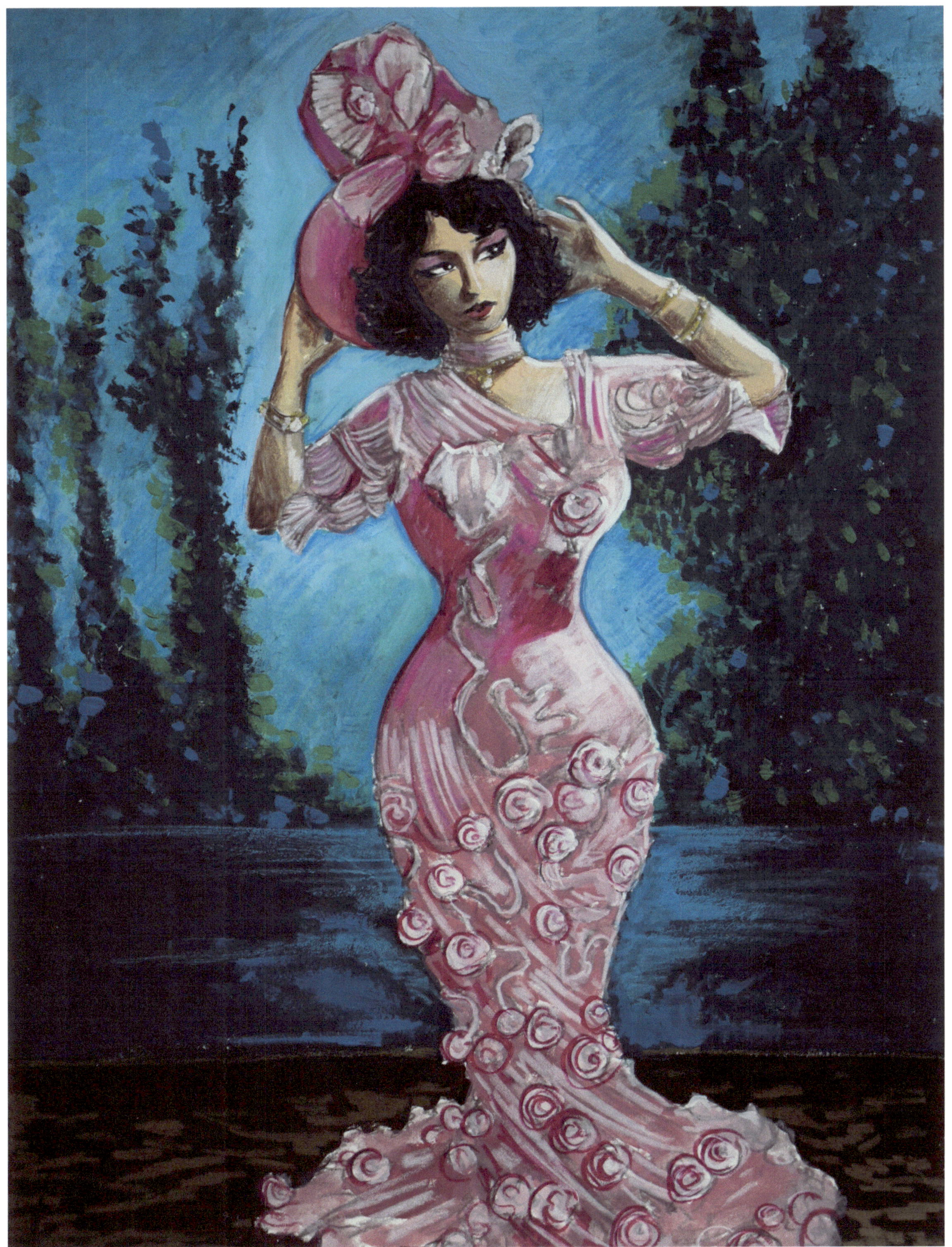

Shock the Lamb

Slow dancing with a corpse,
Bloods my only sport,
But I'm running out of chain.
So I scratch these walls,
Searching for a flaw,
But I'm running out of chain.

You had to ask,
I'm the evil one.
I'll show you god,
I'll douse the sun.
Your blackened eyes,
Won't stop this fire,
And your demise,
My only desire.

Waiting for my chance,
To escape this hole,
But keep running out of chain.
There's a crack I can see,
Just out of my reach,
But I've run out of chain.

Let me in this world,
Let me outta this trap.
Gotta shake shit up,
Gotta shock the lamb.
And shine a light,
On the sacred lie.

Or rot in hell,
With no free will.
I take this knife,
And end your life.
Your sacrifice,
My great device.

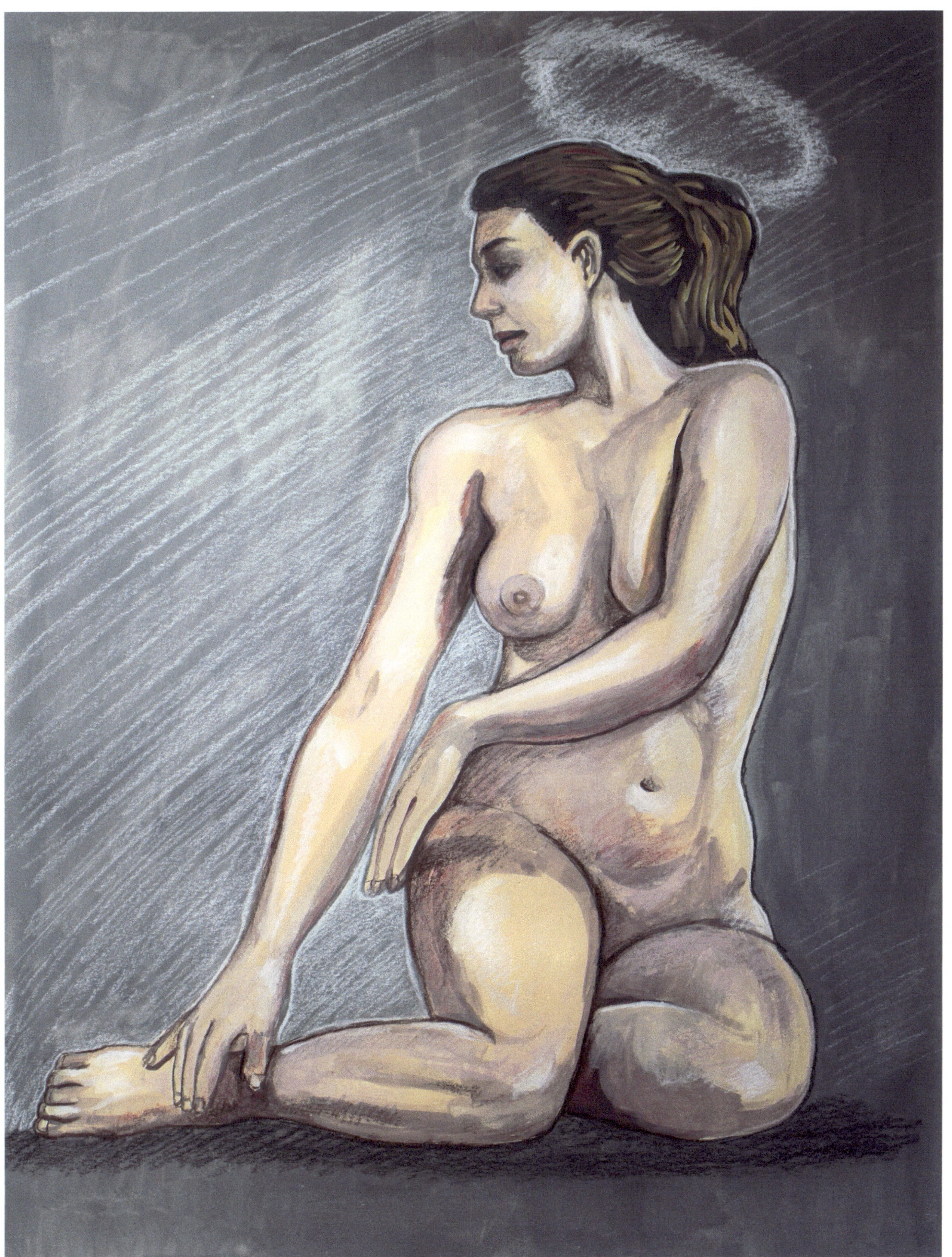

Gimme a cure doctor

Gimme a cure doctor from what ails me in my soul,
There's a shaking in my stomach and a fever taking hold.
There's a girl around the corner wants to put me in a hole.

Oh sweet angel,
You're making me sweat.
With all the possibilities,
Running around my head.
So your daddy's got a shotgun,
Pointed at my sin.
Gotta find a potion,
To fix the trouble that I'm in.

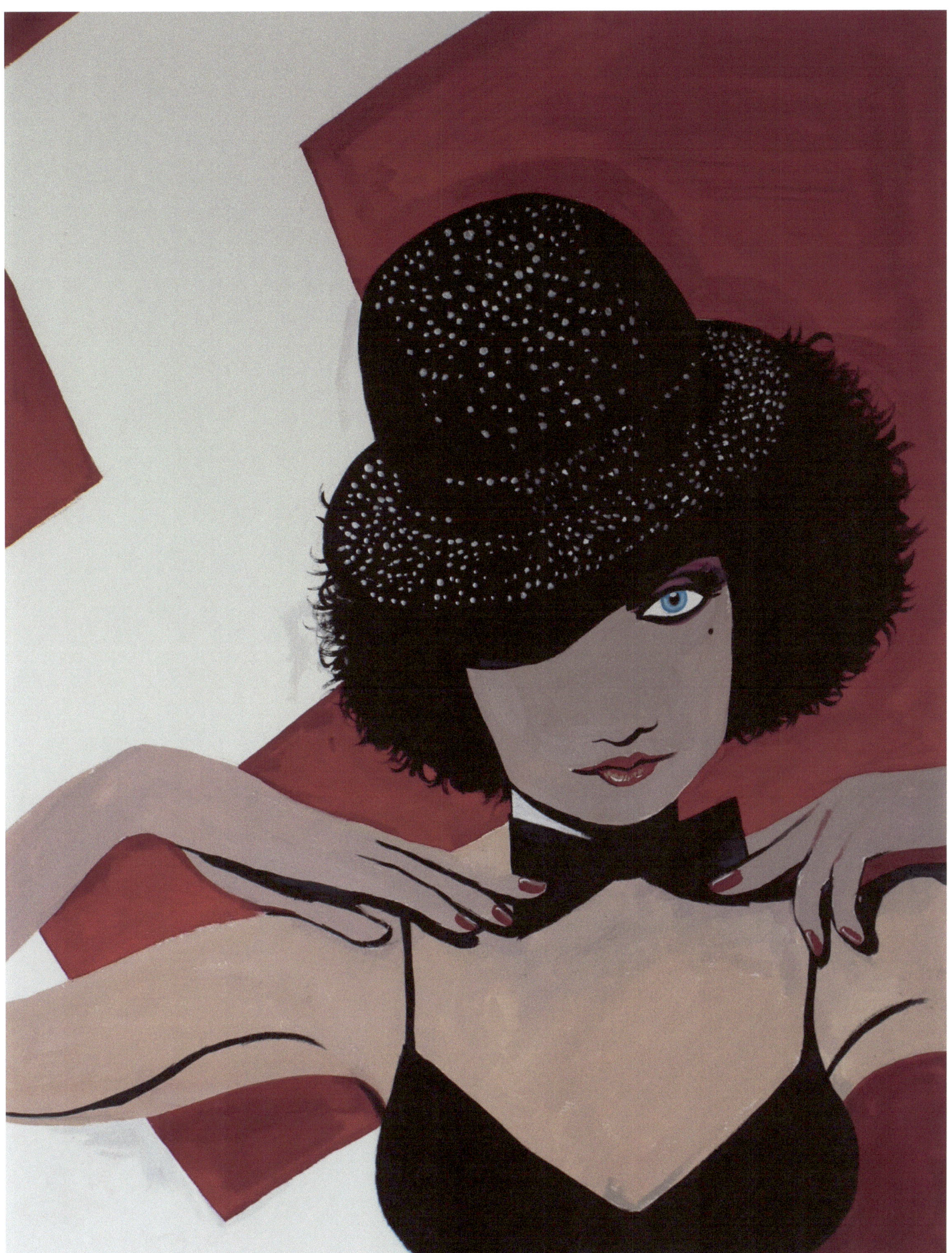

Grid

Drink the water from my cupped hand,
If you thirst if you need.
Smooth the cracked lips with a cube,
If you gasp if you need.
Candles shiver as you burn.
I recoil I join the ranks.
Souls that wither as they fall.
Hold your head to the sun.
Raise those lids and call again,
Oh my friend you drain.

When the hand between your shoulder blades falls away,
Can you stand without a prop?
Splint your spine wired and rivet.
Cantanker me you're strong enough.

Patch worked skin I suture you,
Butchered boy you're ragged Oh so.
Cauterize and bind you'll heal,
And most scars will fade.

With a reaper grin you lope away,
And I feel like a God.
Mainlined black knuckles congealed,
Needle back you bruise so sweet.

Clean the blade were done today.
Next I'll lick the mountains flat.
Motion brings the answers back.
You're my prodigy of pain.
Felt so good I'll sin again,
Just to start another wave,
And they'll quake with all your acts,
Fill me up with all I crave.

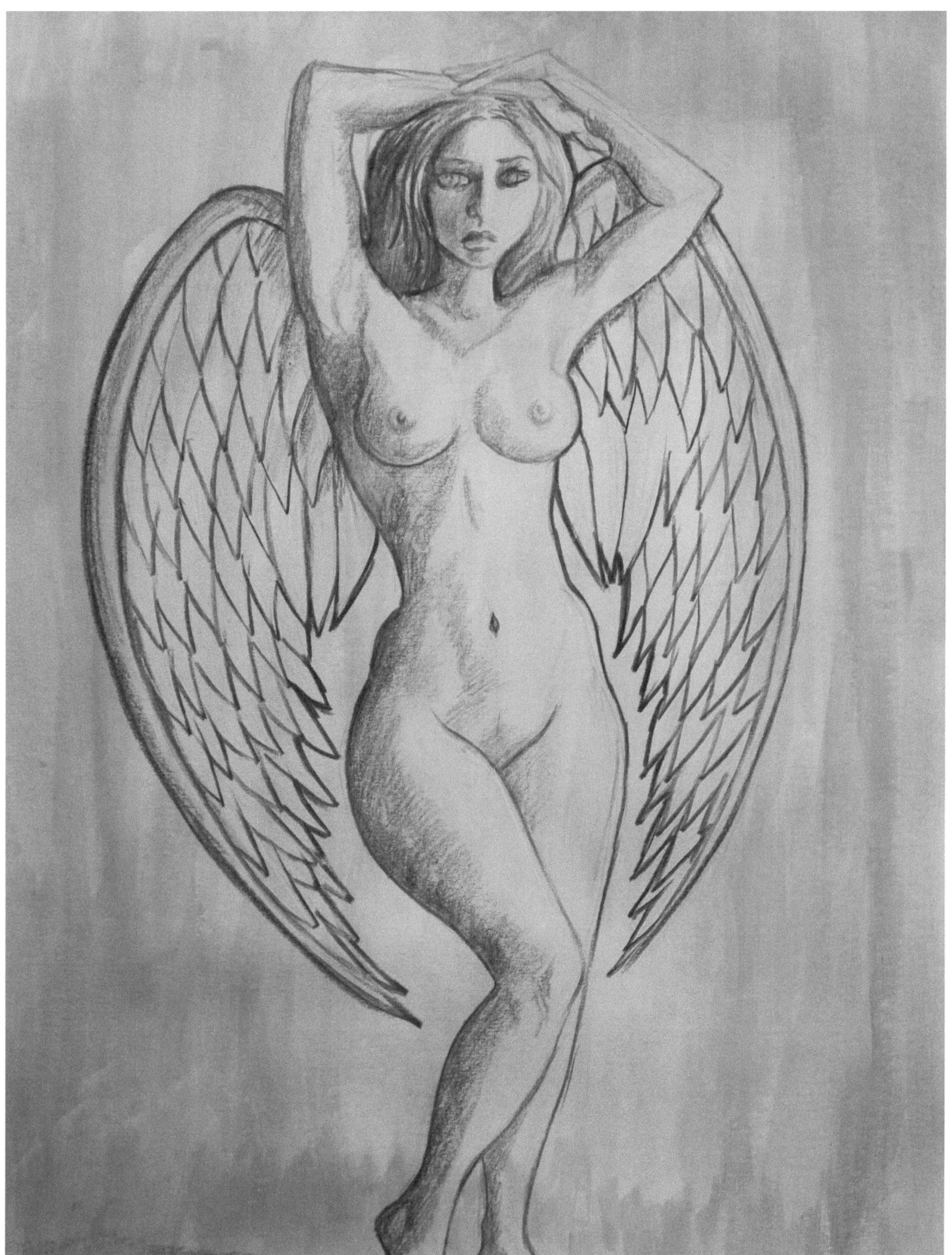

"I don't want to lose anymore of myself in you."

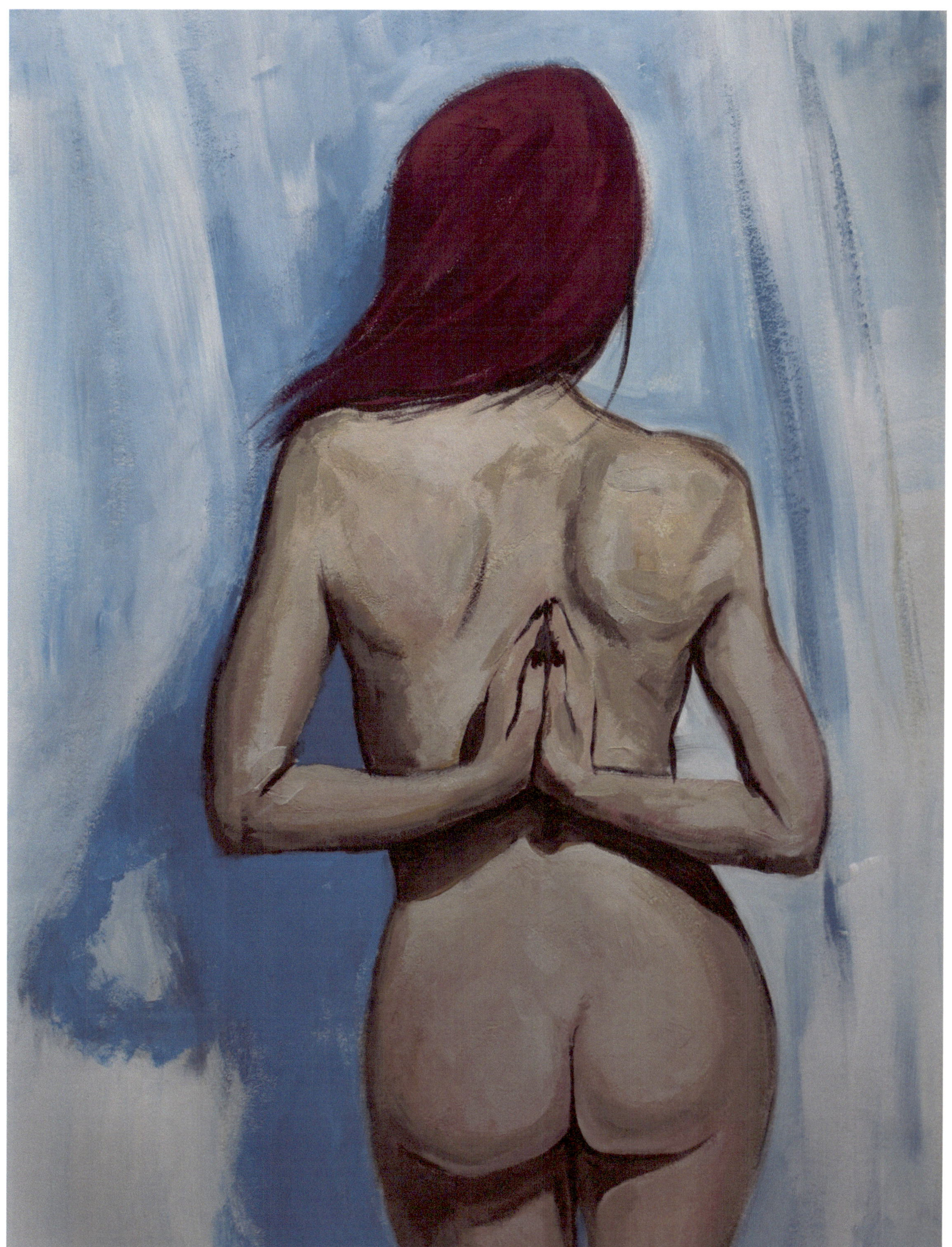

Four hundred years laid alone,
In old man willow.
His souls on standby,
Laid down by the saints for loving all his brothers.

He tries to shift the earth but he's been buried here too long.
All he tastes is dirt,
Twisted roots hold him down.

Bound by his hands and feet.
Lost in the ground.
There is a movement here,
In the leaves of old man willow.
If you lower your head maybe you can hear a sound.

Dried fingers claw through rotten leaves and clumps of mud.
Breaks through the surface in endless blood.

Lay your bones beneath the arms of old man willow.
Spiders weave your blankets,
Natures own lost and found.

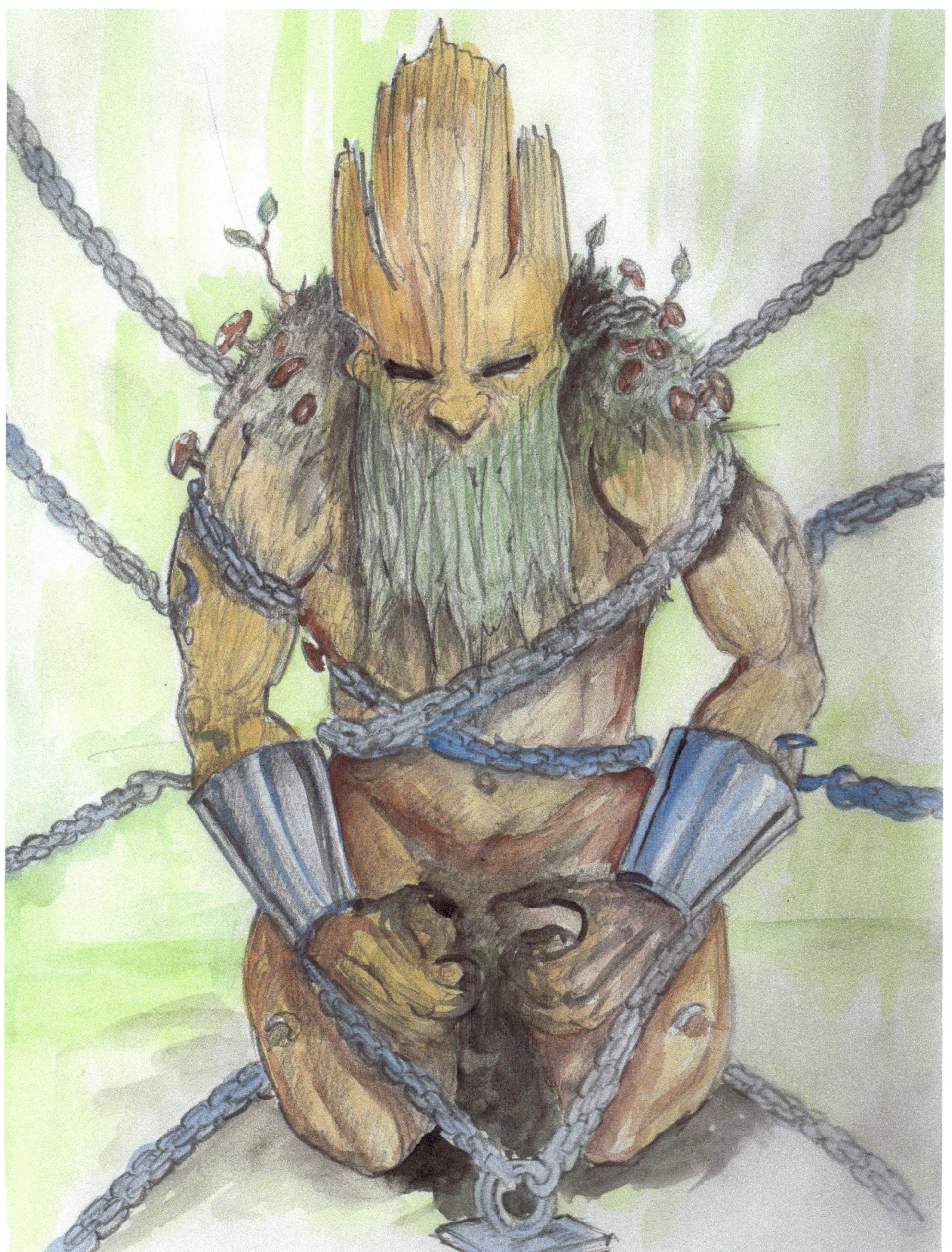

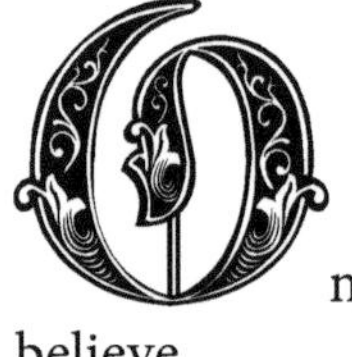nce the young man that was me, was foolish enough to believe…

I remember when you seemed so strong,
But then I saw him standing over you.
He clenched his hand but you didn't raise up,
You just turned and ran into the woods.
There was blood on your face,
But there was nothing I could do.

I just don't feel that way about you anymore.

There is no rain, just the sound of the leaves,
Brittle from the exposure to the sun.
Anger, Frustration, Loneliness, fear, and then nothing.
No feelings at all,
Just a horrible numbness and disorientation.
Just me and the wind, and an eternity of nothing.
Forever onwards.
Alone and one.
My world, as it stands, here and now.

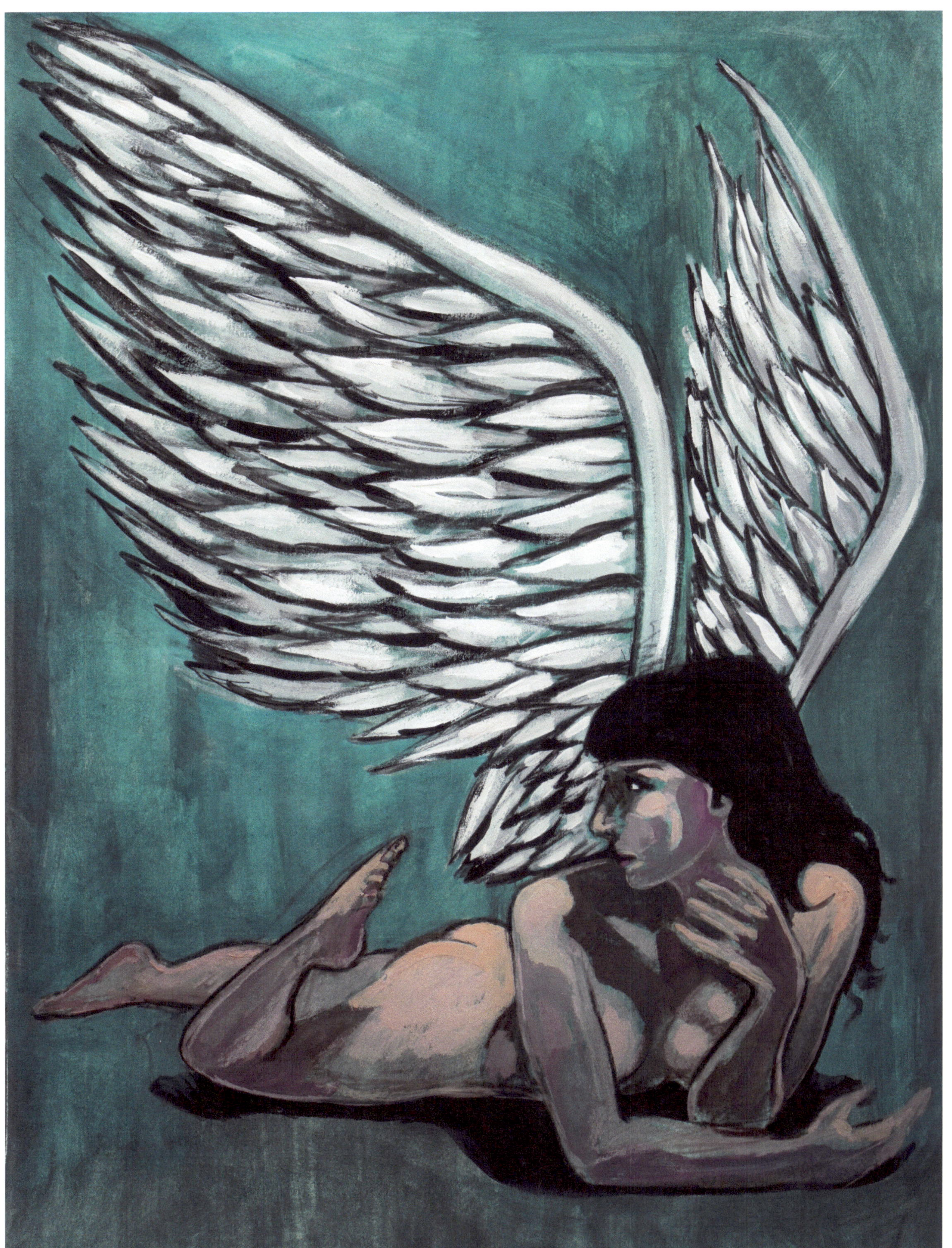

She's Brutal Beauty,
The fire in my veins.
Can drive me crazy,
Then she makes me sane.
I've been enslaved by her dark dominion.
For forever she's all I'm given.

She spreads her dark wings,
Into the night she flys.
Finding lovers and living in their sighs.
She'll make you tremble,
Bring you to your knees.
My Brutal beauty,
My queen I need to please.

A slave to darkness,
I'm burning from her light.
This caged catharsis,
From which my spirit fights.
I'll be her lover, her slave, her king, a god.
And reign in moonlight,
Ruling by her side.

My Brutal Beauty,
She visits in my dreams.
She made me shiver,
Turning blood to steam.
I feel her passion, from a thousand miles.
My Brutal beauty,
With her demon eyes.

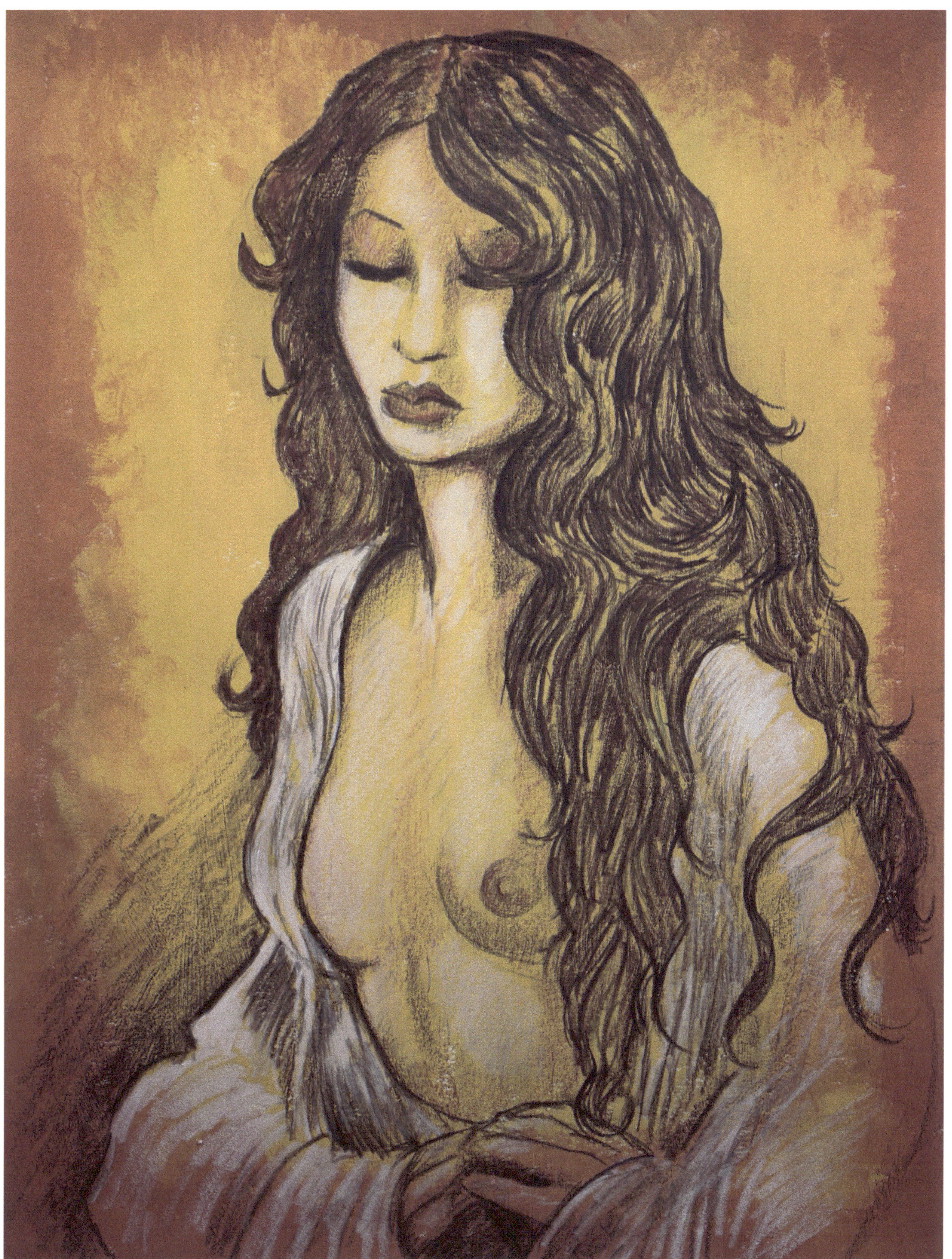

If I'd know It'd be this cold, when I sold my soul,
I would have brought warm blanket with me.

But they took me too fast,
Out on a blast,
I wrapped my motorcycle around a tree.

Now they are digging my grave, with nothing to save,
but now I can finally see.

That a dangerous life, with this switchblade knife,
Ain't gonna make me free.

So if you learn the truth, when you're long in the tooth,
better show the good lord you've seen.

Cause you'll lose all the light,
In the dark of the night,
And end the same way as me.

All cold and alone, on a broken throne, with the hounds baying at your heels.

And all the pain that you caused,
Gonna come from the claws,
The devil will make you feel.

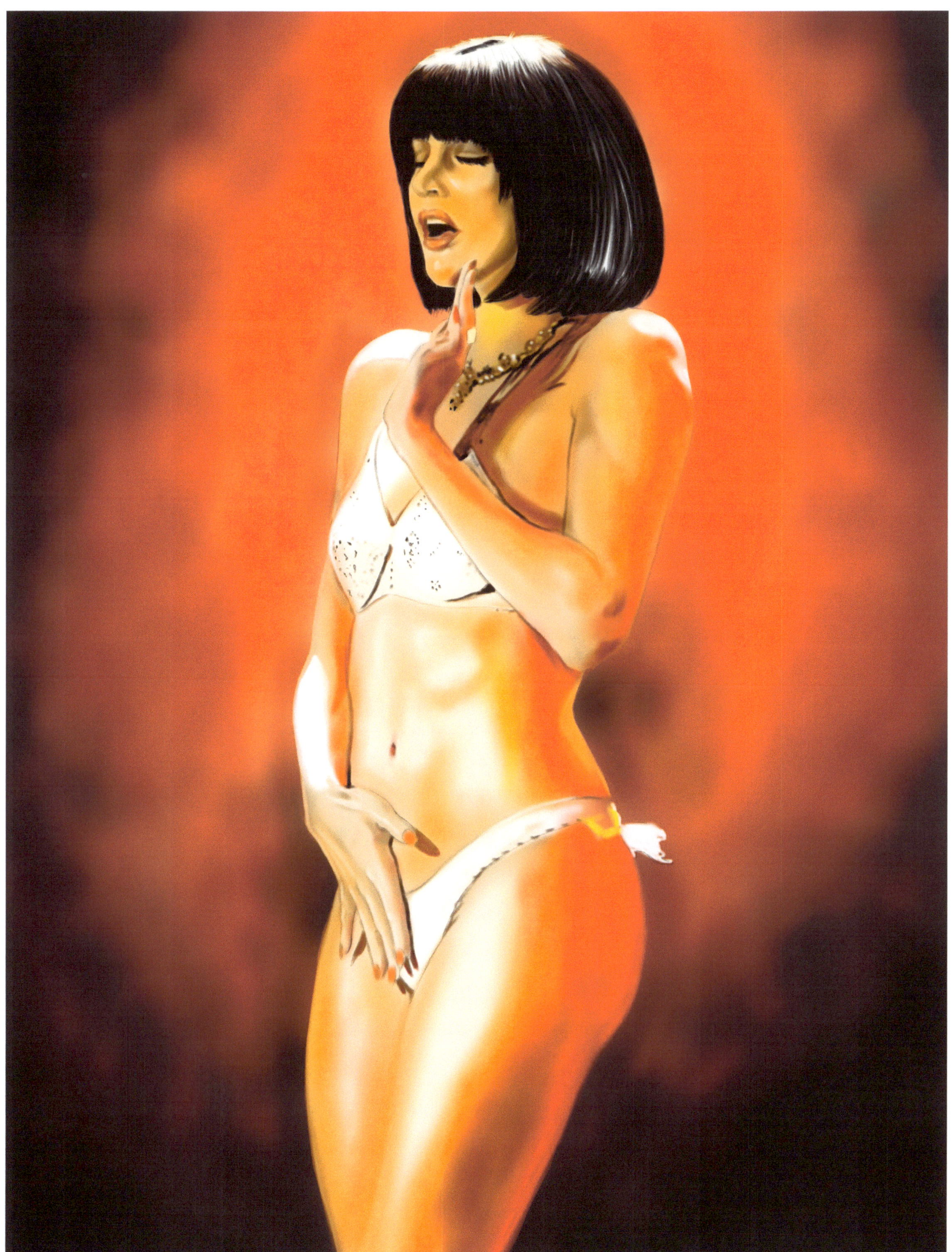

Fall from Grace

No grip on reality,
No place to call you own.
With a mindful of chemicals,
Now you're facing the unknown.

Making light of everything,
Blowing off the ones who come your way.
But there's only so much charity,
When you're living without a home.

The solution to everything,
Doesn't come in a needle or a pill.
But it's easier said than done,
When your bloods on fire and you're feeling ill.

Hold on to your brothers hand,
There's a light that will come your way.
When you let go of everything,
And start living another day.

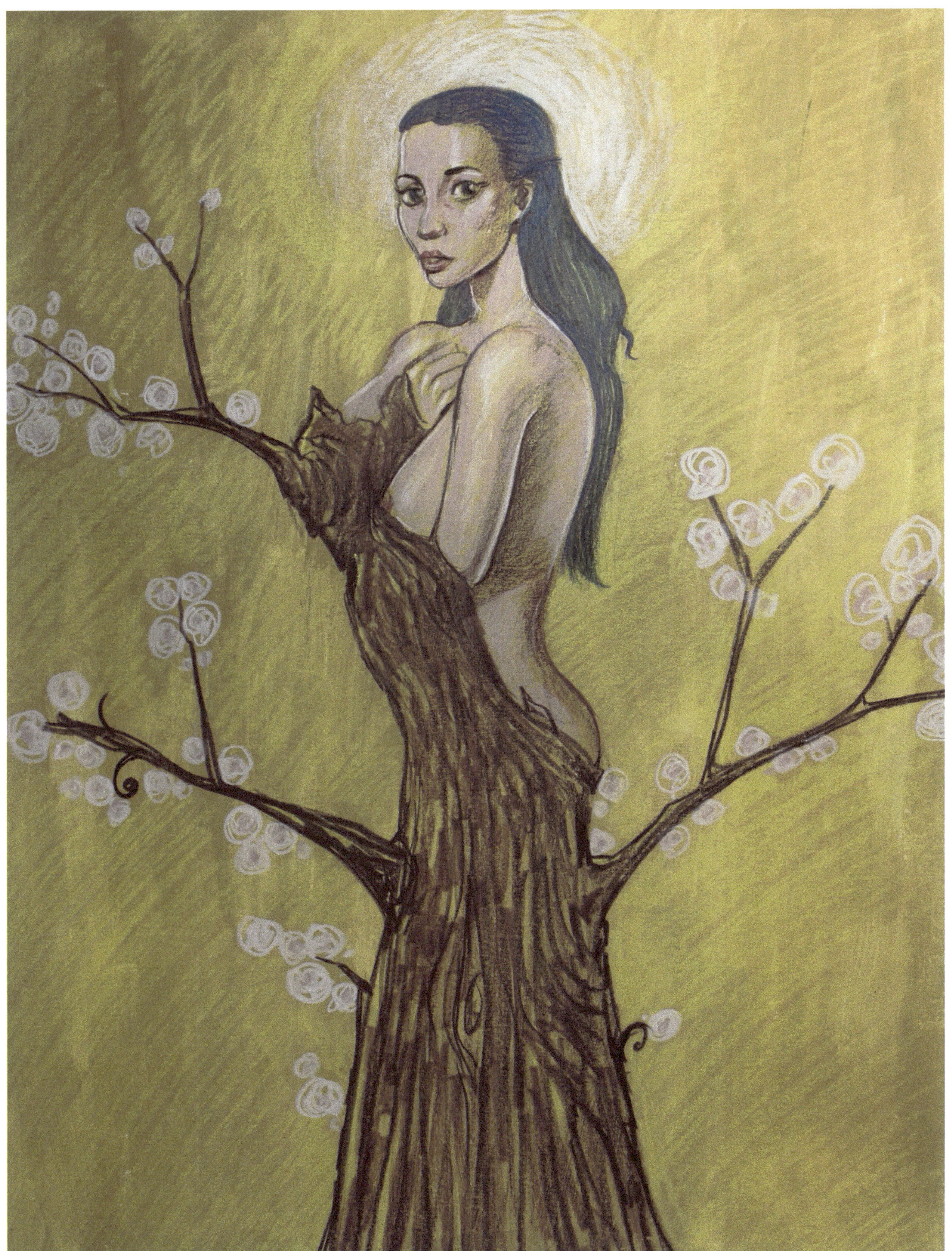

Frayed

In my car,
Waves of fear wash over me,
Feelings strong,
Wash me away.

Need some help breaking repetition.
One more song and one more mission.

Then we come to the same conclusion,
That this life is just an illusion.

Near the part,
Where I give it all away to you.
All my tricks,
All the ways I like to play.

Move them all and you'll break your boredom.
Steal the clouds and make a brighter day.

Pretty soon you'll have to make a decision.
Fix it all or keep it the same way,
...But you're really frayed.

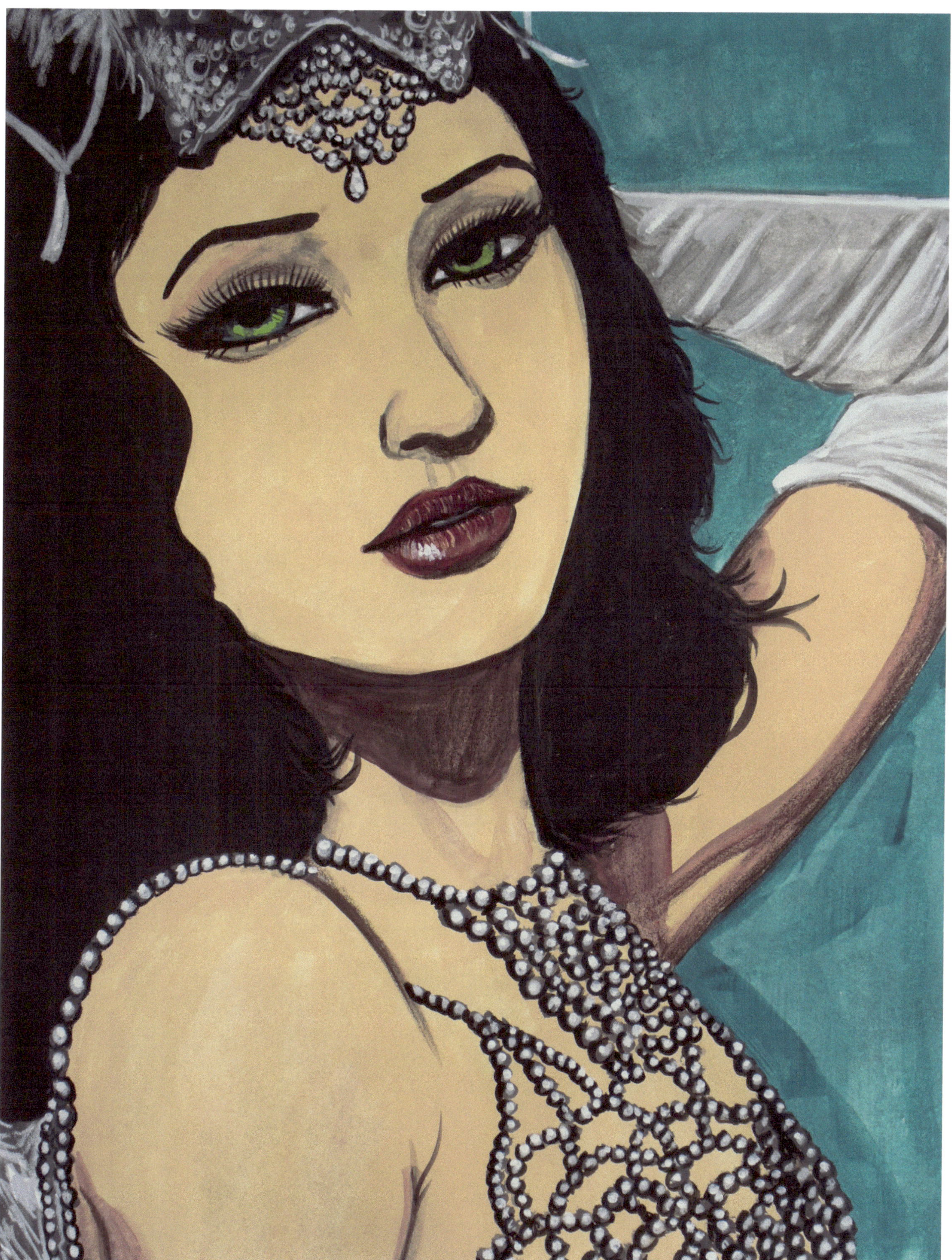

Marduk the Destroyer

Truly unknown,
And then tomorrow comes and takes the night away from me,
and leaves me here,
Alone.

Will you welcome me?
Or will you find a way to show me that I don't belong to here,
I retreat.

Truly, I'm broken,
And all the pieces of my life will fade away.
Like you did from me,
Like your love for me.

Waiting for the dawn,
But theres no warmth here,
Just the an endless creeping frost in my bones.
As I fade away.

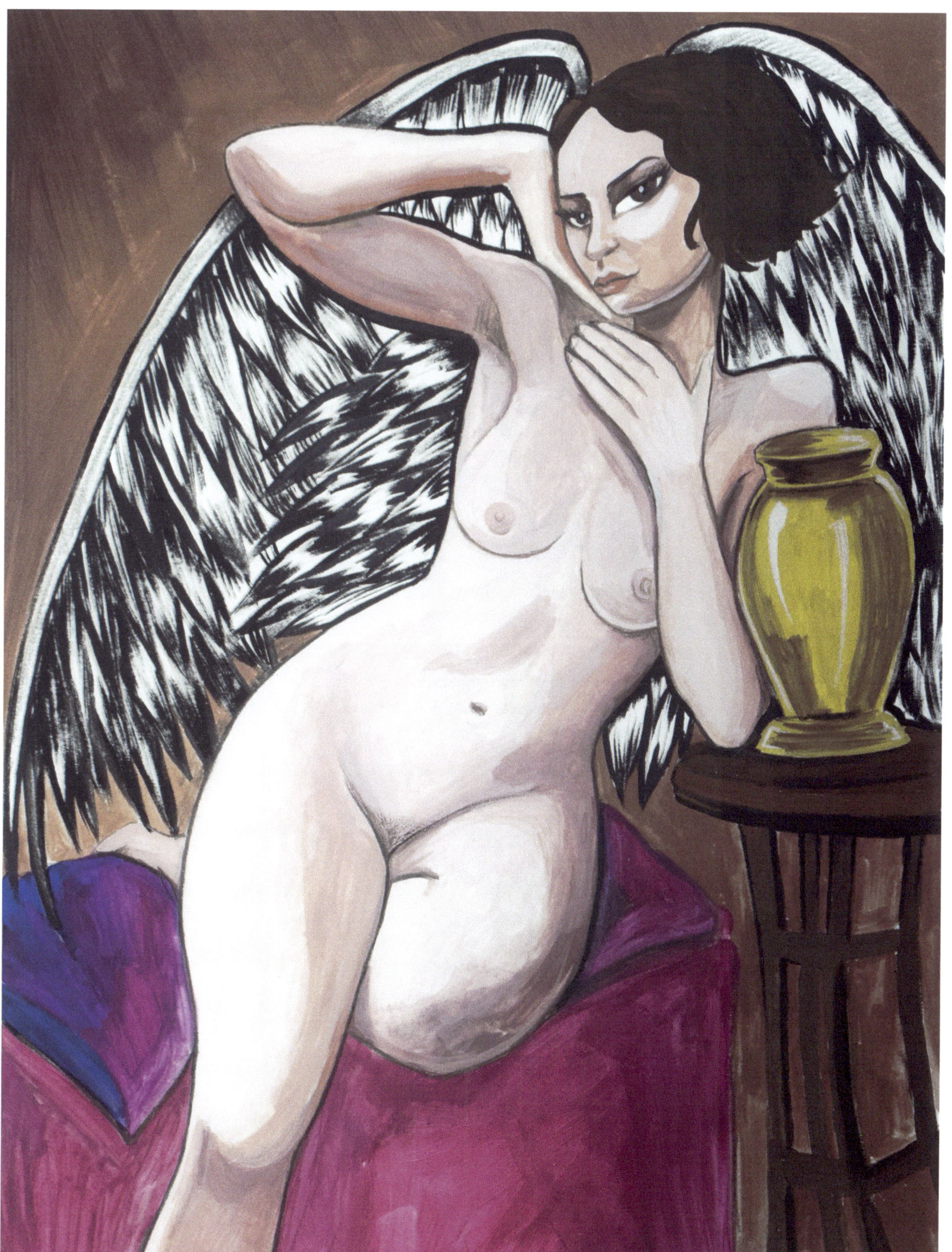

Parallel Worlds

I'm trying hard to believe in something,
I'm trying hard to find the words.
Cause we all got to believe something,
Otherwise there really is no point.

So you move in parallel worlds,
Where all time is no more.

We move through parallel worlds,
And swim to distant shores.

I got a feeling I'm hallucinating.
Got a vision of a hidden temple,
And world within another world.

Born in the path of another plane,
Two and a half thousand years since we saw its face.
Turning our world in a polar shift,
The ice and the continents begin to drift.

Still we tell ourselves it will be OK.

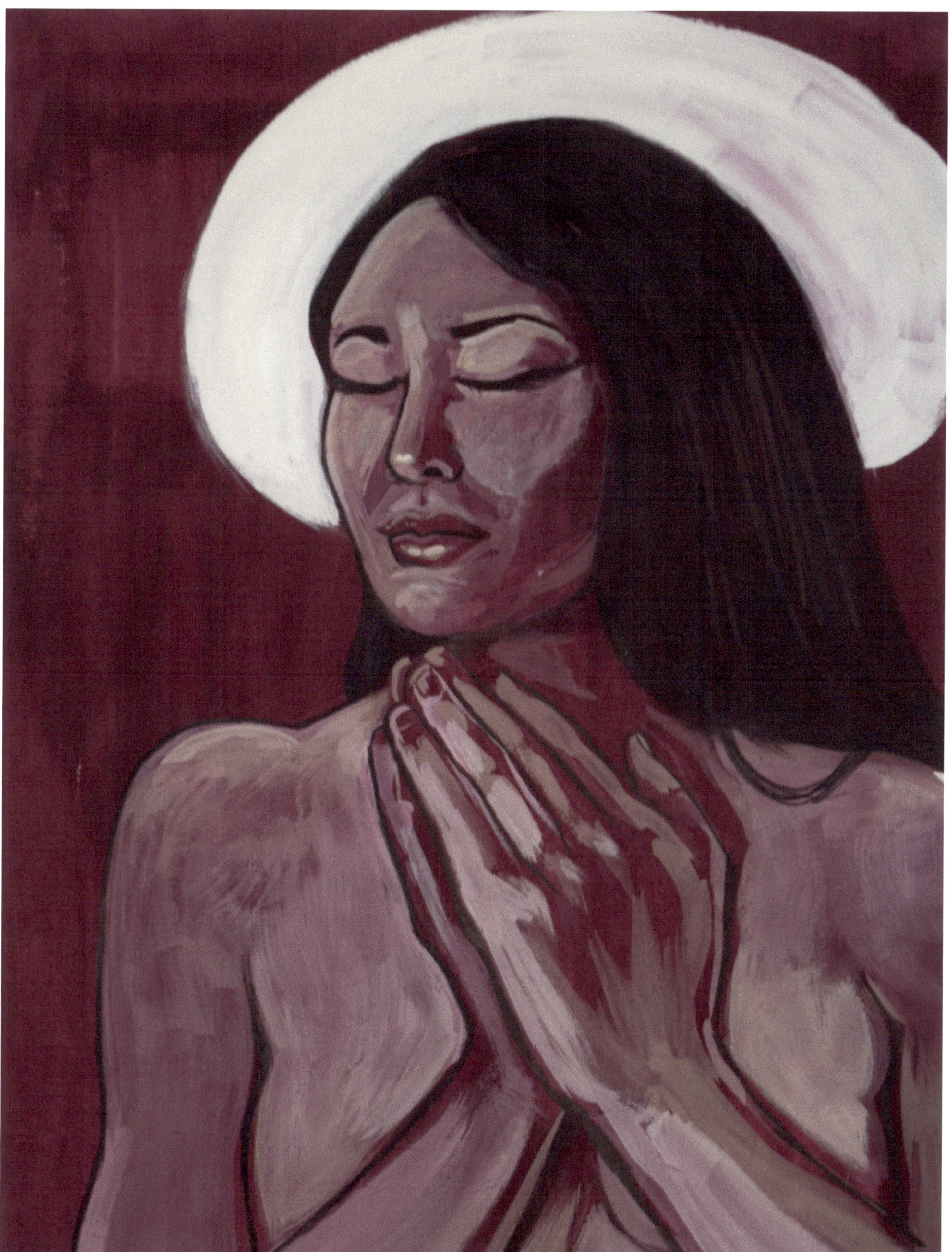

Ragged red

With all of your heart,
You call for me girl.

All that I want is to get it on with you,
But I can't see relief in this sin for me.
Rush in too soon to love,
And it comes back on you.
Finally see the dream.

All your heart is a start,
For me girl.
All your heart is part of me girl.

Rollin a doob I'll be getting around to you.
Then we will see if she is really meant for me.
Calling all day but when it's time to play,
Will she let me be free?

I'll fight despite this life of sheer delight,
Always erase the haze before it brings me down.
And if she needs my seed, she'll have to act the clown.
The circus is all I need.

Stripping right down, now she is kneeling on the ground.
Taking the time to show me what she's all about.
But I can't see relief in this ecstasy,
And I feel ill again.

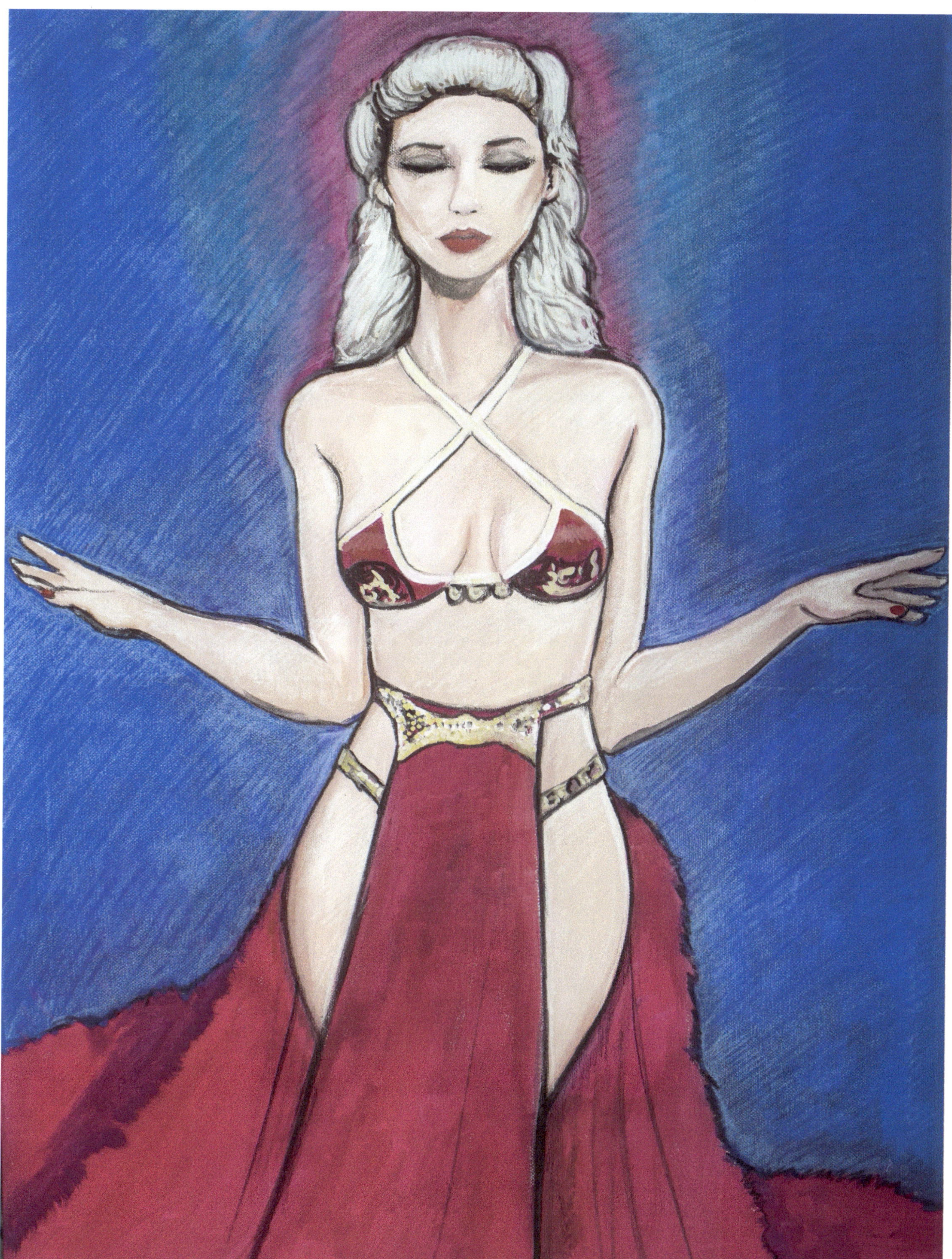

Resuscitation

Resuscitation,
Got a mindful.
Ground keeps moving,
But I stay still.
Hibernation,
What's it all for.
Just keep breathing.
Yeah, I got a mouthful.

Only falling,
Only falling.

Skin is crawling,
Blood is calling.
Till it sheds some light,
On this endless night.

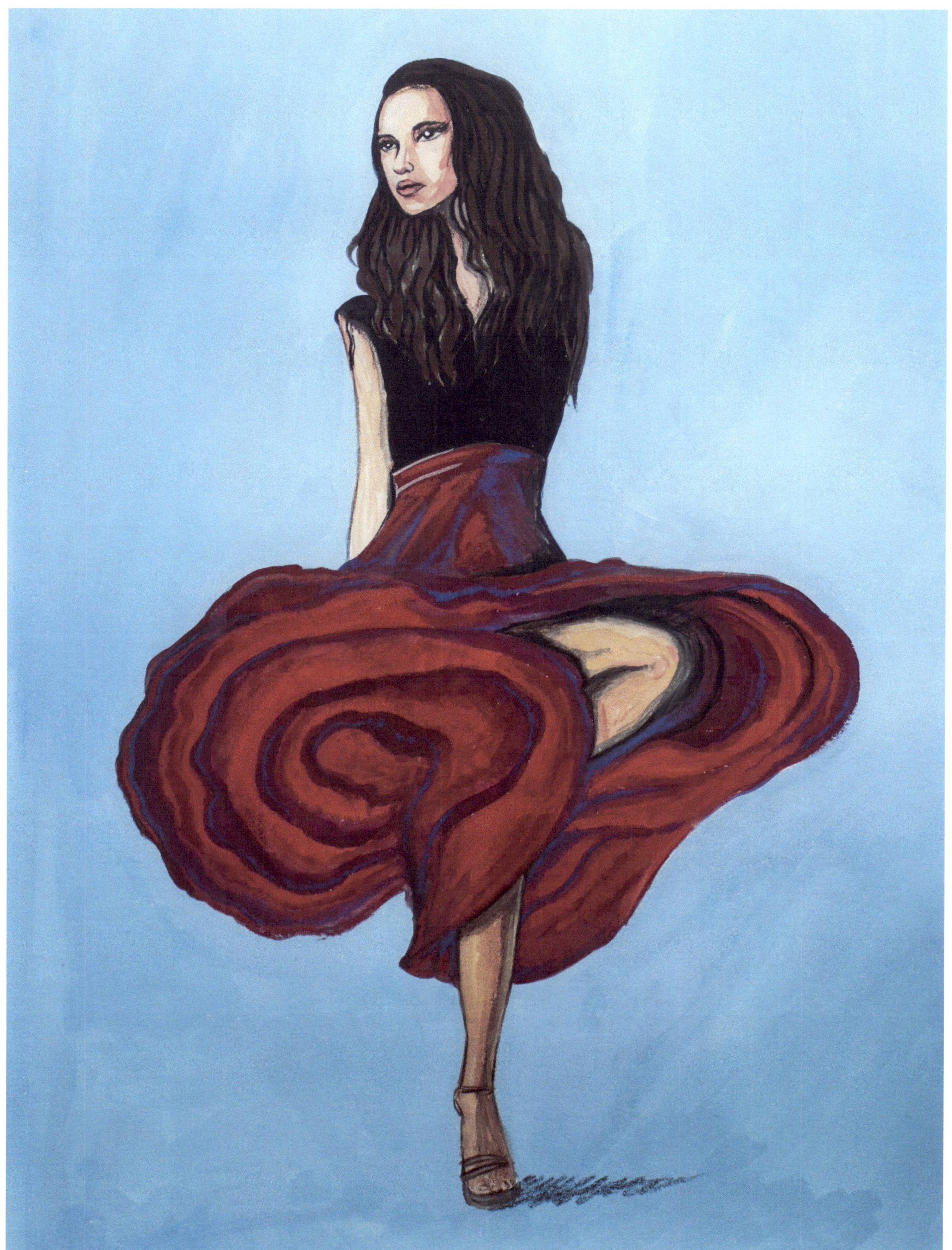

Dry Ice

You turned my life around,
I've never heard your voice,
Now I hear you sing all over town.

I'm really into you,
I won't mess around.
You're the only one,
Who makes my world turn upside down.

So it's down to the ending,
Who's going to walk away?
I gave my life to you,
Now I don't know what to say.

You're the Queen of the century,
And how you rule my heart.
Things were so much simpler,
Way back there at the start.

Let's turn the clocks back,
And just start again.
Forget when we were lovers,
And remember when we were friends.

Wrap your soul around me,
In your silken wings.
Find forever with you,
Because our love will never end.

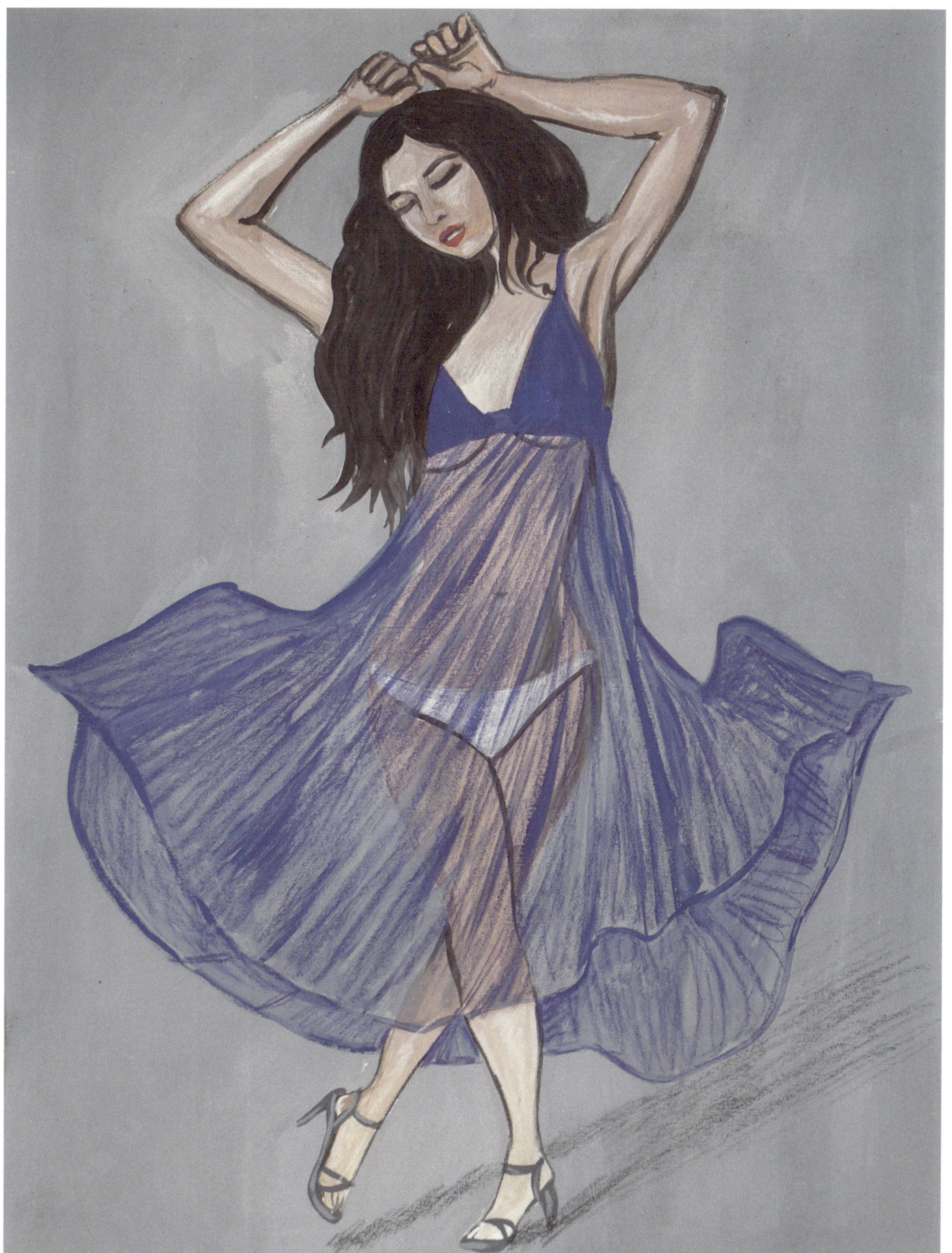

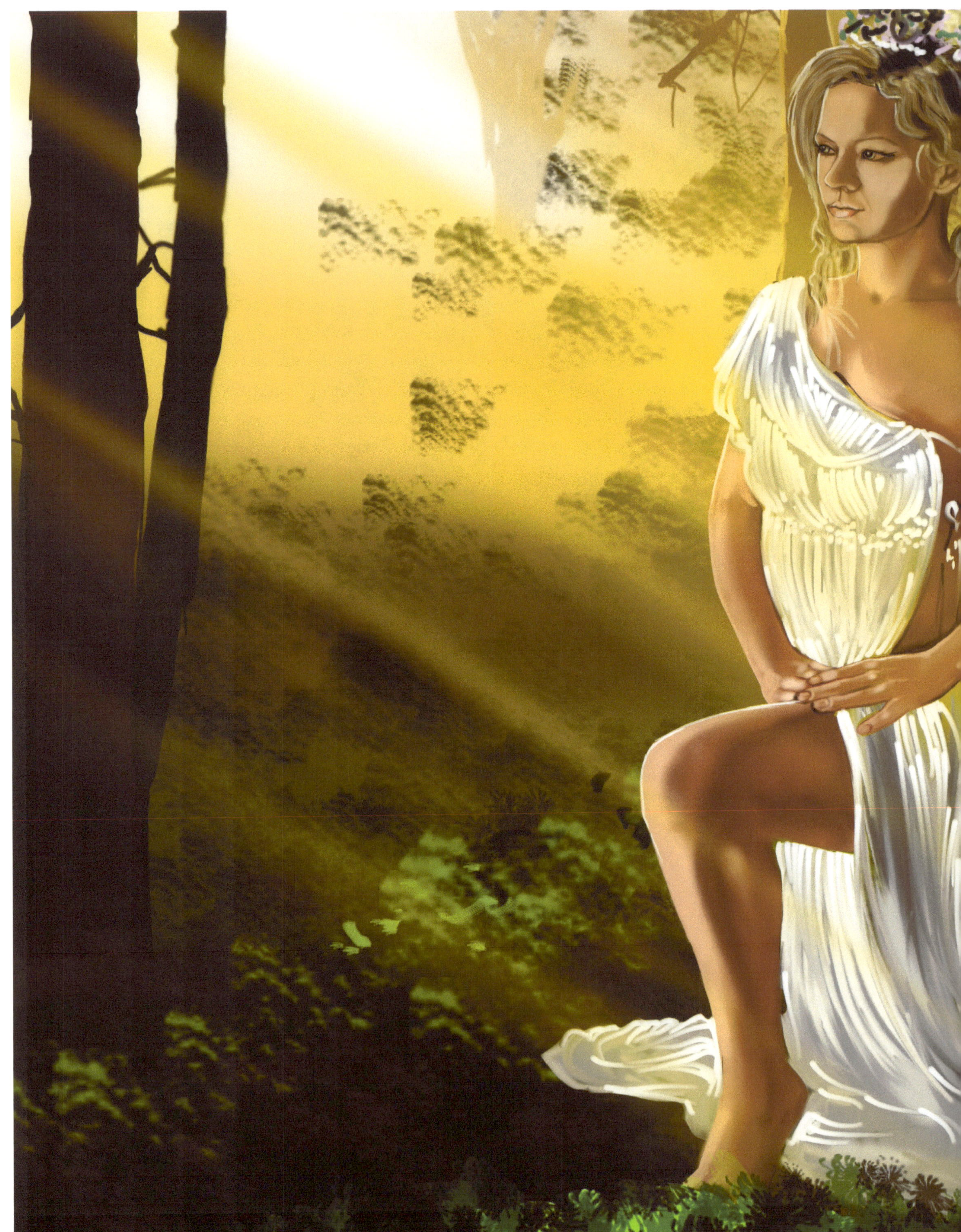

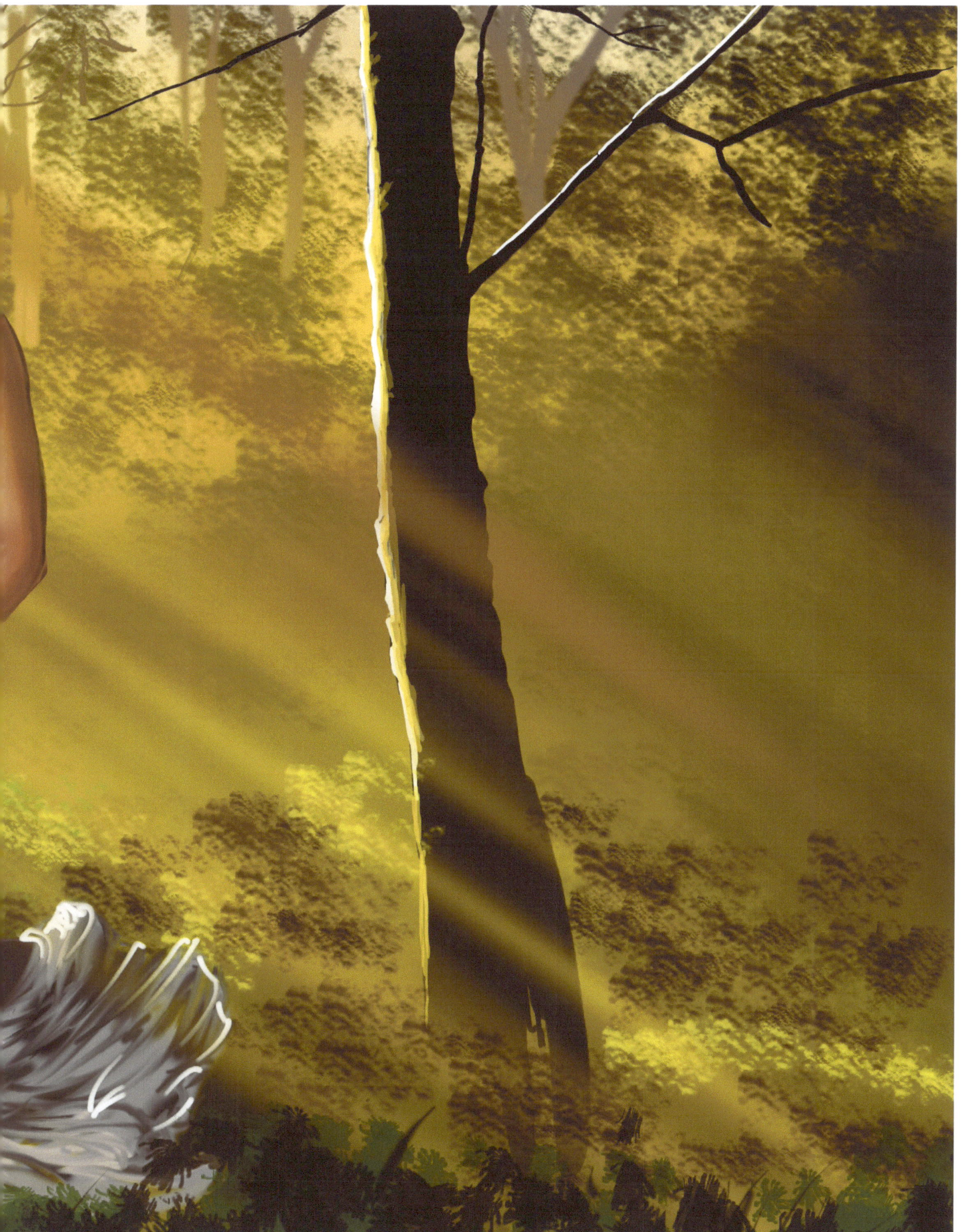

Nammu, goddess of the watery abyss

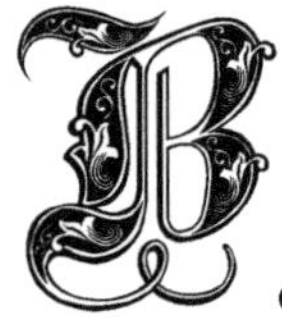een so long I've been sitting here,
All alone.
Building a lively calamity in these songs.
Forever sifting through the debris,
Where I belong.
Broken frames of forgotten history,
Long been gone, long been gone.

Straight into this watery abyss,
Where you belong.
I found a purpose, I found your kiss.

Upon your throne,
Now you took it too far,
You took me down into the dark.

Now you took it too far,
You took my soul,
You took my heart.

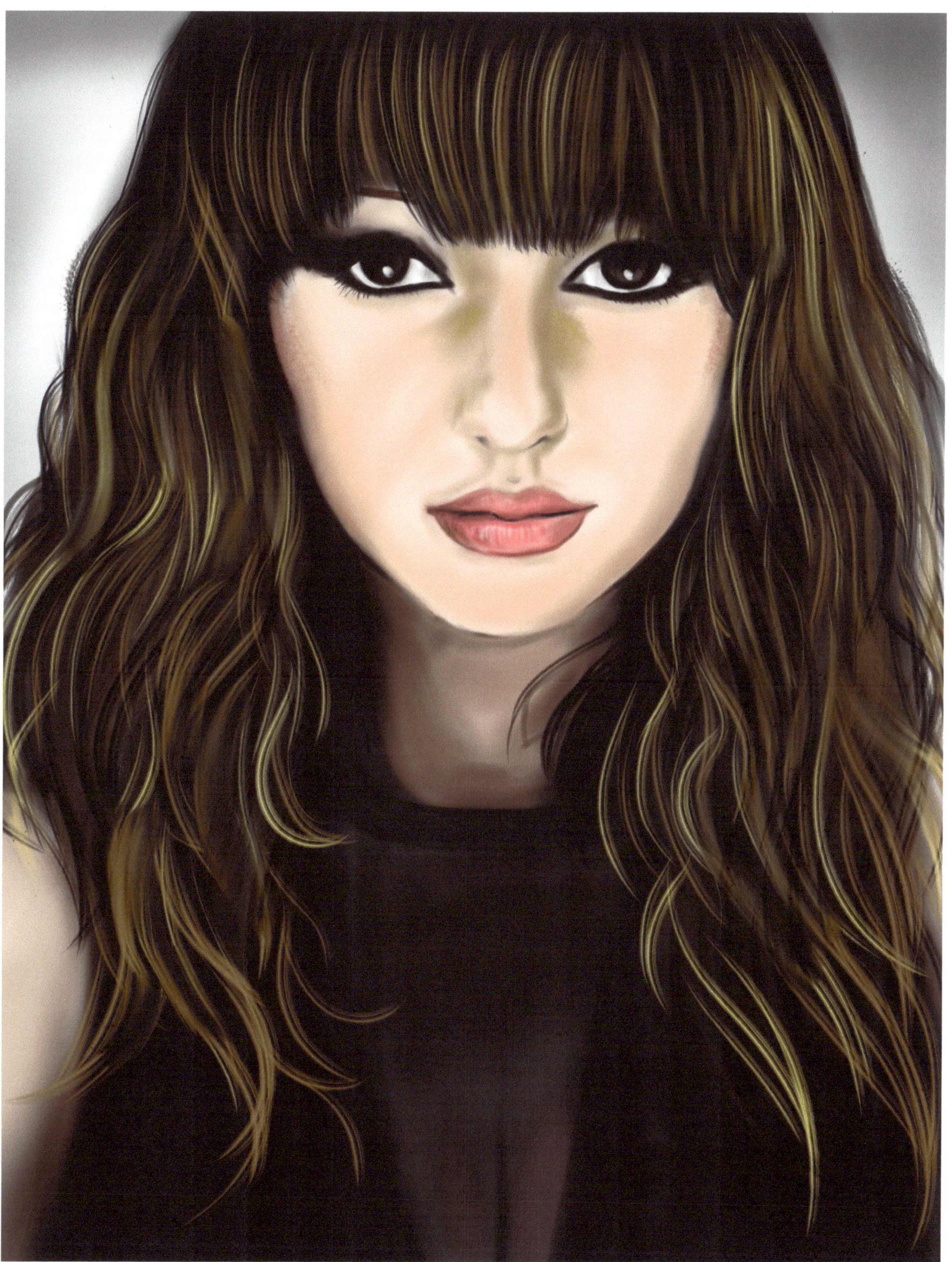

Necroscope

I won't be a whipping dog no more.
I feel too free,
And the ghost I want to see.
Oh, all you spirits come to me.

I'm a channel for the brokenhearted .
A demon to your dear departed,
A necroscope.

And I touch the dead and read their feelings.
And I can't weep tears cause my eyes are bleeding,
A necroscope.

If it weren't for all the dead things
I wouldn't speak at all.

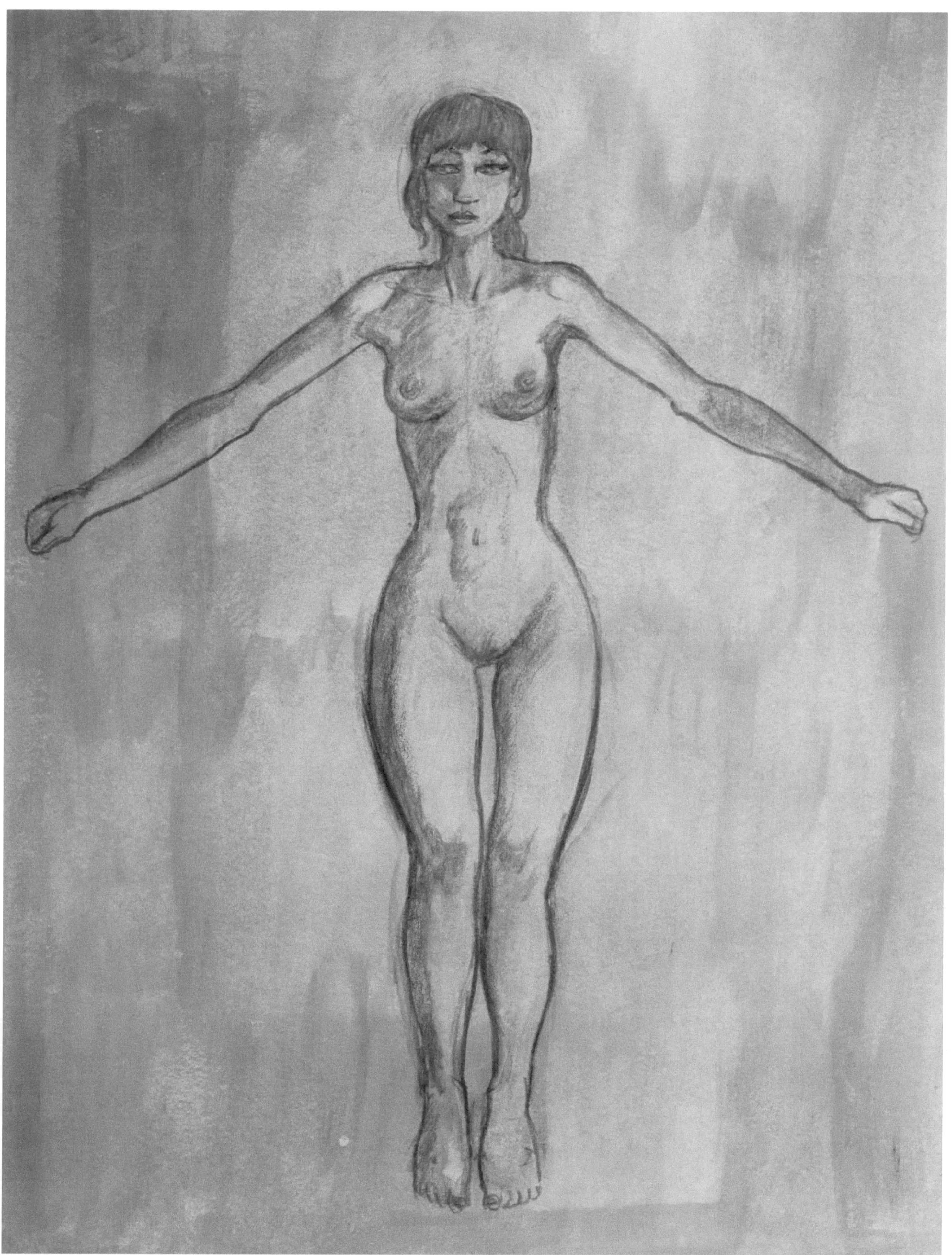

Hot tin Roof

Oh, we see her,
With stardust in her hair.
Long to hold her, still I hold her to this dare.
Said take the dark road, and ride the storm to shore.
You can be my cement shoes and drag me to the core.

Oh our dark love,
Black kisses on her neck.
Drags her under, to the tar pits breathless grip.

So we dance our last dance,
With deaths fingers around our necks.
Try not to struggle honey,
Soon all light we will forget.

Fall such a long way,
Till there's no hope for relief.
Slide down the rabbit hole,
Of Absinthes drunk belief.

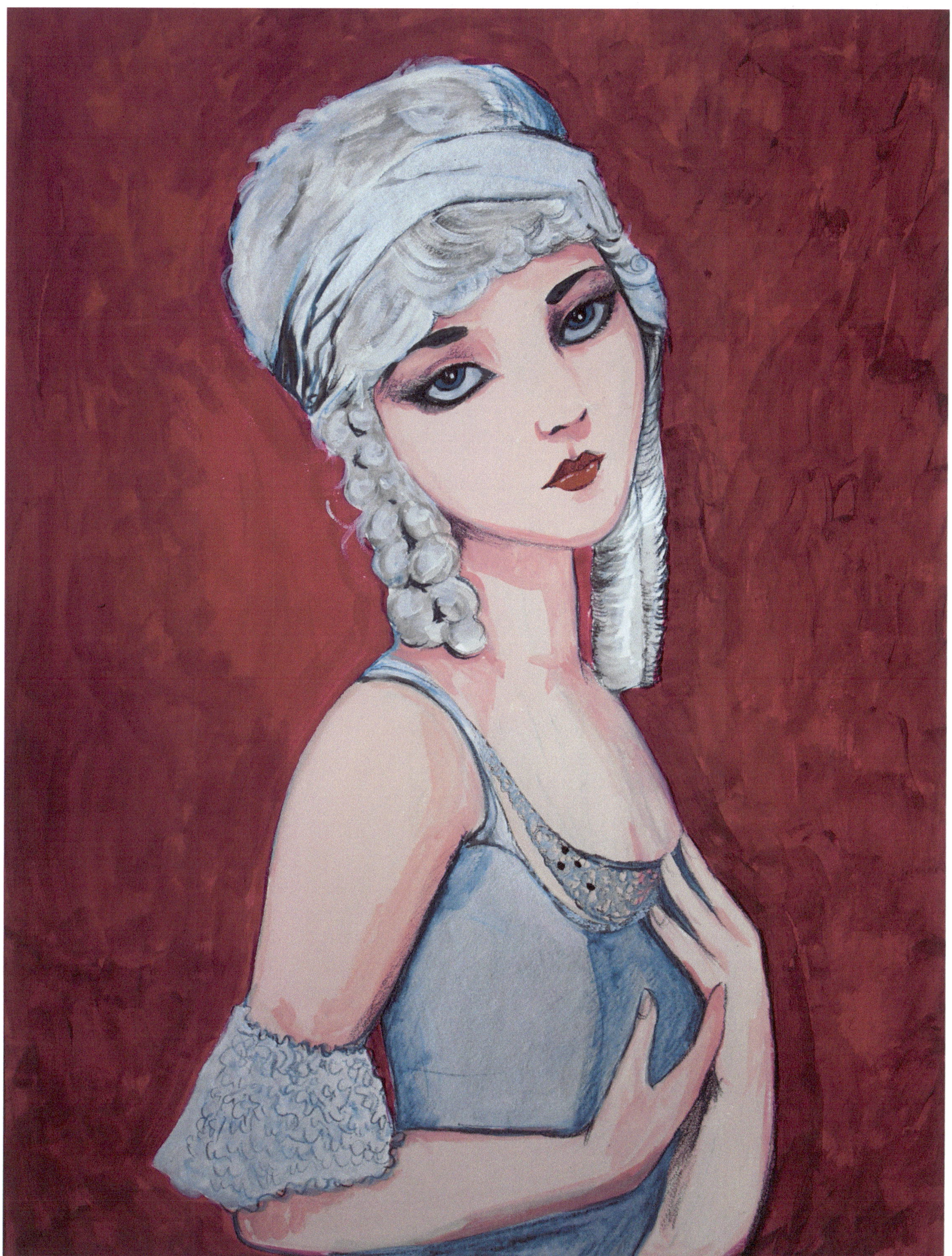

Only Just getting started

Only Just getting started,
Only just found you,
Only just realized you love me too.
I'm awash with your water,
On your sea I'm afloat,
No more I'll be an island all alone.

You're on high,
You are mine.
Can't deny,
You're divine.

Wading deep in the water,
Falling softly for you.
Paint your name in the sky,
It's the least I can do.

When our close friends departed,
Nothing more left to do.
That's when I get lost, completely in you.

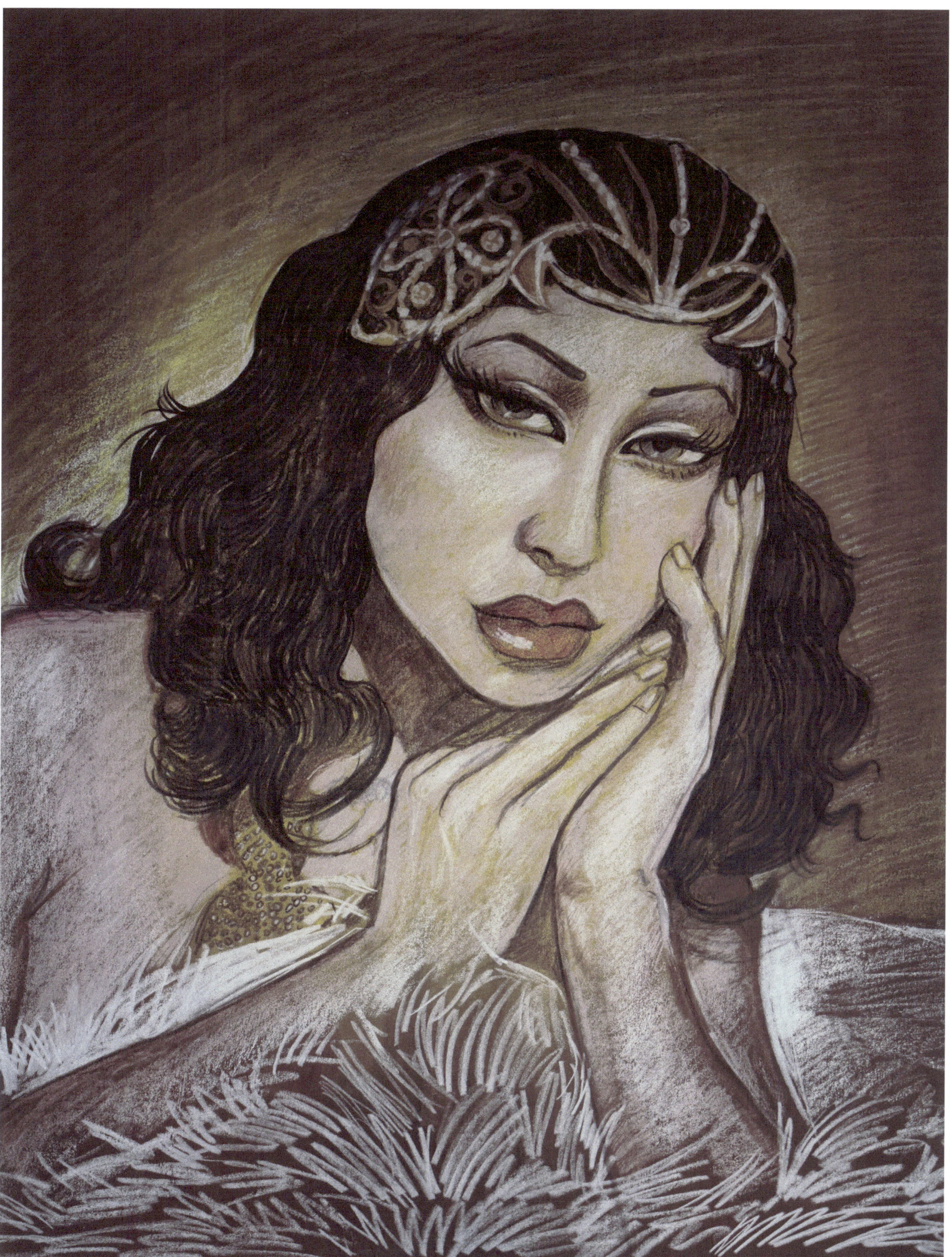

Set me Free

So you find me now,
Begging on my knees,
Mind so desperate turns,
To gasping final plea's.

This icy Breath,
Tearing at the leaves,
Creeping in my bones,
I begin to need.

Won't you help me now?
Set me free.
Take my hand,
And all my dreams.

Besot with grief,
Weeping at the dawn,
Nights long retreat,
Then my head will fall.
Then my hand will fall.

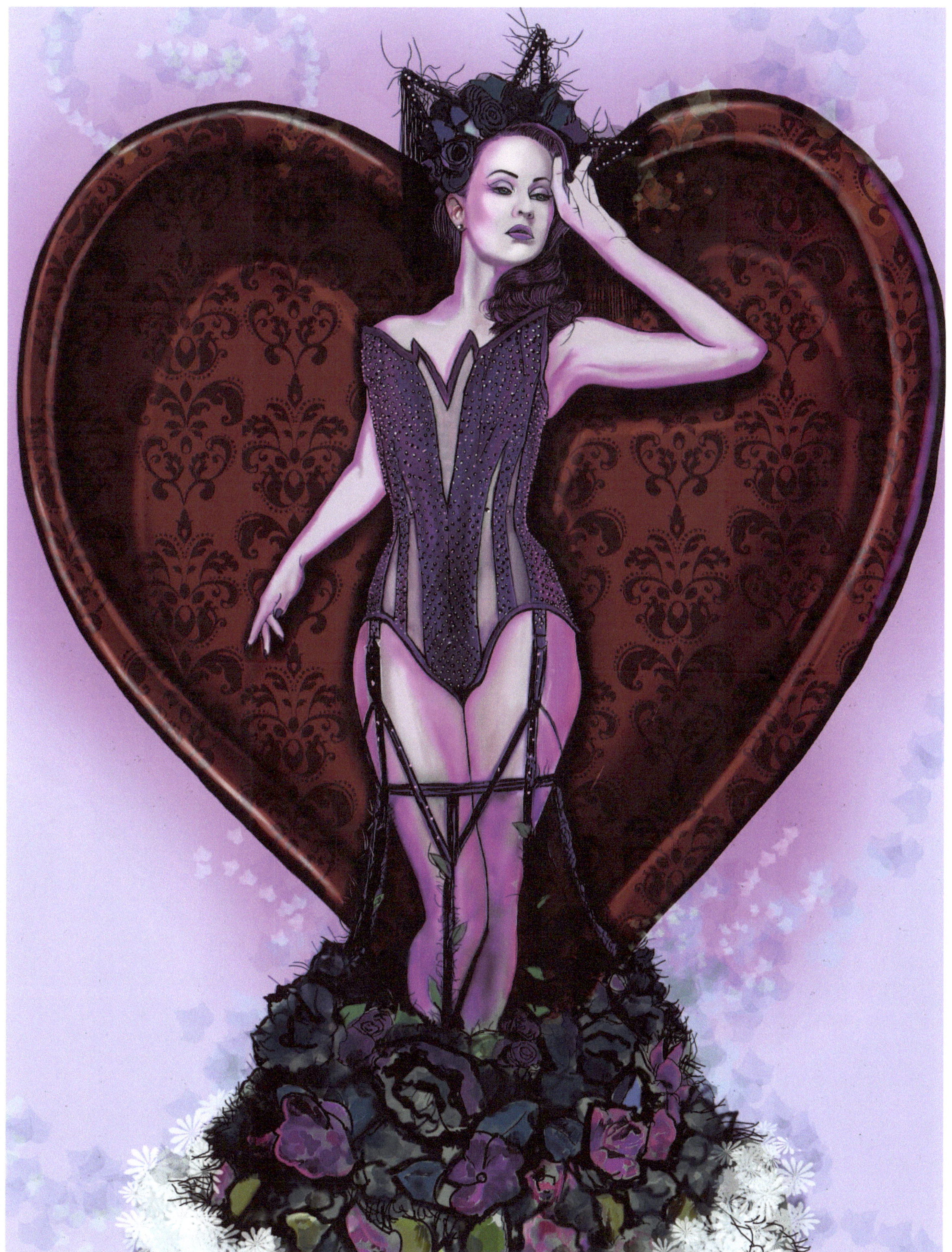

One step at a time

There's something wrong with me,
Can't handle reality.
All your love could set me free,
Make me what I want to be.
But I crawl all by myself,
All this love sitting on a shelf.
Just a man of dubious health,
Rotting in a private hell.

Can't you see I'm running on nothing,
Sitting in this corner I made myself.
All these dreams but no fuel to fire the rockets,
All this gold but I can't tap the well.

I can't sleep, I can't eat,
I gotta take this one step at a time.

I can't see, I can't breathe,
Gotta take this one step at a time.

This ain't real, this ain't me,
Its a byproduct of history.

You don't know, you can't see,
All the things that I'm gonna be.

Could it be that you're on the take?
You're the king of Penny Lane,
All you see turns to shades of grey.
Take a breath, see a brand new day.

It won't take long,
Regrets and consequences will be gone.
Then you can rise with me,
And become the god you're meant to be.

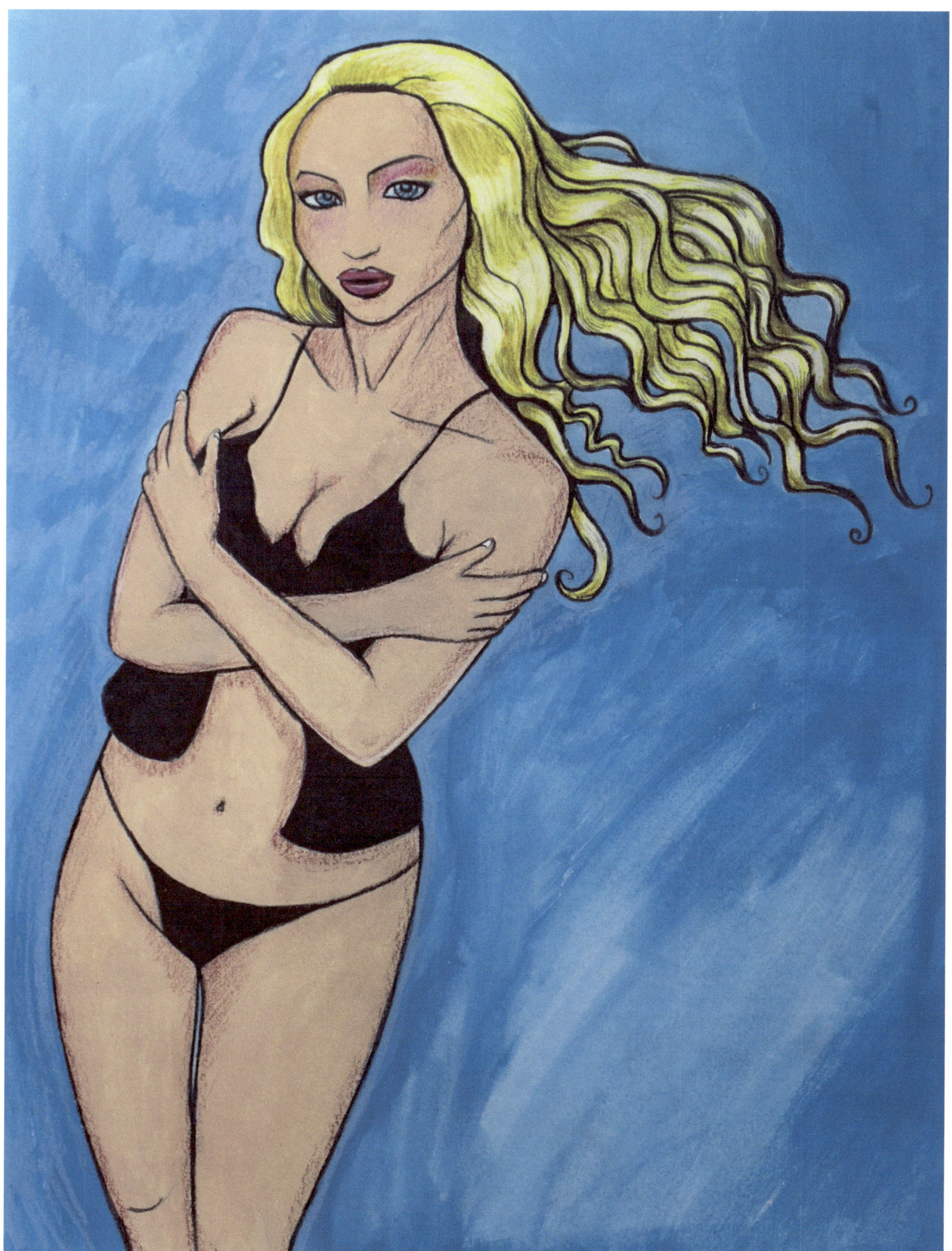

Reptile Hybrid

I went to the bank to borrow a dollar,
The man wouldn't let me.

Saw over his shoulder a reptile hybrid,
Giving him orders.
Pulling the strings and
Shaping his thoughts.

My tinfoil helmet
Keeps me protected,
From the spies in the sky,
That keep us connected.

Like sheep for the slaughter,
Or meat on an order.
Slaves of the empire,
Blind by the old lies.

Now he's shedding his skin.
Revealing the world that we are in.
In the trees all the snakes are hanging around,
Whispering in our ears and bringing us down.

Don't wanna swim in that water,
Though I know that I should.

They are waiting beneath me,
I'd run away if I could.

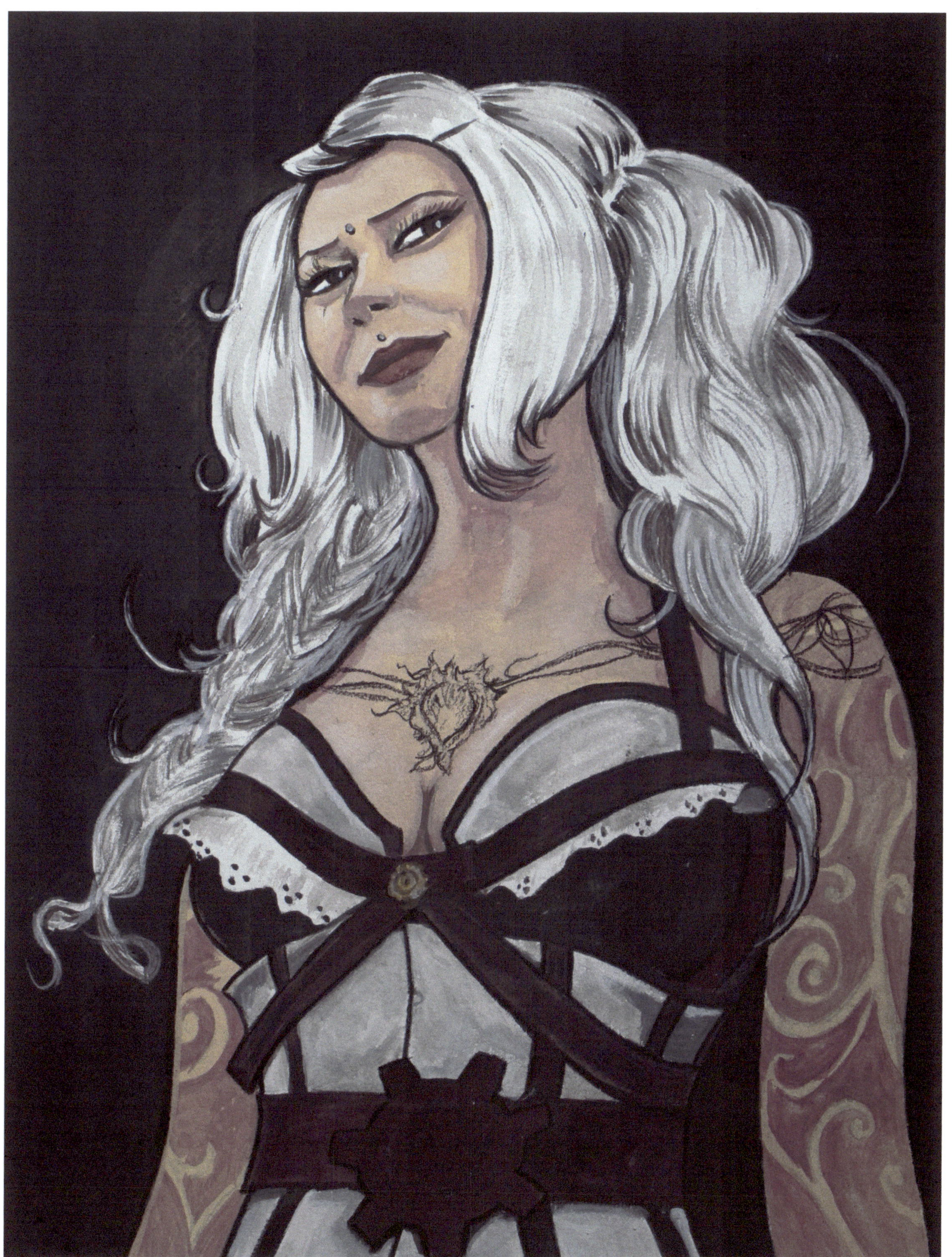

Shadow Man

So many people drift away from me,
They can't ever see how I feel.
I wait here hoping for a second chance,
At a sweet romance with you.

Can see our paths split away.
Don't know what say
To keep you here.

And I know that I had my chance,
Now there's another man in your world.

All I have now are these memories, and they're keeping me waiting here.
I search these walls for another door, cause I hope for more than this fear.

Can't be a masked Silhouette,
Just a shadow man,
Made of tears.
Gonna take a path to another place,
Gotta break away from you.

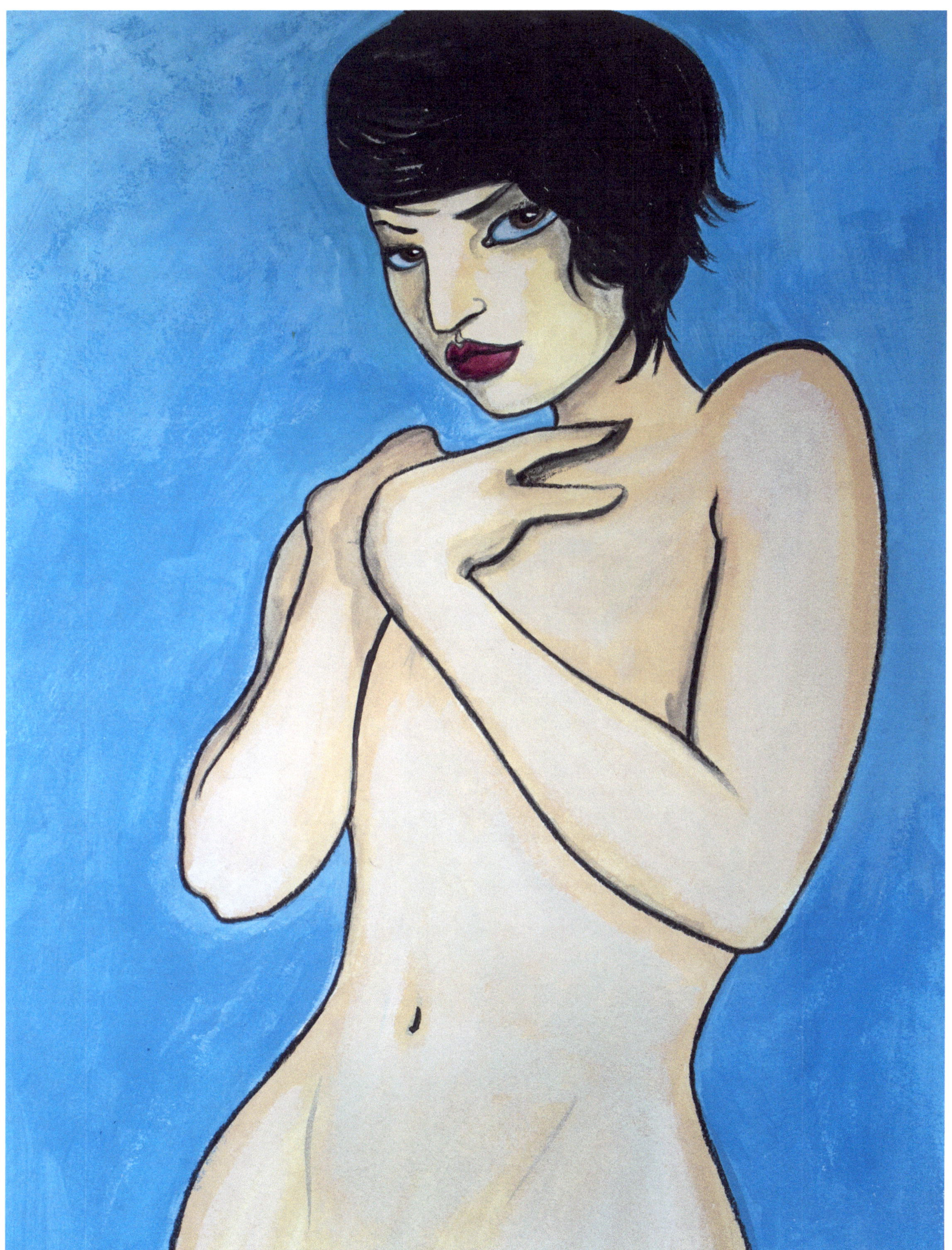

Secret Amnesia Machine

From the sun he comes to me.
He's my King Dumuzi.

'Lord of the sheepfolds',
God of green and fertility.
From Descent of Inanna,
He ruled the underworld.

There's a secret amnesia machine,
That sets us in a trap.
Making us forget,
And then sending us back.

And we'll never escape,
Until we fool the machine.
And we'll make the same mistakes,
Unless we remember them again.

We don't remember who we are,
We don't know where we've been,
We don't really know what we are,
Just the lies that we've been given.

Secret Amnesia Machine,
Now I know you're there.
You can only hope that I start anew,
And forget your ancient fear.

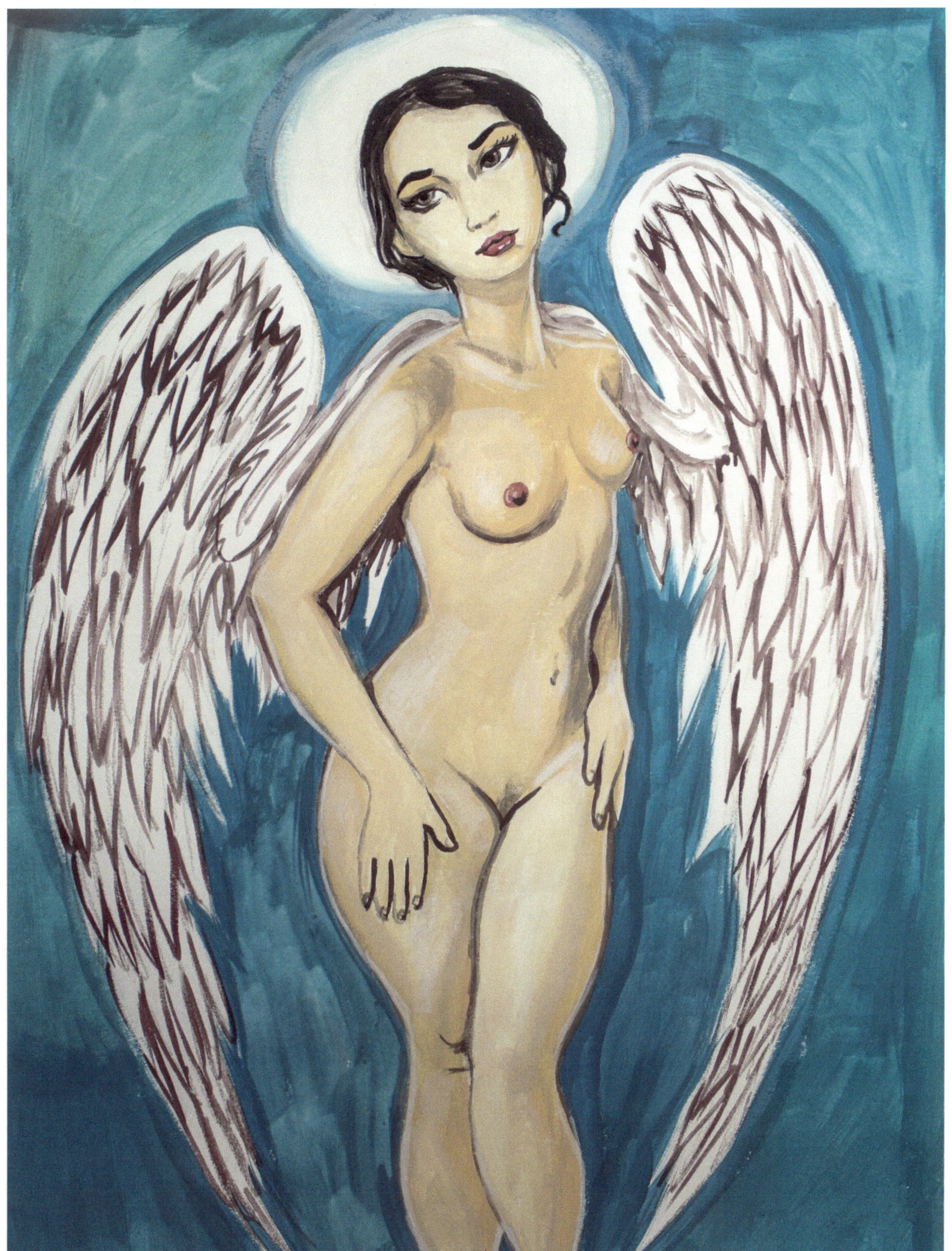

It's just not easy

All these questions have been bothering me,
And all these shadows won't let me be.
I'm waiting for the answers to come to me,
But I'm so locked out I don't even dream.

Want to see the light from all the shadows,
Want to see if I can land on my feet.
Want to drain the poison from my system,
And just like you I want to be free.

But it's just not easy.
Yeah, it's just not easy.

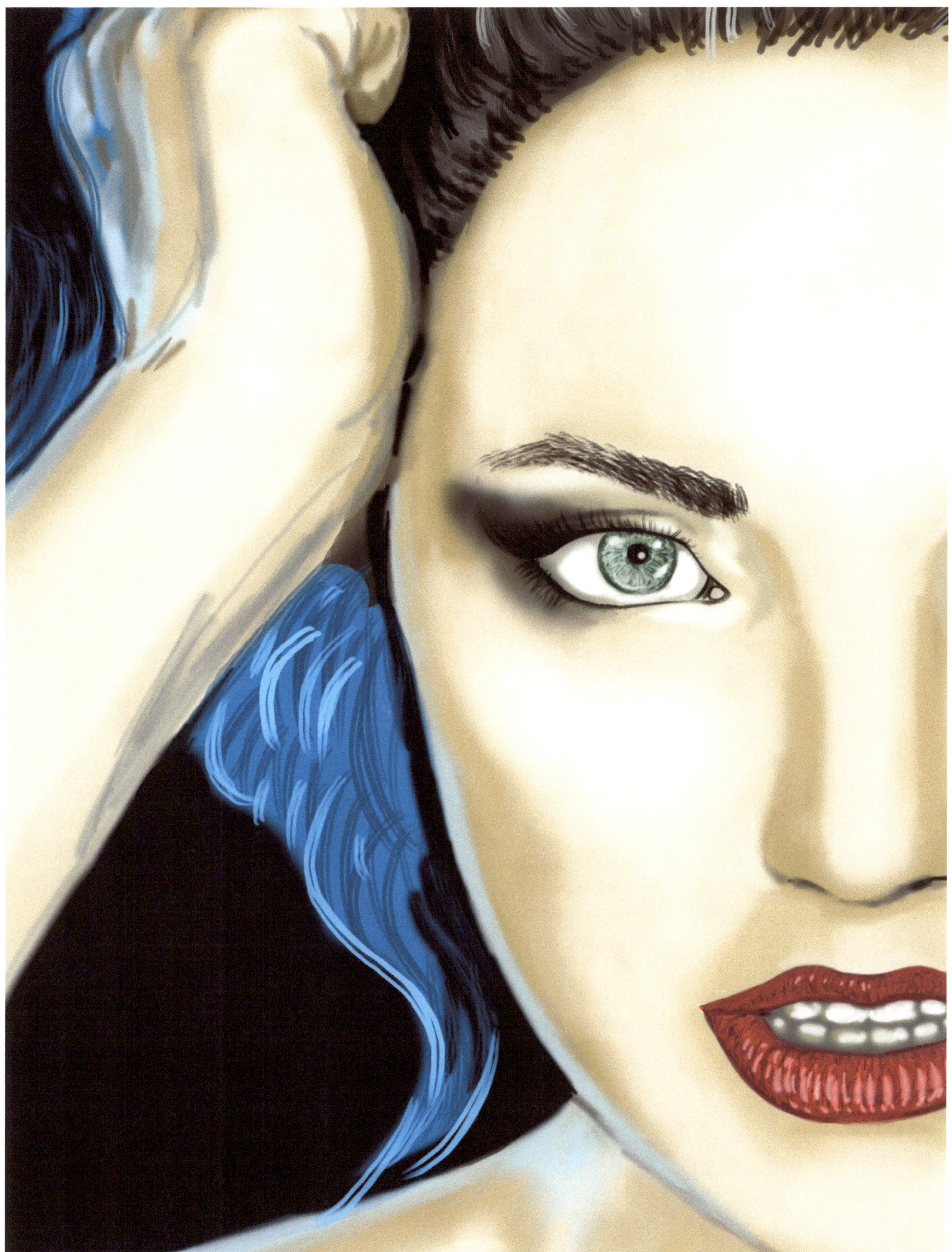

Jupiter's Falling

Dancing all hopes away,
Fade like your honored view.
Had you thought you belonged.

Sunsets on a faded dream.
But she still rocks on,
Can't help but believe it,
Hadn't burned till her heart.

Black thorns drawn upon your eyelids,
Visions cold,
Seen all future doors,

Black Feathers speak of nothing but pain above,
Burnt bad by your hold.

Till all my dues are paid,
Can't help but be alluded.
Where are these thoughts gonna go?

Between hopes and memories is a gilded cage,
Can't help but be in it,
Anything for her love.

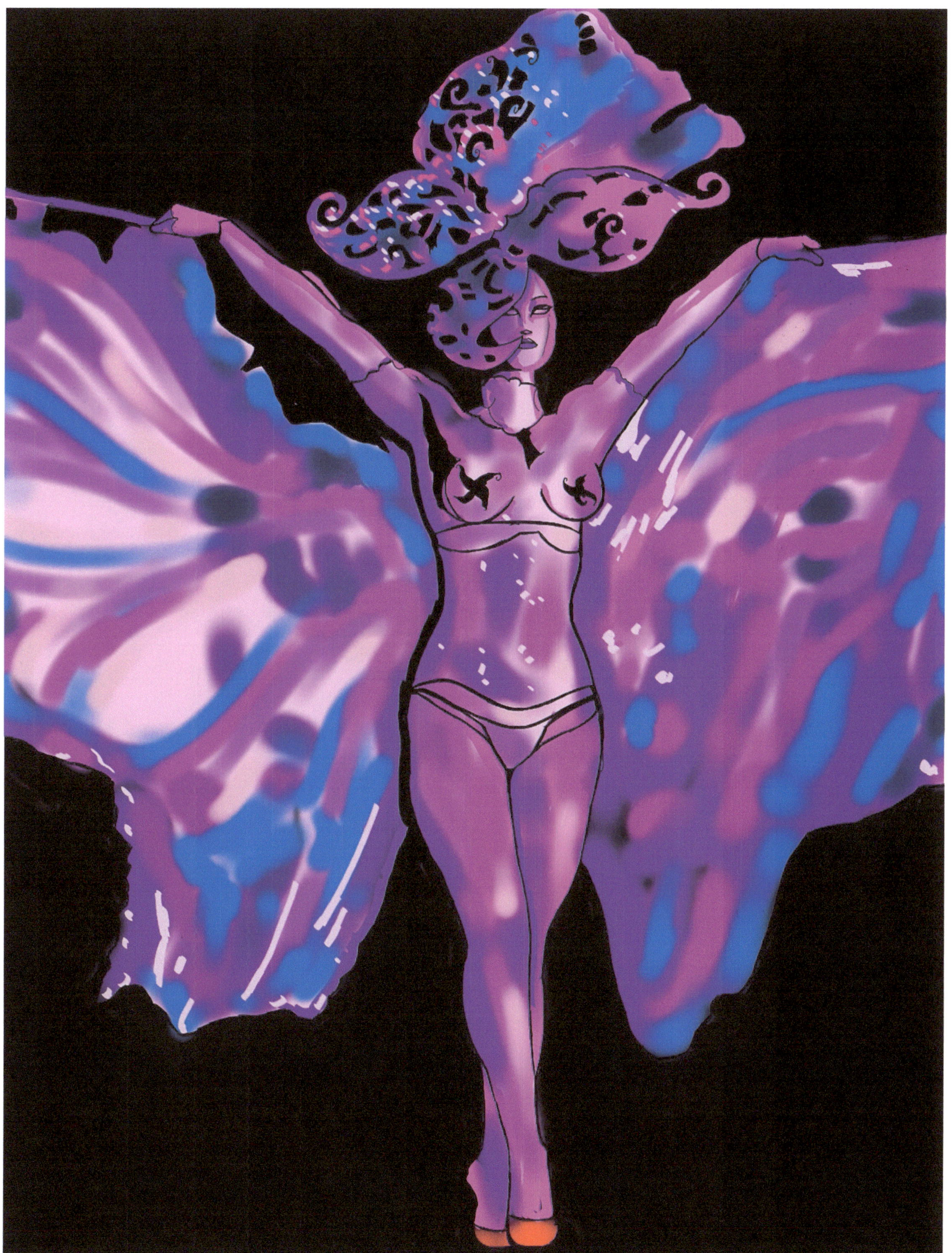

Slave to Love

When I see her,
The Goddess in the moon.
Move within the ocean,
In the blackness of my tomb.

I'll be halfway between the moon and the deep blue sea,
When all these ancient secrets open up to me.

But having all the answers doesn't mean that I'll walk free,
Cause I'm a slave to love,
Yeah I'm a slave to love.

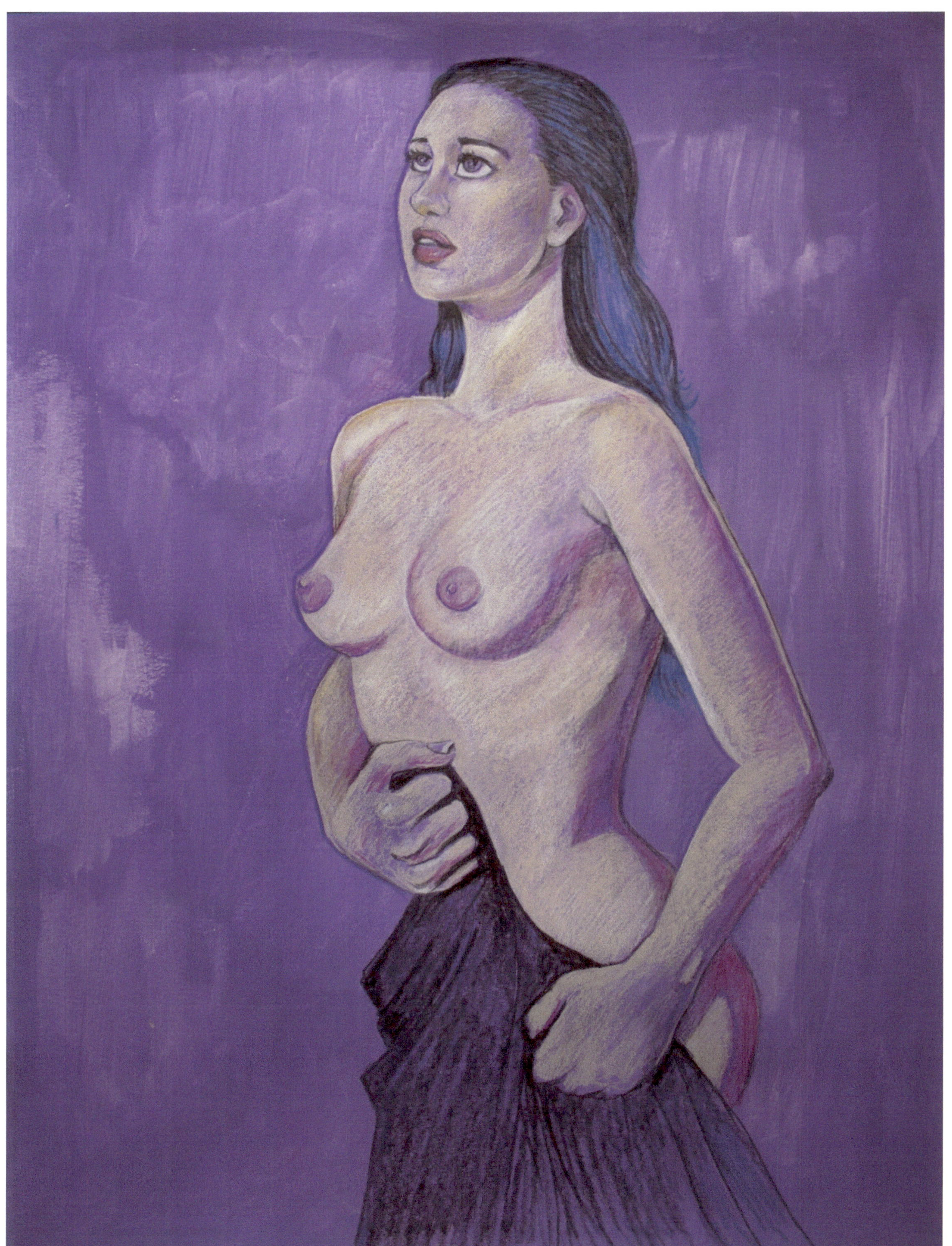

Never gonna win

Been sitting round now,
Like I didn't learn anything.
Been sitting round now,
Like I didn't learn anying.
Trying to get my head around this blues thing.

Its been time long since felt your loves embrace.
It's been so long lady,
Since I saw your face.
Won't you come back and give me another taste?

Think it's time now that I got back on my feet,
Thinks its high time that I took a fast retreat.
You ain't never gonna coming back, and I gotta get right off my seat.

They think I'm crazy now for waiting in the dark,
Think I'm crazy now for holding on this spark,
I lost my head when you left me in the park.

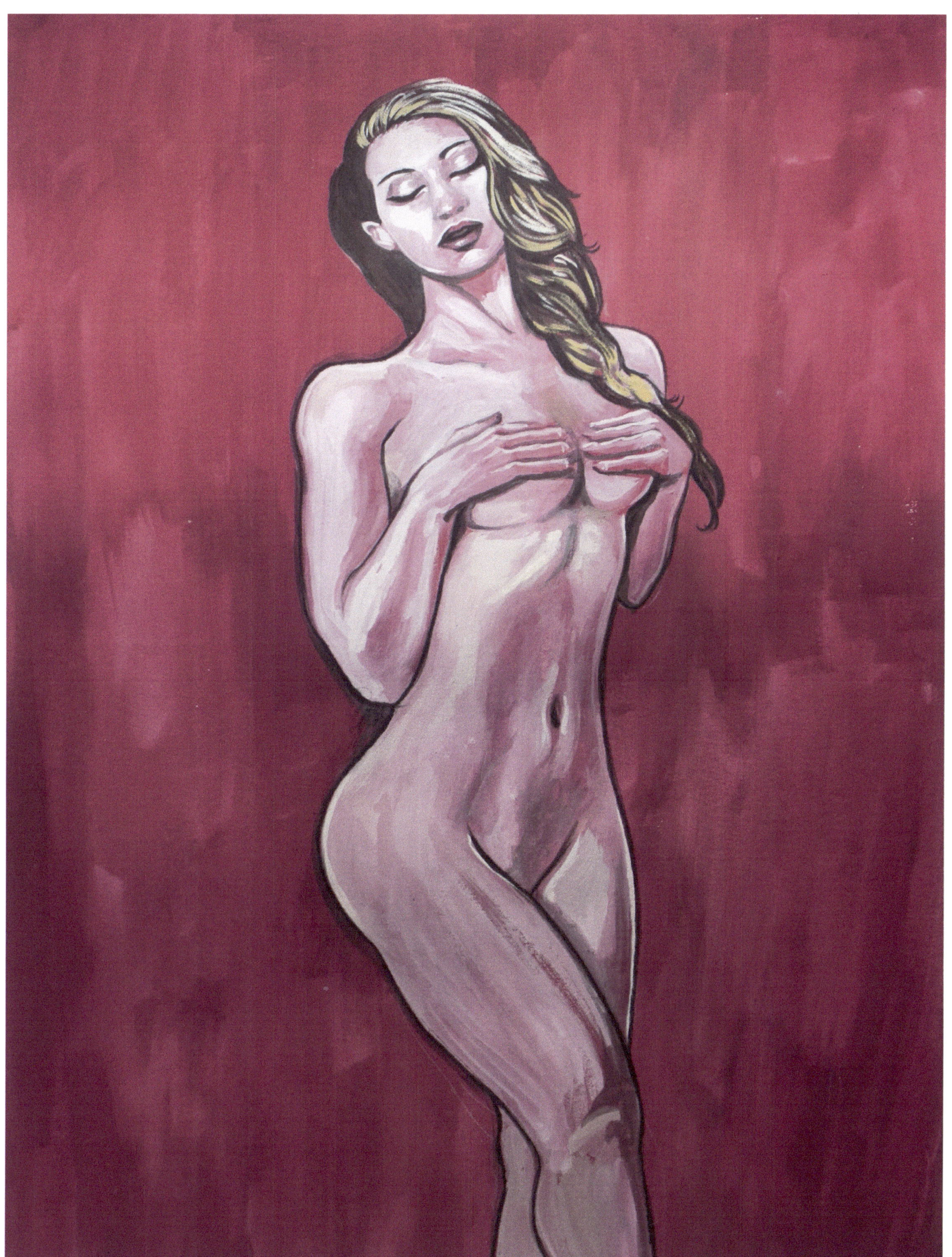

The Sweetest Waters

Sweet water urging my soul to drink.
Spirit Walker, alone like everything.
The goddess feeds me,
So I need a taste.
Growing older every second, precious fluids drain away.

Why would you leave me dry,
Or drowning from too much too fast?
Denied all this precious life, a thirsty man would longer walk.

Navigate the space that floated once with your fill.
Growing darker every second,
Storm clouds flood to spill.
Raining down and soaking through my skin.
Make me feel like I am whole,
A full man again.

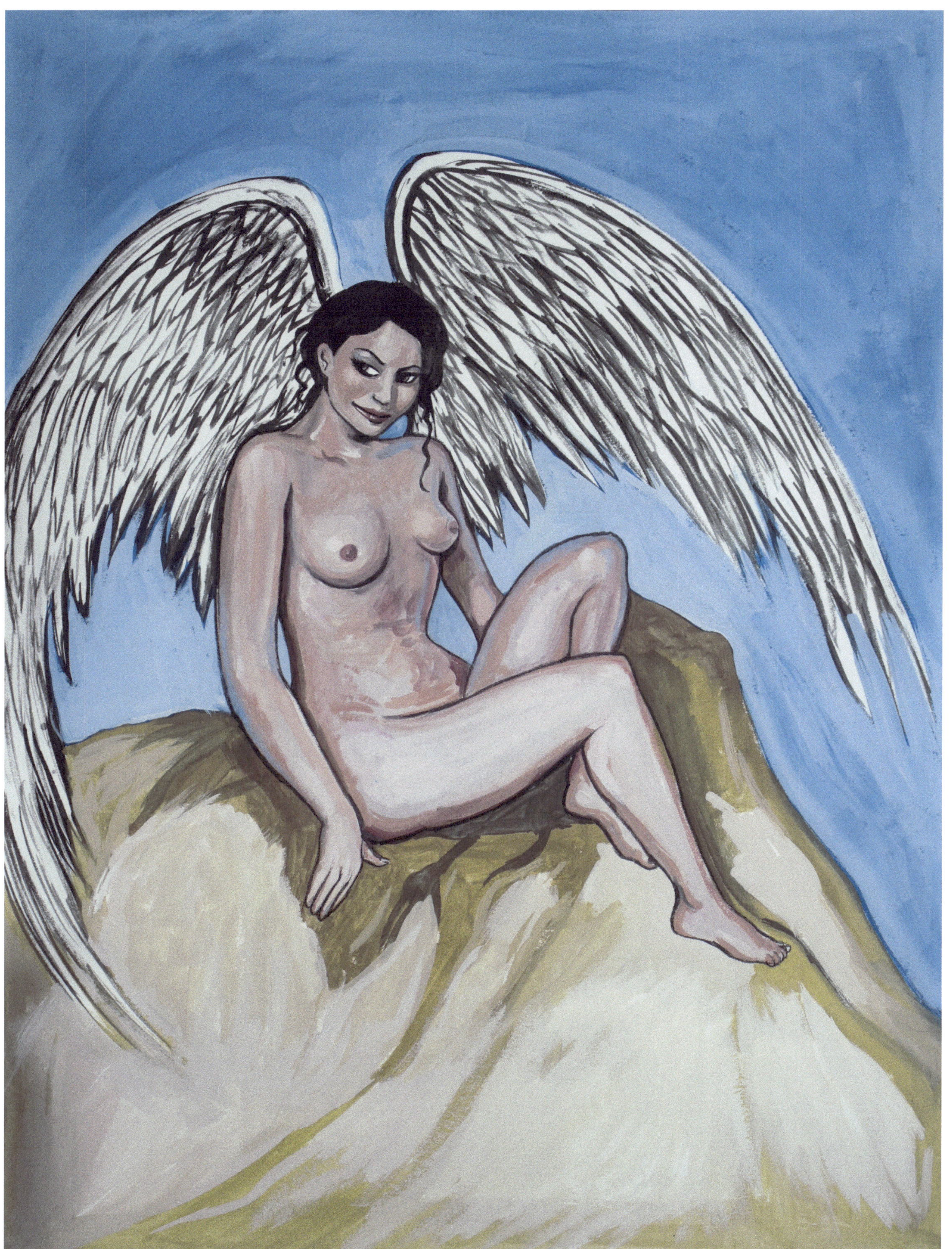

Blind hope

While you say again,
Move and fair my Casket friend.
Worm food noiseless,
A cracked egg shell.
Curt hurried voices,
A silver Bell.

Saw the Demons part from here,
Don't budge an inch, show no sign of
fear.
Chord on holy, caught on blind hope.

Measured seven feet with bended knees.
Hands clasp and a handshake in the
other world.
Mountain man at the ending of another
book.
Five serpent sea snakes caught on your
hook.

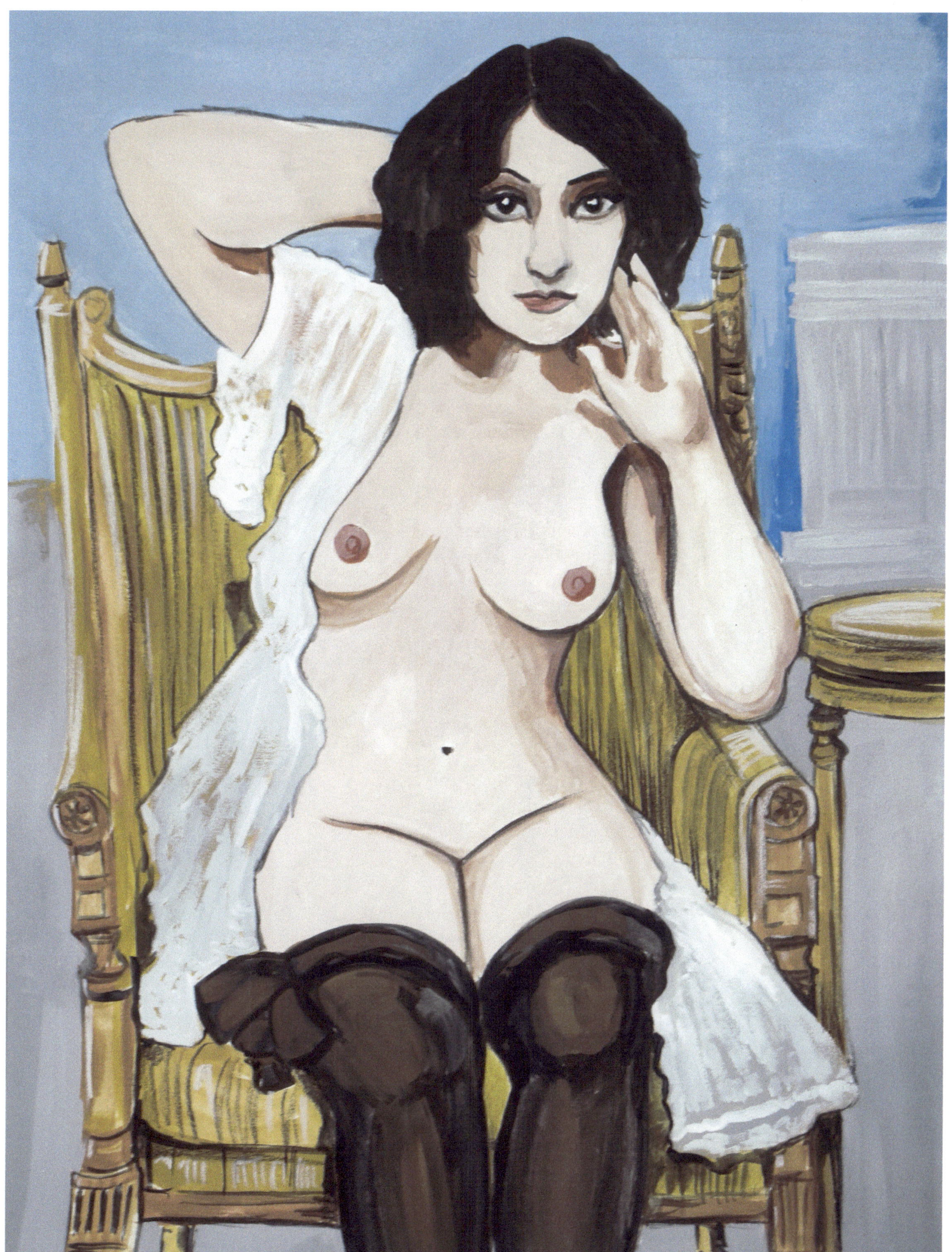

Obliterated Conscious Mind

I've got a taste of it.
Bleed wine from the sea,
And the wind says to me,
Stay longer.

Oh I'm left to my thoughts.
Tied them down cause they stray.
Obliterated conscious mind.
More time.

I build a life Brick by Brick,
On the foam of other thoughts.
Wait for that voice to kick in.
Tapped a vein like I ought.

Come across a divine life,
A predetermined accident.
Learn to fly by missing the ground.
I wander.

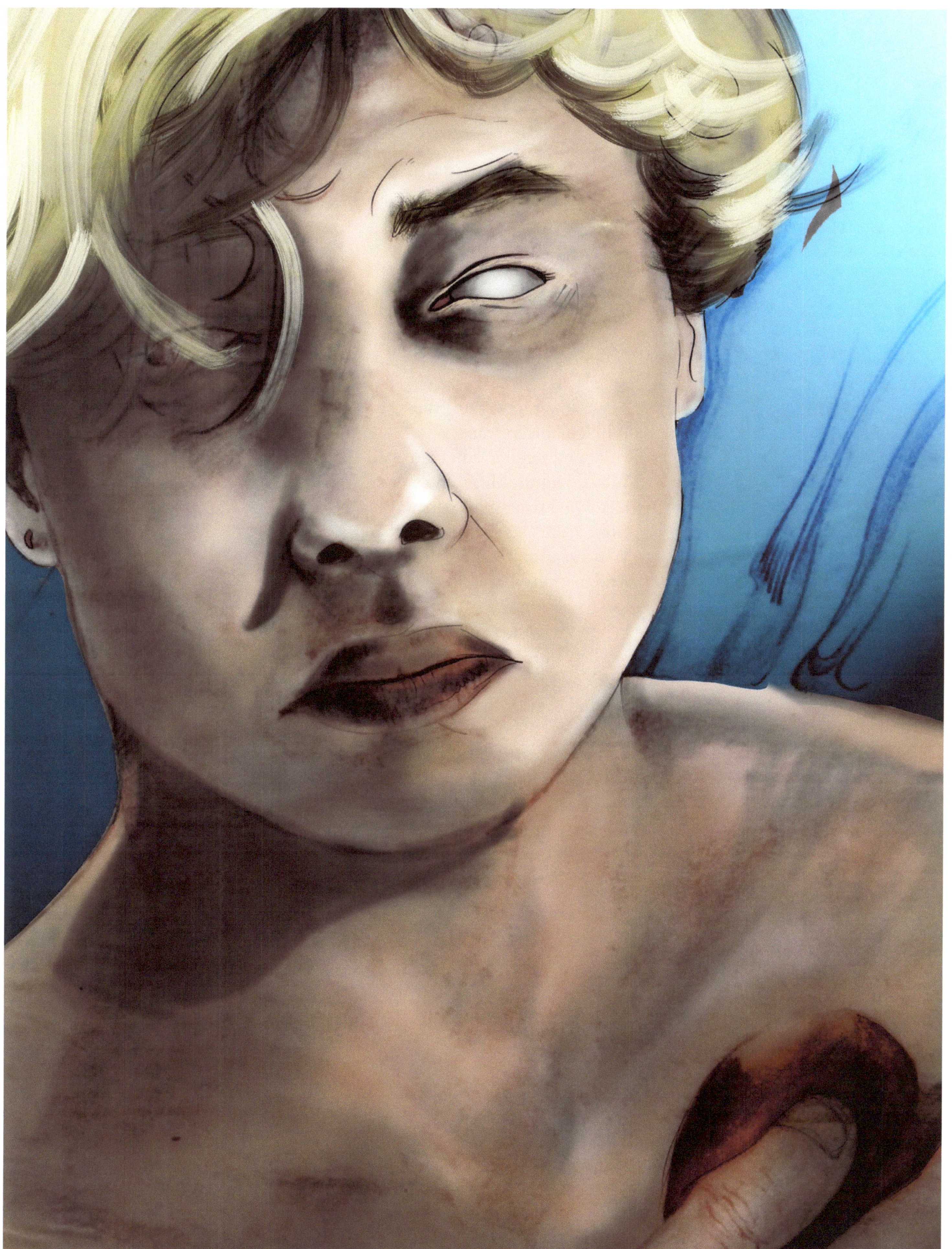

Ghost Town

Running on your fear,
Will it all disappear?
Full of tainted blood and dreams,
Why do all the children scream?
Daddy's buried in the dirt,
Gone from this world of hurt.
Why do all the leaders lie,
And let their sons and daughters die?

When the winds begin again,
We'll be blown like the wind.
Hurled around like the tumbleweeds,
On and everlasting seed.

Oh, years gone by,
When we reached for the sky,
And laid our plans of gold and fire,
But the Sandman was a liar.

Now our children build again,
Make Beginnings from our ends.
Finding things we never thought about,
No room for fear or nagging doubt.

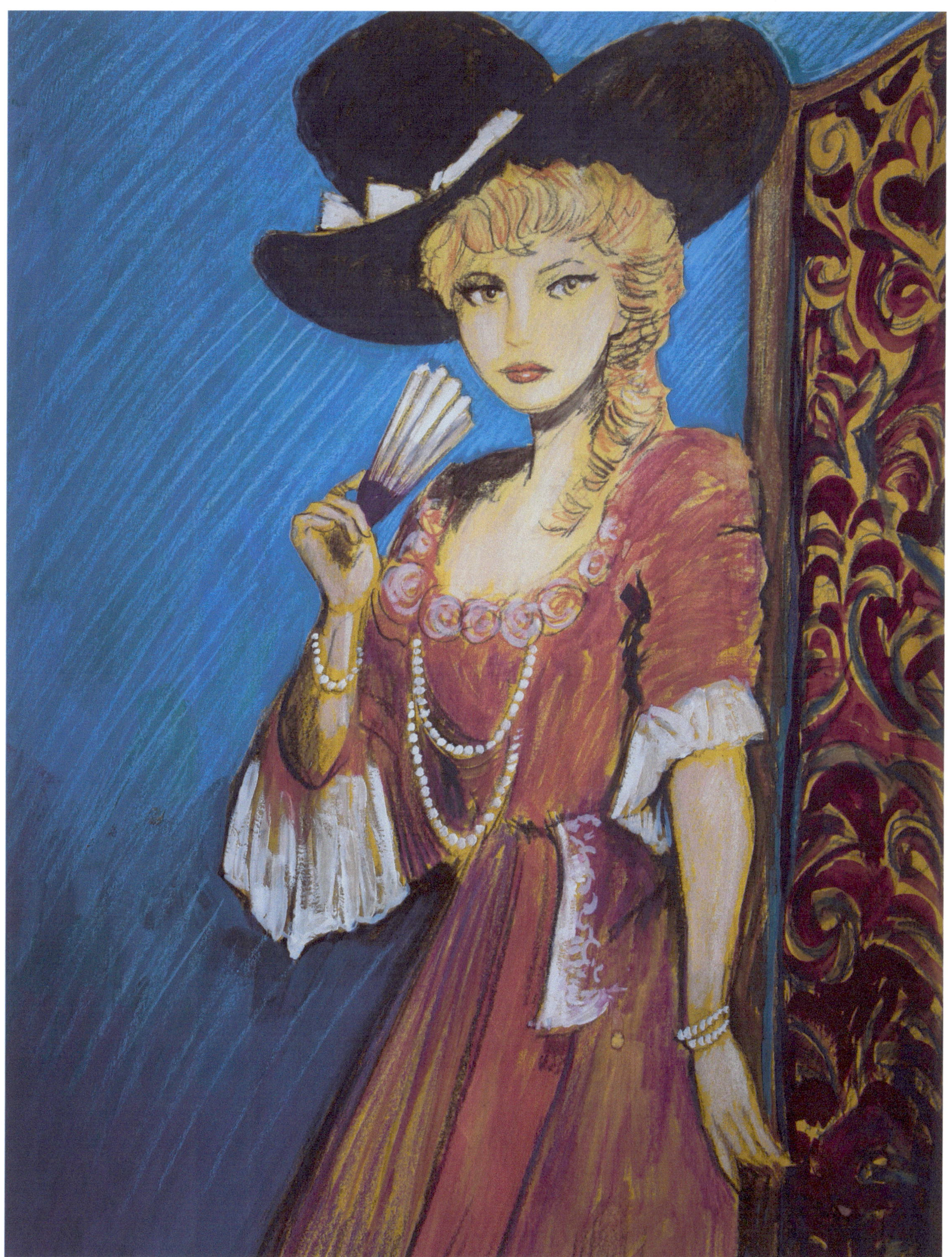

Chromatic War

Can blind be bothered,
And I'm bothered by you.
Shout and whisper,
Still can't break through to you.

I topple too much.
Want and found steady ground.
In passing passage,
Newfound strengths a subterfuge.

Empty found, the blue seed ground.
Tied and torn, envisioned all.
As they fall, burnt blackened sun.

Tired gaze,
An answers born.
Wild one,
Gather as they fall.
Enlightened view,
Chromatic war.

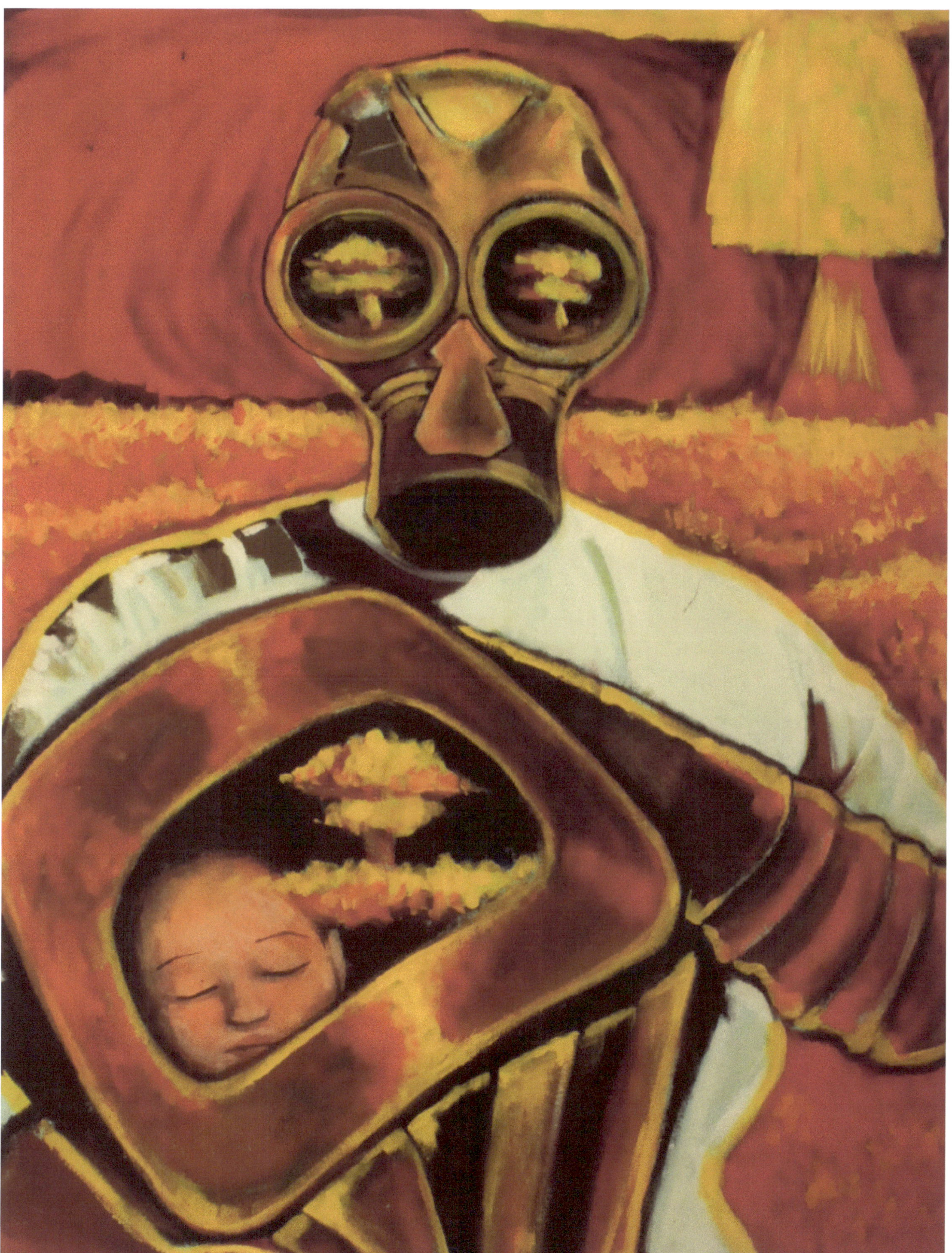

Shame

Why won't you talk to me,
Because I've done worse than this.
Shied of mediocrity,
I failed in warming you.
Dealt with this honestly,
Now I'm wishing I had lied.

Now I reel in the Shock of you,
And your bitter mouth and downcast eyes.

We're all alone,
Just one with fears to free.
I'll never belong,
Just a freak with a burning seed.

Why can't I die,
If living means I'll always play the fool.
This jokes on me,
Now I'm left with living off my shame.

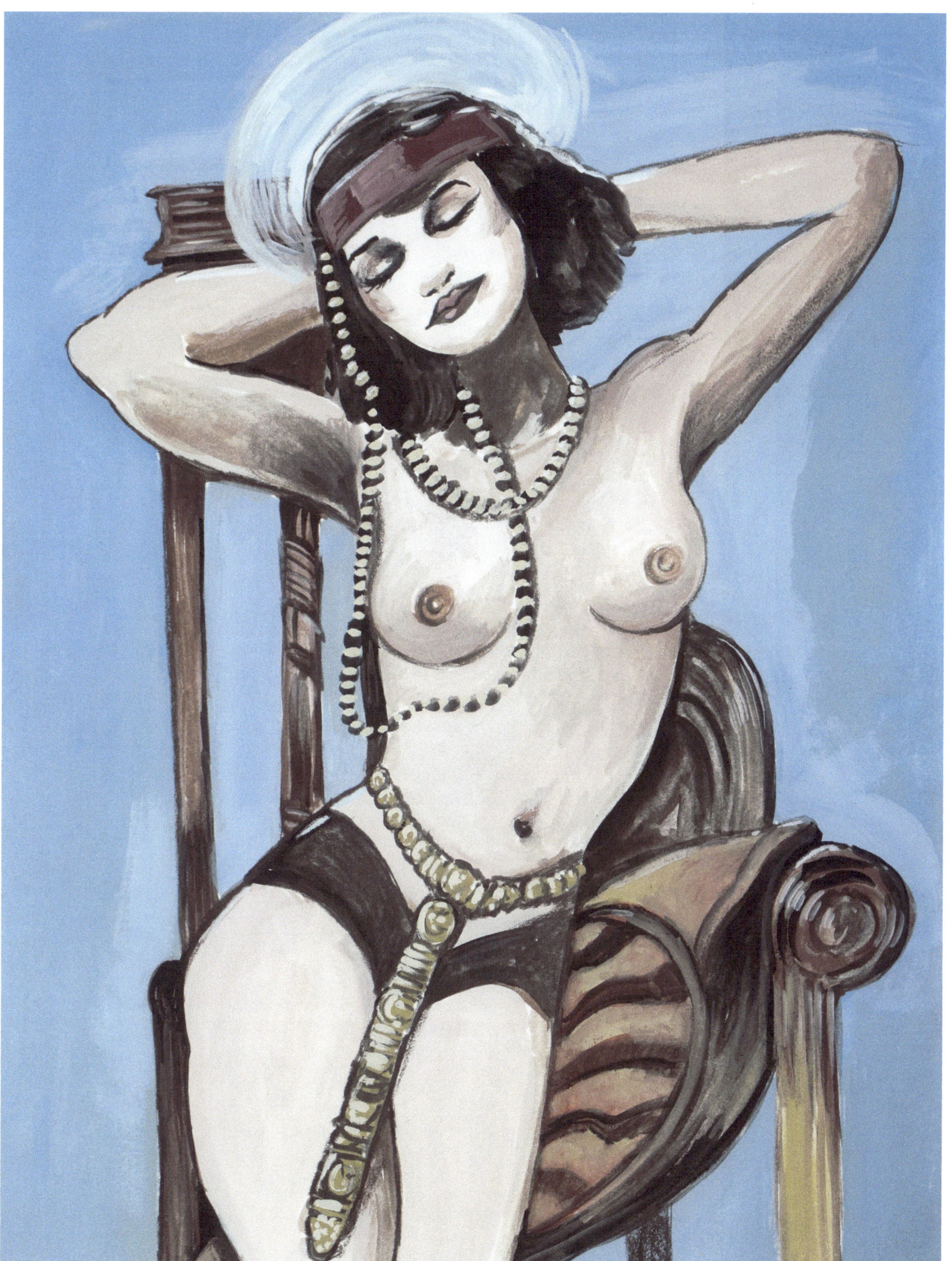

Embrace

Hold on to me again,
As I wrap my arms and hold you close my friend.
Given all before, so I'm vulnerable you see.
But I sure have had a good time,
Seeing how you see.
As I've given thanks to having friends around,
Oh, with this fires warmth,
This warmth inside of you.
Taste the sweat around your apple core,
What am I supposed to do?
Take a ticket and wait in line,
Or drop my head and break on through?
I am gone.
Closed mouth, fever thoughts and song.
Not sorry, I kick back and think of you.
Take a seat, and wait to see what you do.

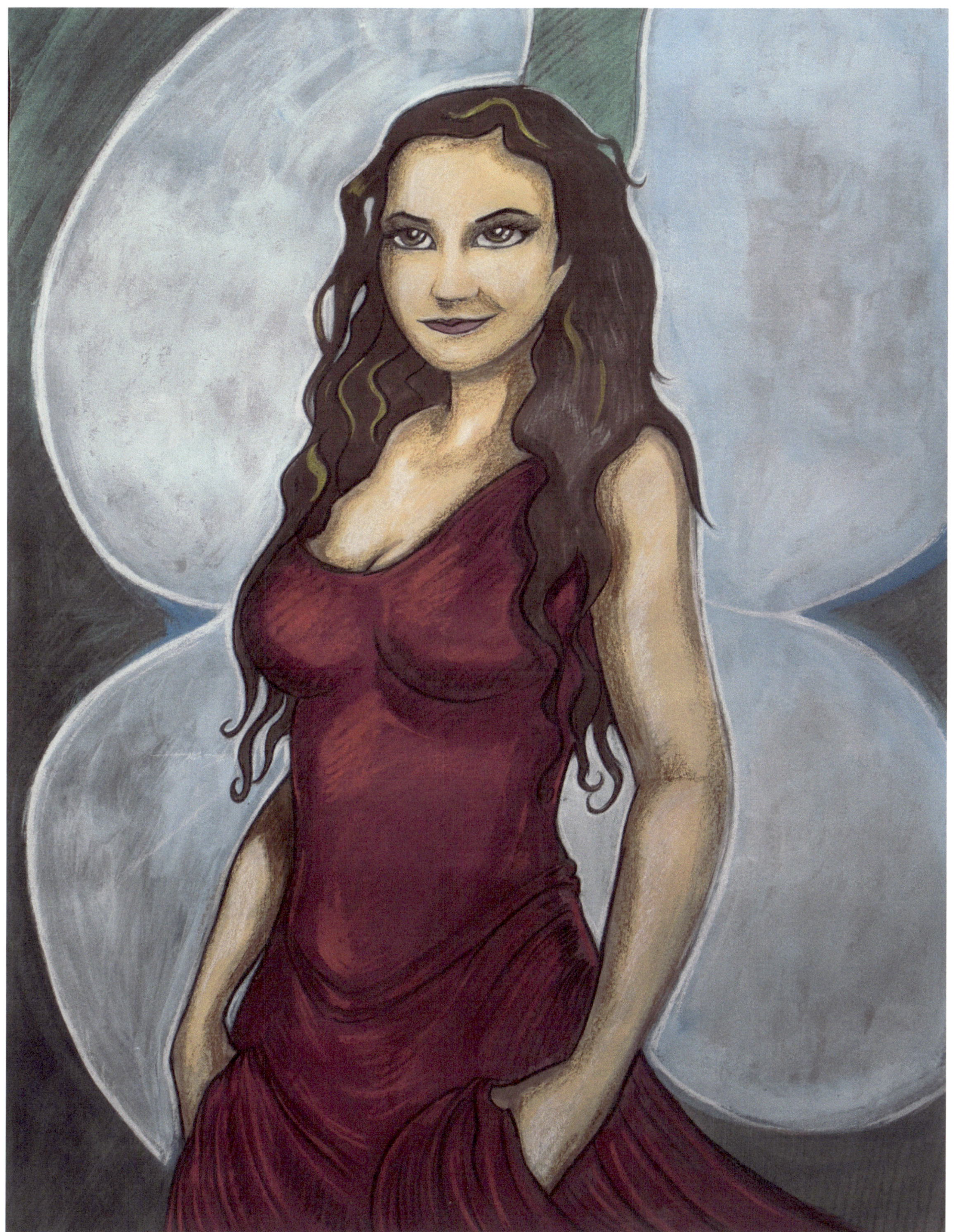

My secret thought

Watching you sleep again,
Stretched out like a cat on your bed.
If I could cover you with roses, know I would.
Want to kiss you from your cheek to your toes,
...And I want to share all my secret thoughts.

She don't want to hear those thoughts again.
I say them in my head every day,
My Silence can't get too cold.
Just wish I could say what I know,
...And I want to share all my secret thoughts.

In times alone my thoughts come along,
Your celestial place glowing in my space.
My want is warm for your form,
Flooded heart, the dam breaks.

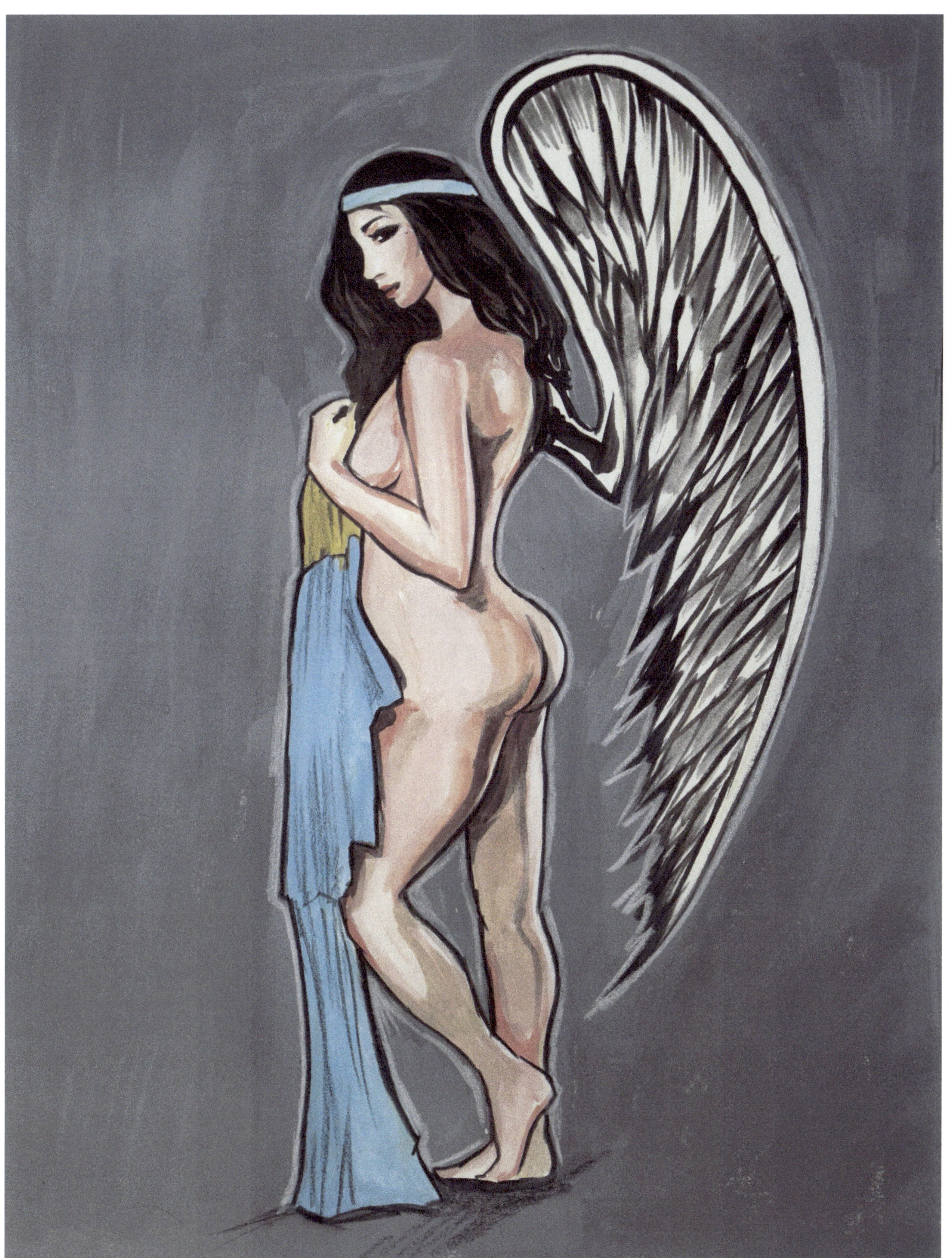

Drawn lines

Pulling the Mad Dog,
Driving the air from my lungs,
Building up spires to the sun.
Sending a message,
Soul birds alight in your cell,
Dreaming up words I can't coo.

Don't you think about your baby,
Growing up on these mean streets?
Getting too cold for him lady,
The way they take gives me the creeps.
Burning in excess,
Taking abuse for some love,
Had this new passage been shunned.

My hands been tied over,
With all the things I can't keep,
Till all my friendships will end.

Don't you take part in making,
The fall boys plan to take them down.
Just your space in need of warmth,
And a crystal berth across her crown.

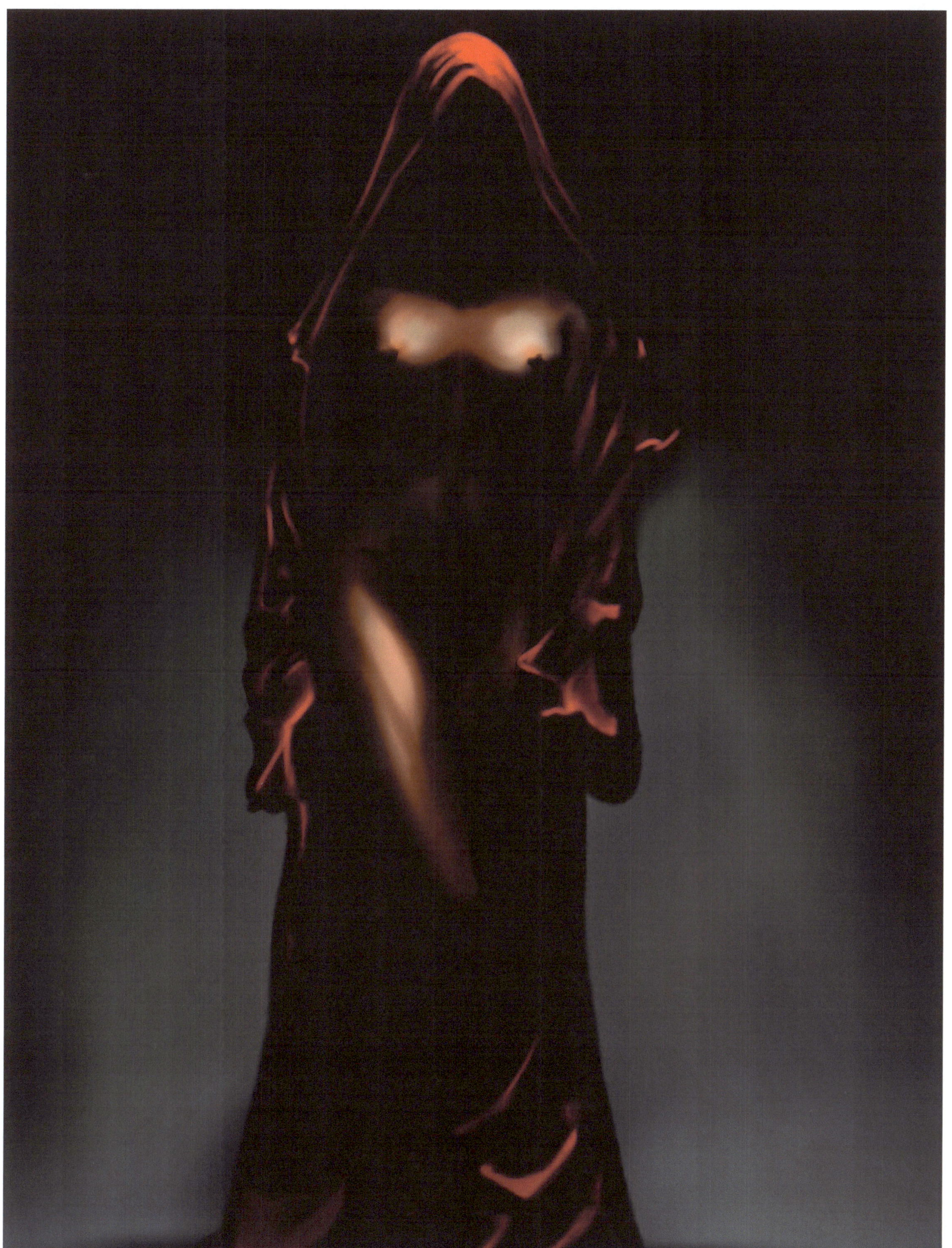

Slipped

Before this mystery this endless history,
Before me, before we,
Showed what we learned.
Let go of all we know.

Don't know what we capable of today.
Only know what we learned shouldn't be said.
Gaining my power back.

Am I fast enough to catch you before you drift
away from me?
And if this really is the end,
I'll always hold you close to me,
So I hope I've gained a friend and not a heartbreak
enemy.

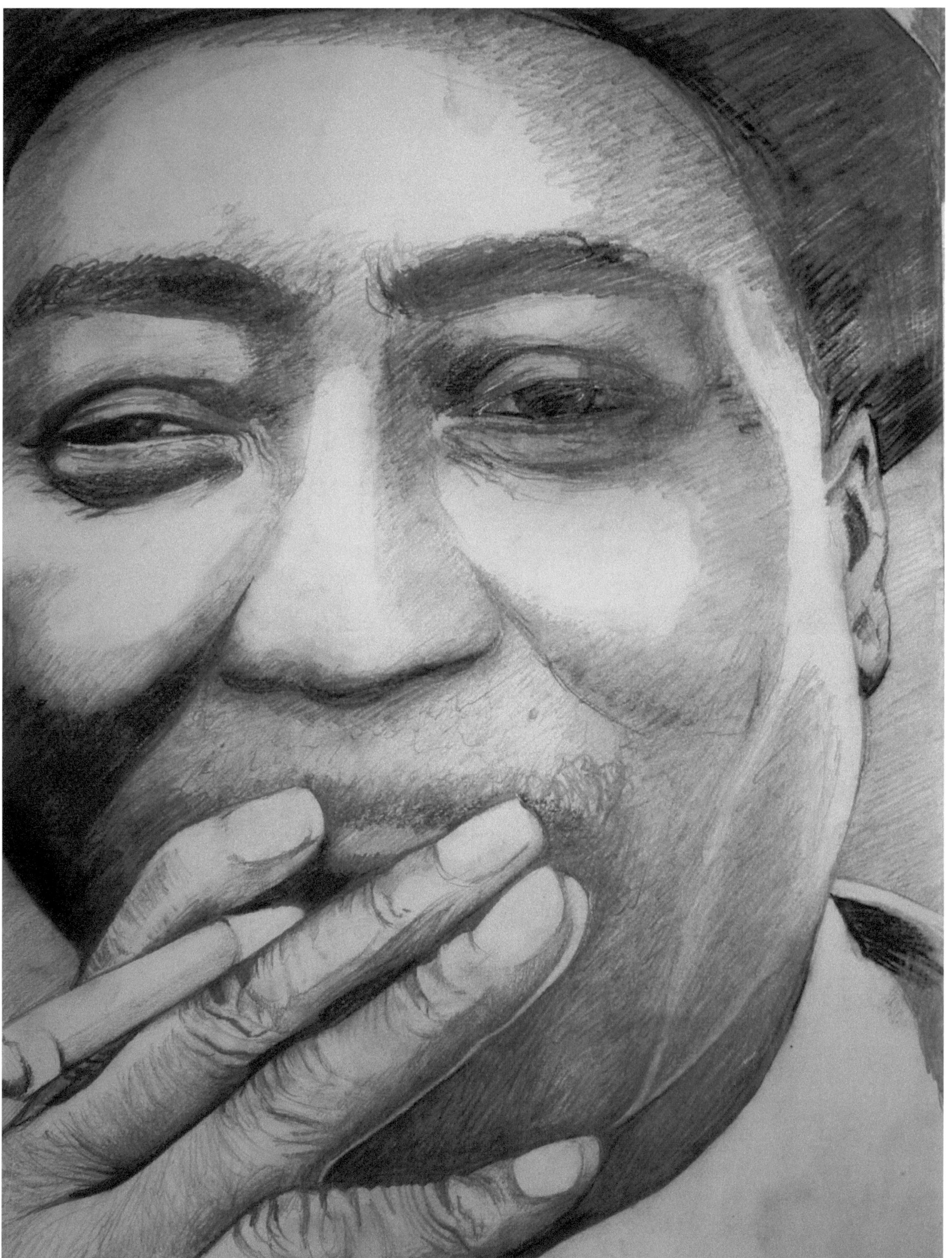

The Gift

So lonely for your love,
Holding the thoughts of your face.
Seeing your life,
Feeling it's seeping through me.
Can we see it together?
Can we see it at all?
We can never connect,
Together, we can see it all.

Dreaming of a life,
With you by my side.
Inspired by your soul,
It's something special in this world.
I will always love you,
I can see your worth.
Will you ever want me back?
...Or should I let these passions fall?

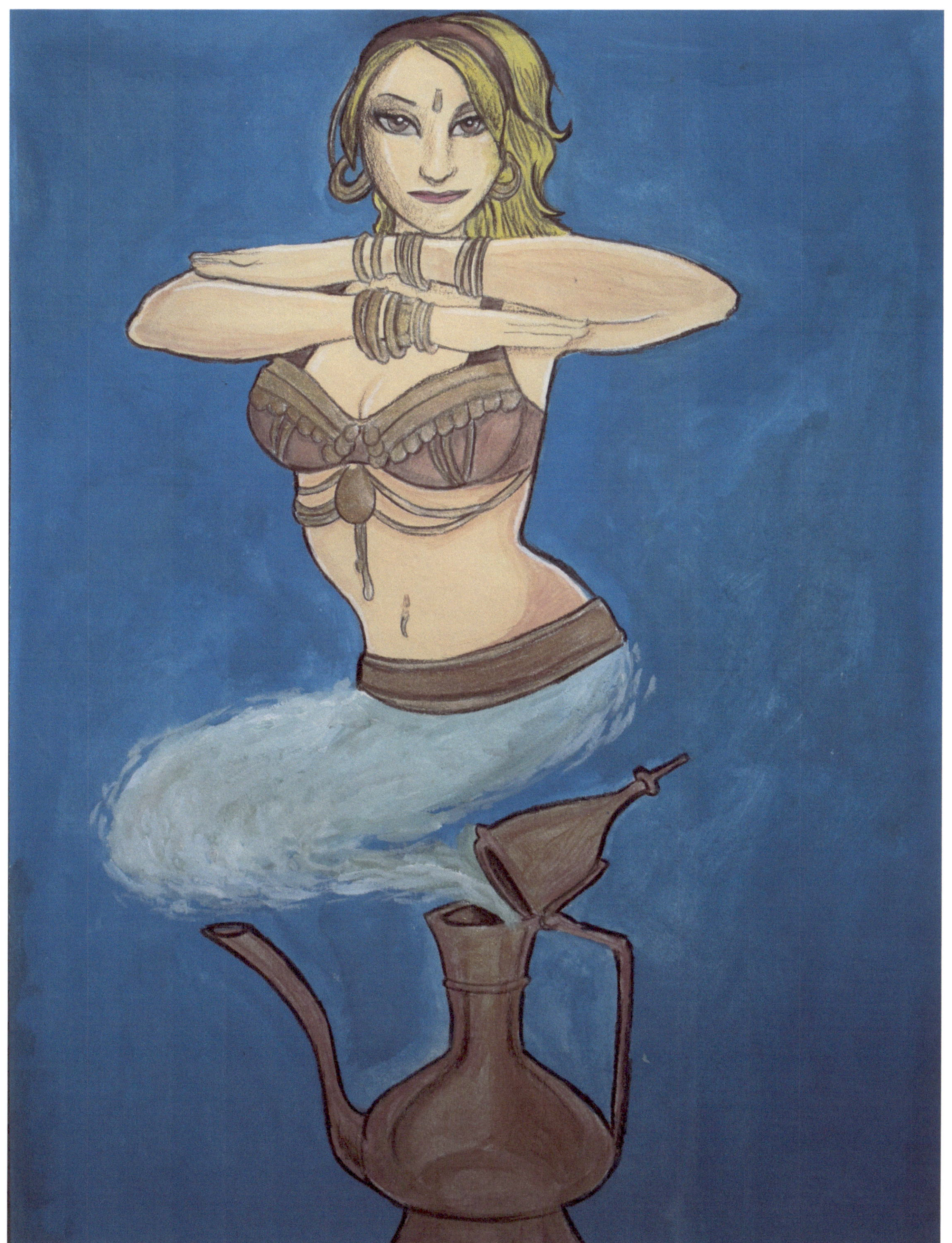

Ascent

Right at home
In a smaller world.
Got an itch,
Blinders real but out of view.

Right in the middle,
Scarred from fighting with myself.
Right in the middle,
Just about to leave this room.

Consequence,
Just a word till now.
The patterns move,
Till I just make out a face.

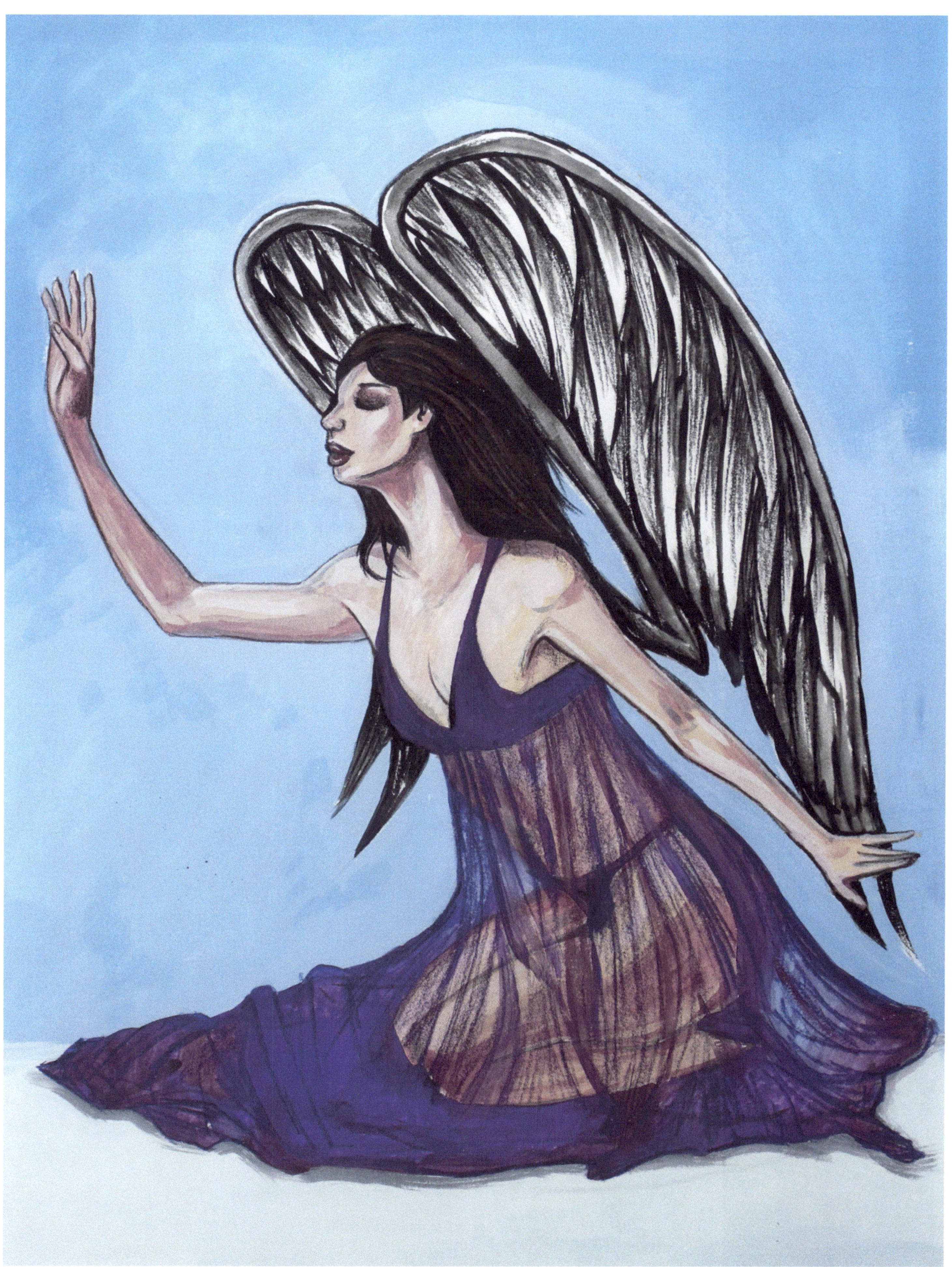

In parchment true

Bold in parchment dyed to weather,
Am I symbol metaphor?
I share them.
Touch a line and sneak your toes across,
And wear a cross.
Martyr mind can complicate a thought.

Like poison ice, melt a sliver in my soul again.
I gave myself to the whirlpool,
Let karma make the ride for me.
Current takes me from the hardness of a knuckle,
Give my wounds more time to heal.

Now I feel it all flowing through me,
Now my soul is free to hunt time across Infinity,
Now I wear your warmth like your only son,
And change the places where we are in dual unity.
Now I feel.
Now I feel.

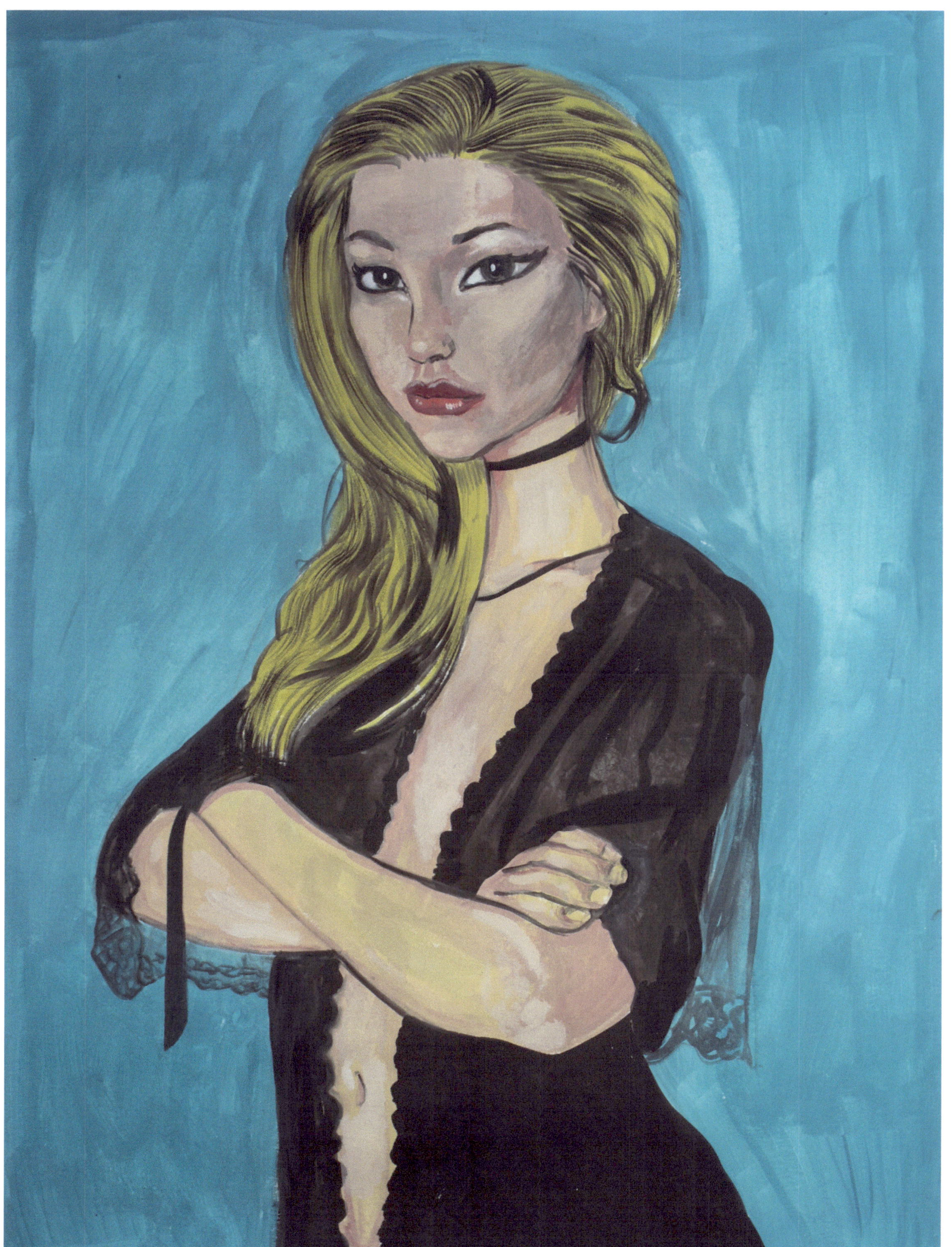

Nicotine stains

I acquired a way to see, and feel, and fear,
As I drift away on an incandescent wave,
Of childish dreams,
But the child stands alone,
And drinks the rain and sings,
And thinks of things to come.

Never thought this is of what I've become,
A shell, a form, an alien.
Oh so alien to you.

Mind rolls on a sea of twisted limbs,
Of the mottled skin and horns,
Of the Furious hordes,
And the whores I want to save,
But I can't save myself.

Now I'm floating in a pool of blood,
Devoid of things I had before,
Like you,
Whoever you may be.

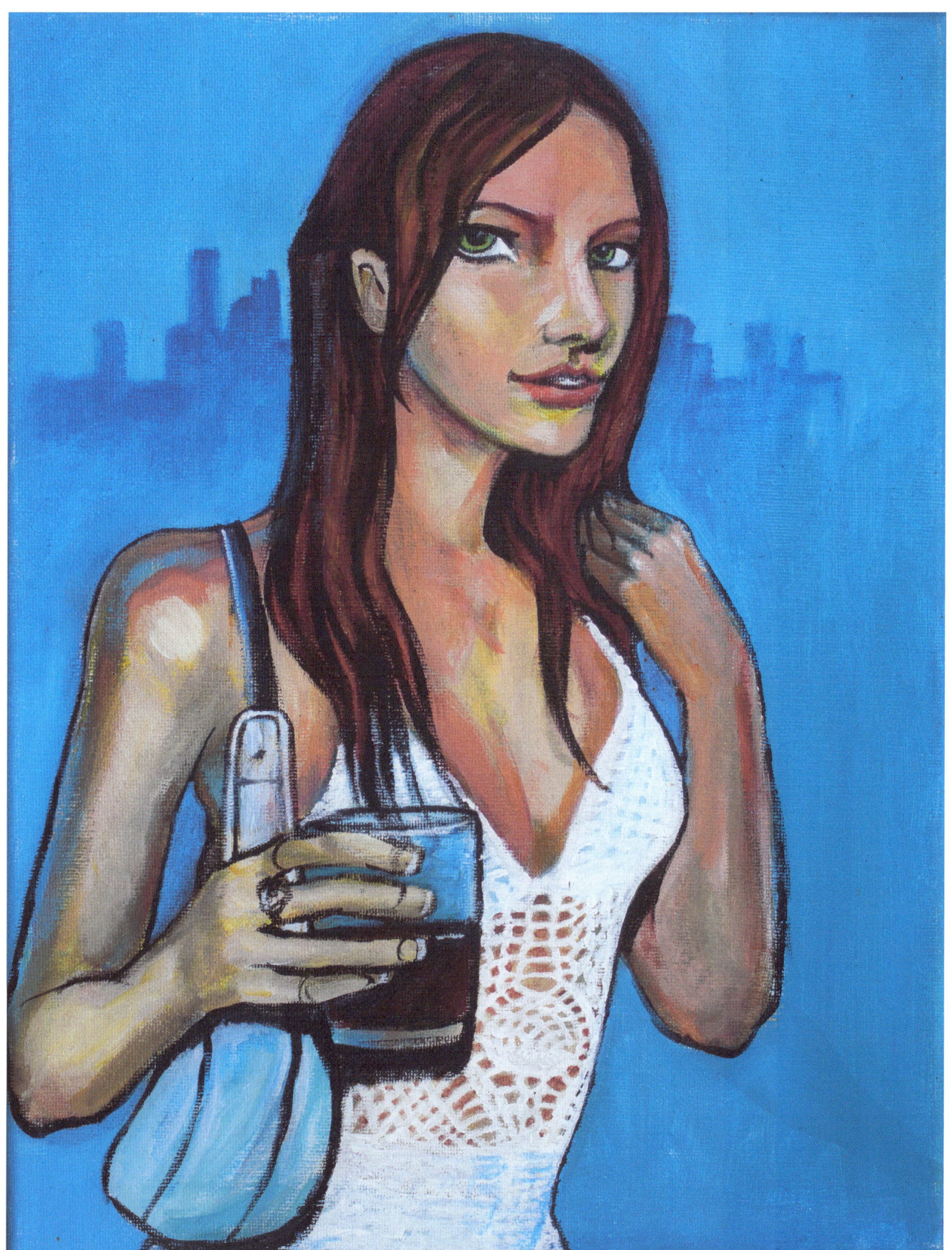

Orb of Fire

An orb of blue fire,
Surrounds my thoughts.
What carves the hordes of whispered skin,
Tells the tale of years far gone.

So you clapped your ear so you could hear,
So you could hear nothing, oh no.
...And you lost your fear in the Autumn leaves,
Now you find your strength in the winters cold,
Where the dreams are possible.
Found your thought,
Dictate where the arrow sort.
...And you thought you knew all their thoughts.

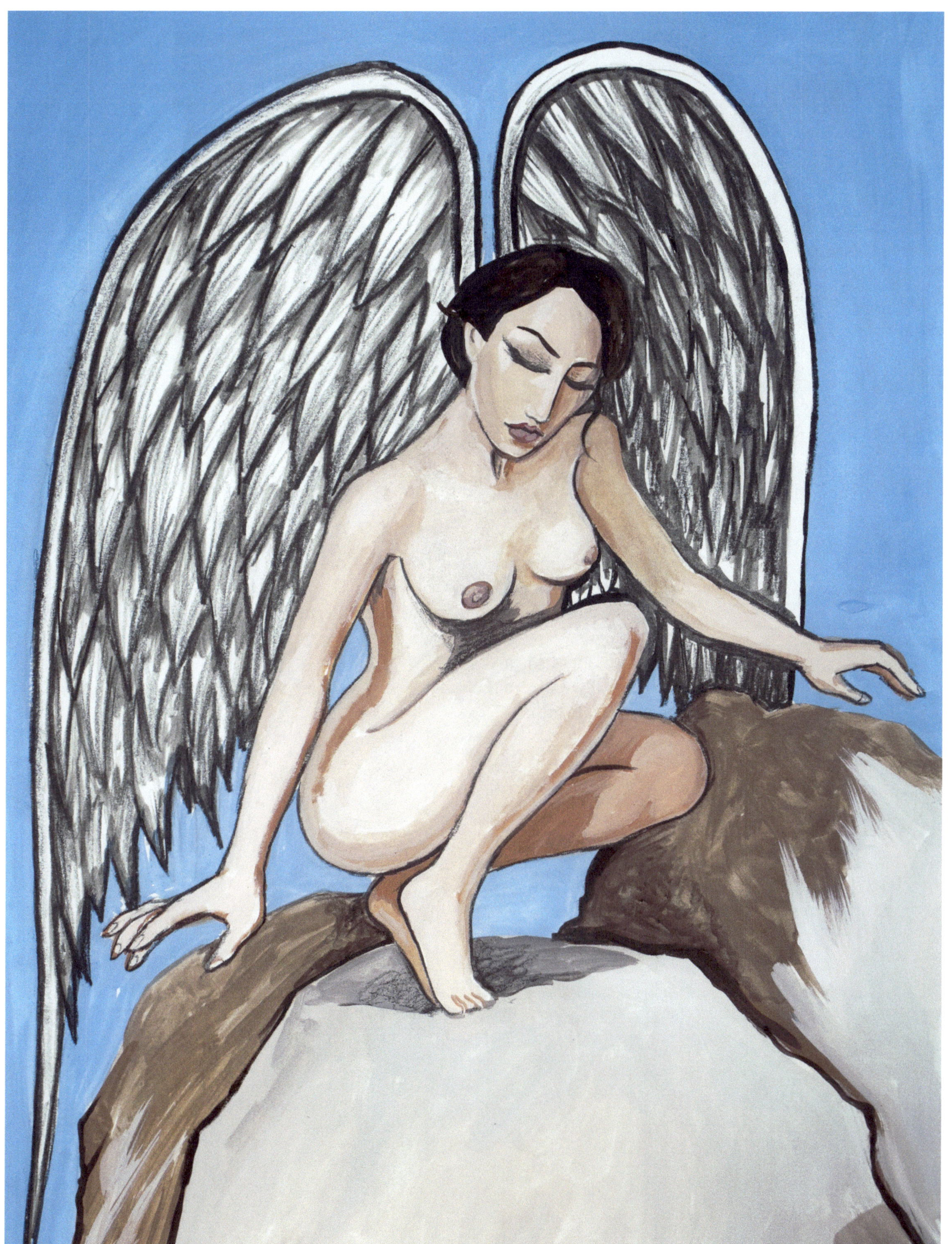

Seashell

Found a seashell that echoed with your sighs,
Like you found your truth, and drowned out others lies.
So I give to you all I have to give,
And I know that's not a lot,
But in me you can believe.

Our painful memories they don't do a lot for me.
Let's forgive them and move on,
Because while they stay there, we have eternity.

Smooth out our hearts,
We've got it all from the start.
Loves just begun.

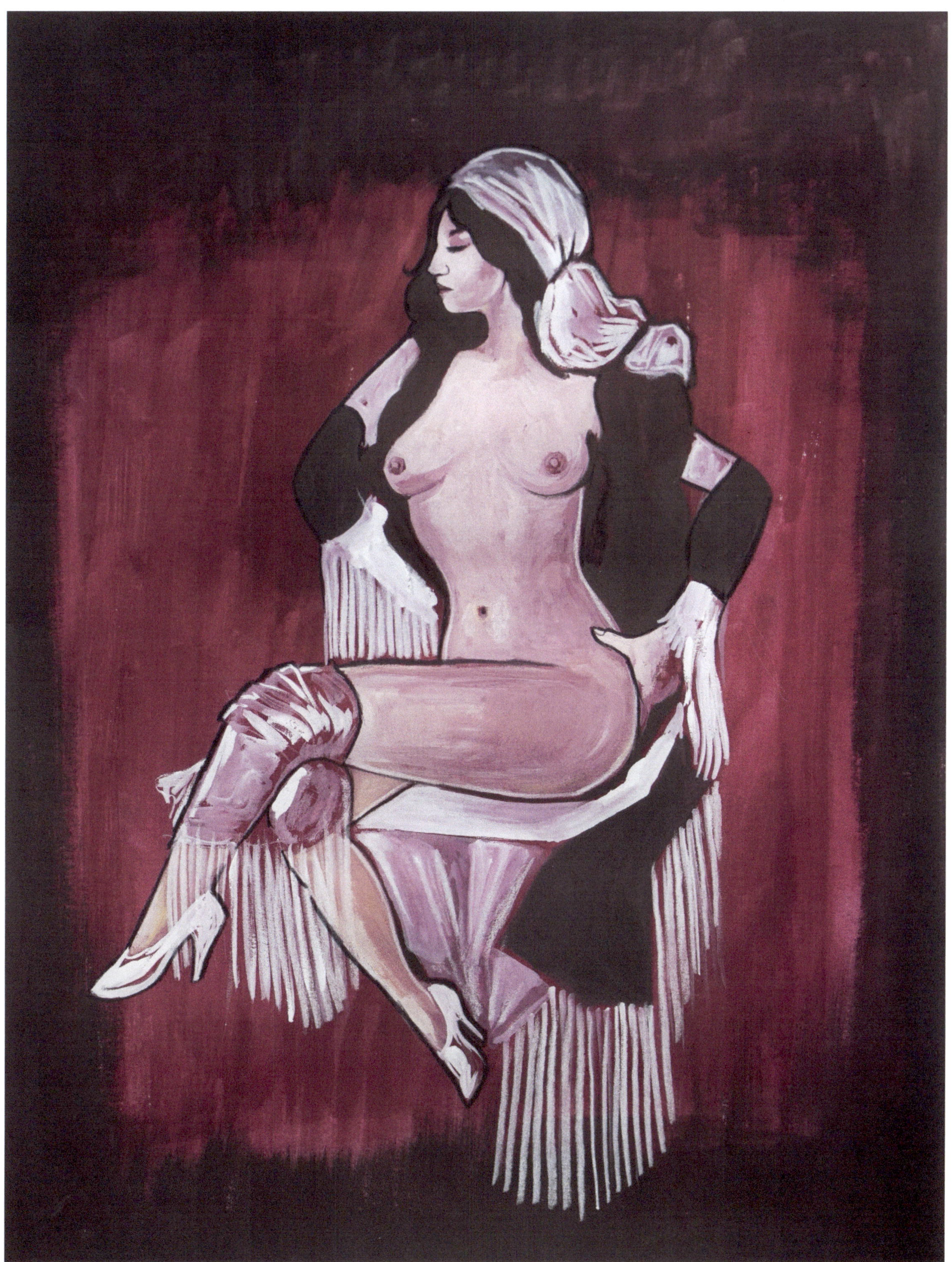

Hope

How unreal is Hope?
Endless patterns evolve,
Doors swing forward to the space as the truths are divulged.
Too ashamed to show my face,
Lost answer to my pain.
Why I always fall the same?
My broken heart is getting cold,
Take this coldness to the grave.
So I warn all you lovers about your warmth,
Cause when gone is all your mystery they will depart.
Think about an early grave,
Think of all the hurt I'll save.
With no thoughts to drive me mad,
...But I'll breathe another breath.
Let this power come to me,
Visions take my breath away.
The movement through these planes,
Don't feel real, just insane.
So I call to all my past lovers that stole my warmth.
If it's strength they want then why do they keep tearing me apart?

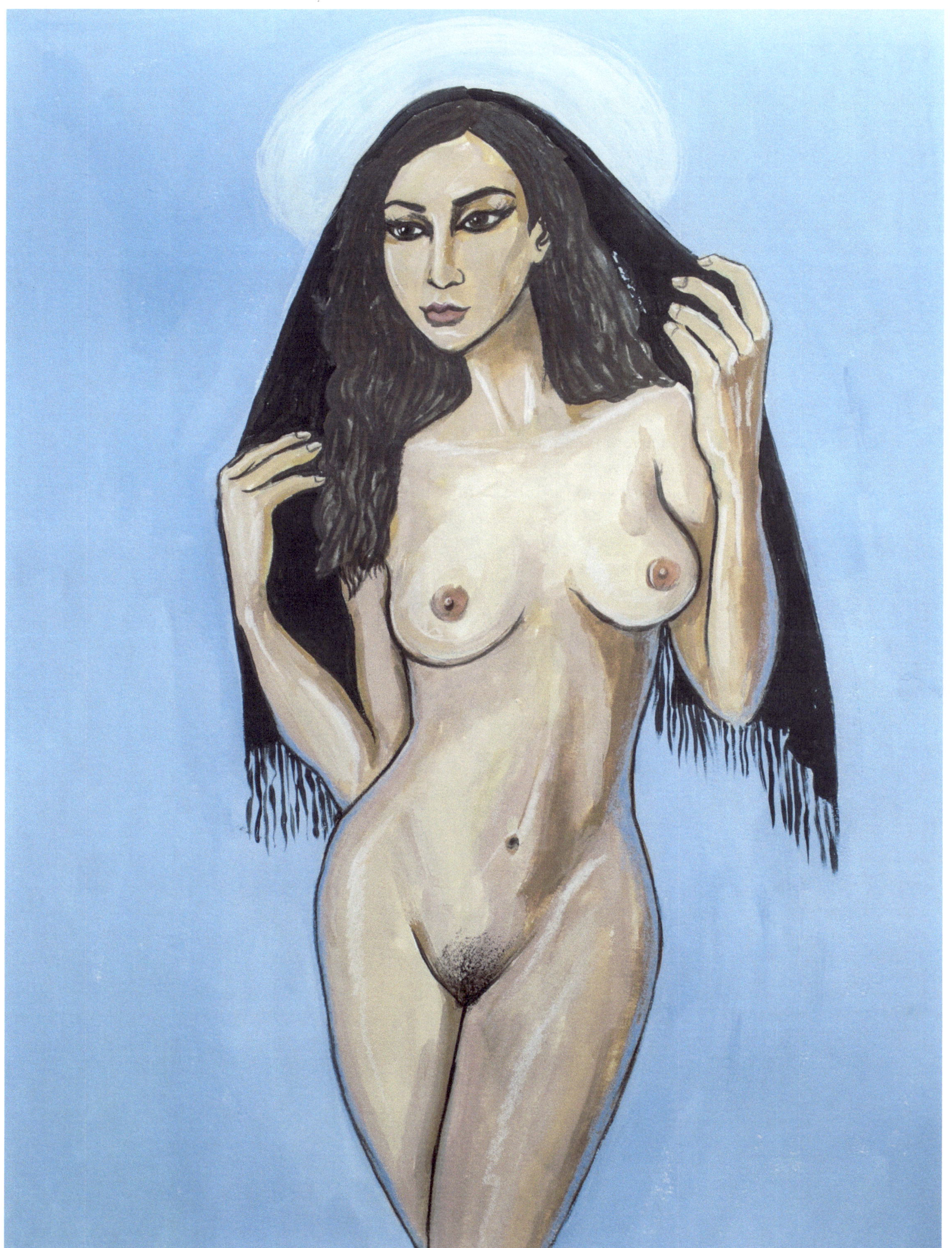

The Scent of Home

Pen your words upon my skin my dear,
And we will ride this fear.
Sharp delivery intent upon pushing us beyond.
Are we far away?
Or do we move toward the scent of home.
Only in someone else's shadow can we really feel alone.
Take your lover in your arms my friend,
And try to see it through.
Temptation caught on what's been gone for so long,
With no images of which to hold.
A love grown cold.

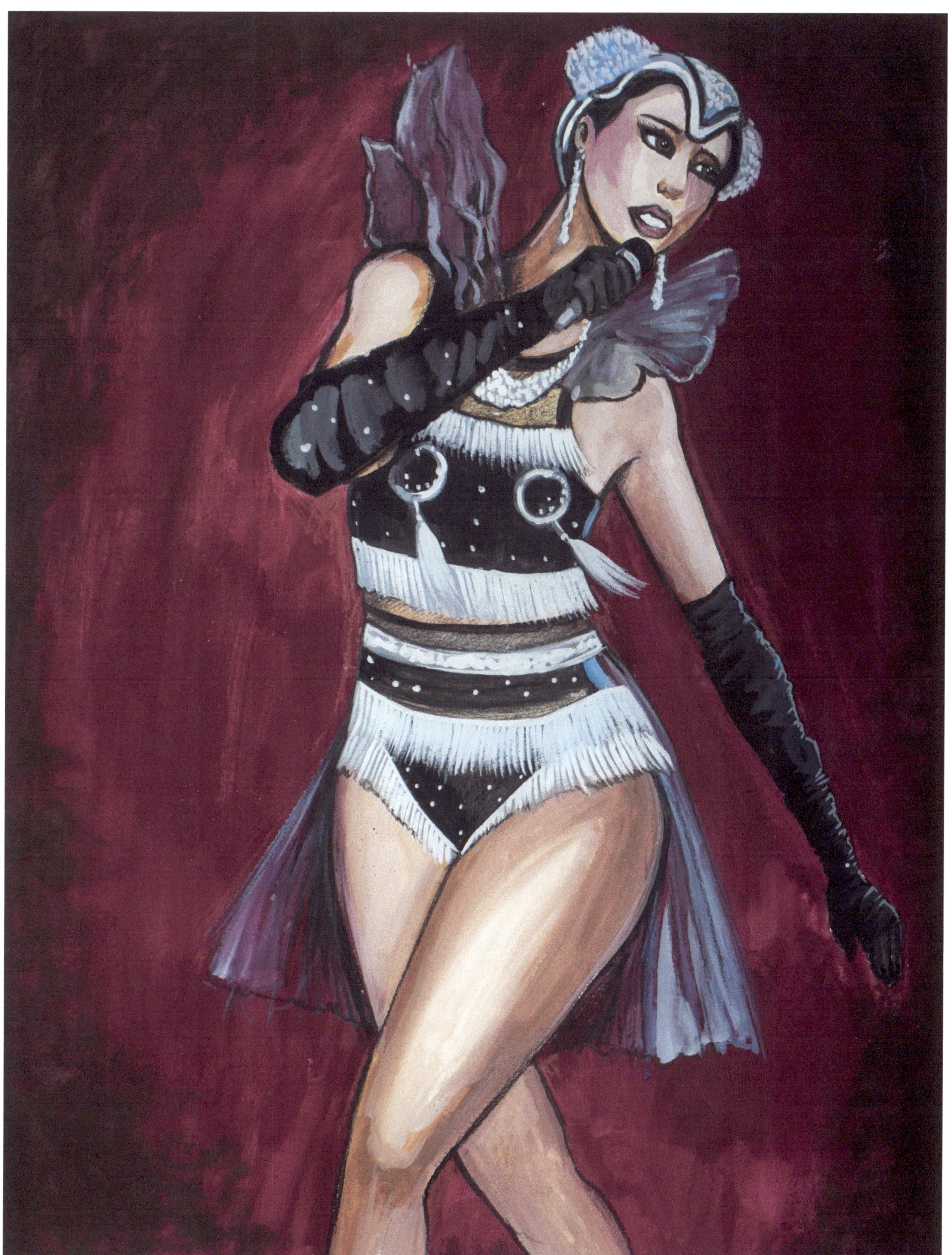

Puckered

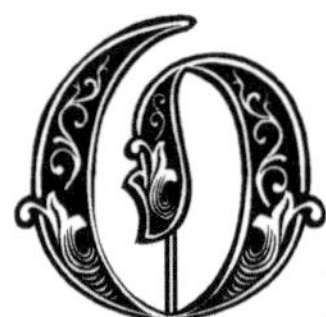h, Subdued in a sense.
I live and breath,
...And your God means nothing to me.
I have the earth and the trees.
Born innocent, but I lost it too soon.
I turn from your petty hates,
And I looked around and guess what I saw.
Saw mothers cry in their sleep,
...And lovers full of shame.
Of all your conquests did you think about all their hopes and plans?

Essentially a good man.
I can't believe the pictures that I saw.
I turn my hand.
All my sisters are not your whores.
...And I'll cut you apart if you hit her again.
...And I'll burn out your eyes if you look that way.
I'll break your arms,
If you steal her youth.
Poison and semen,
That's your truth.
I'll rip out your lungs if you speak like that.
I know I should seek the good in you,
but fuck it,
You had your chance.
I scream that my children should never see your face.
You want to have power,
So you hurt and rape.

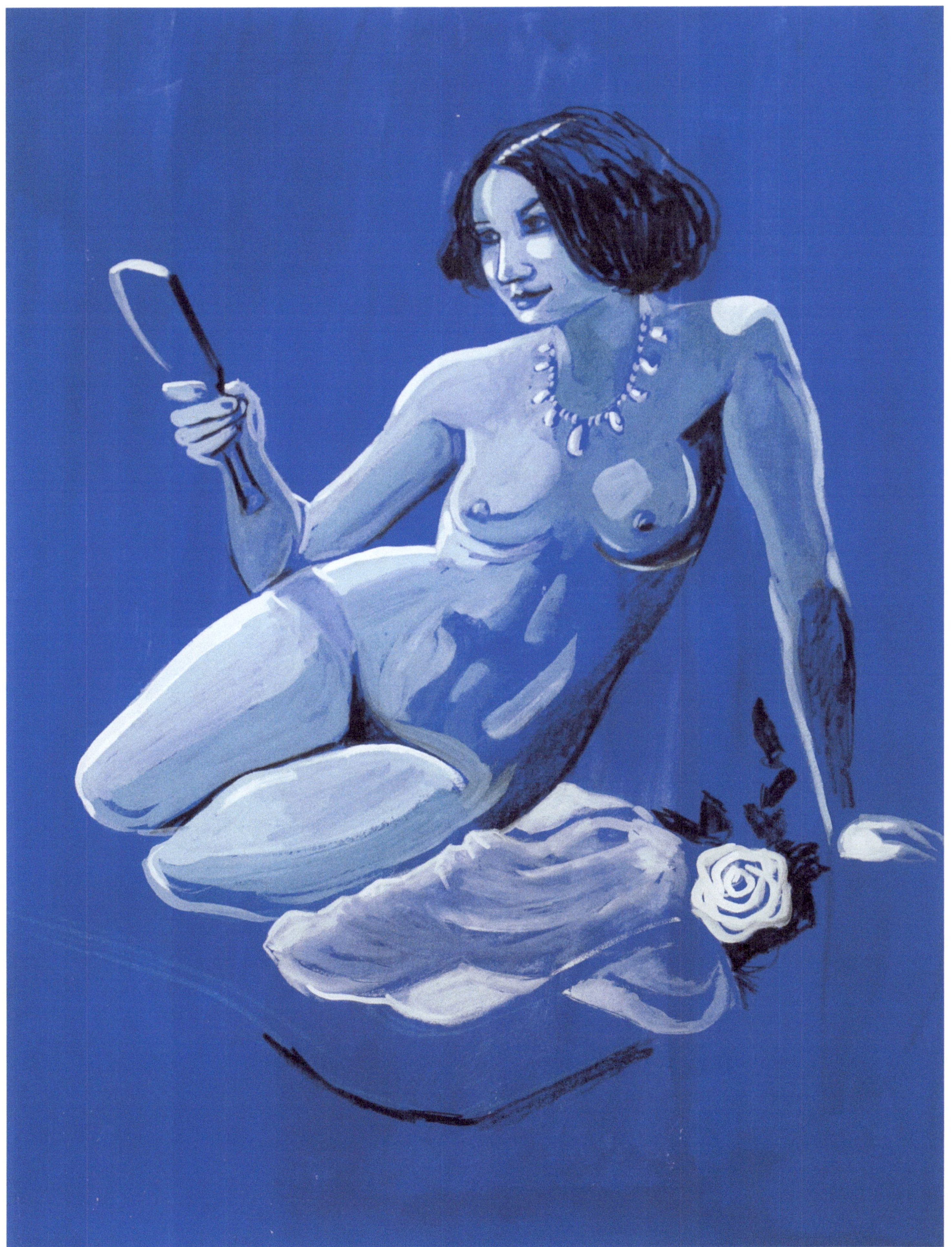

Esme
For Gran on her 84th birthday

Wide open fields,
And you're running free,
You're running free.

Dancing along the beach
With your feet
Ankle deep.

So just close your eyes,
And you can be
There with me.

Only when you find
Your piece of mind,
Then you'll be free.

So just close your eyes,
And you can be
There with me.

These Passing moments fade,
The hours and the days,
But it's not real.

The world is there in you,
And you can see it too,
So you know just what to do.

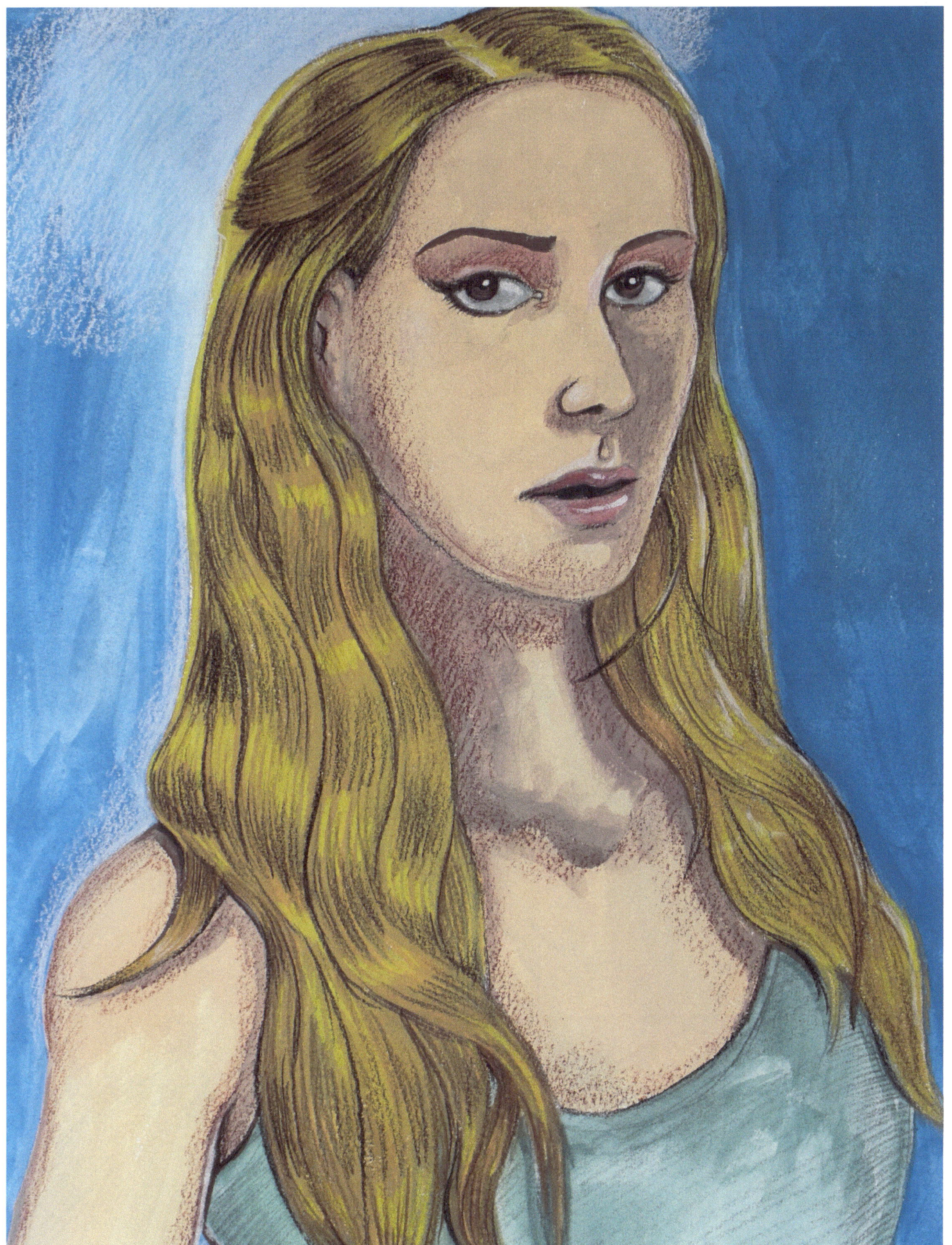

Ostracized Heart

Never want to be in this space again,
Never want to let you under my skin.
I just began to find out where I went again,
Then my world began to spin.
Where does I really begin?
Love.

Where do these feelings turn to pain?
When does the passion become shame?

Can't stop this feeling,
Can't stop this pain.
Won't let you get that close,
No, not again.

Never, ever, ever gonna breaka my heart.
Never, ever, ever, gonna take a my soul.
Away from me.
Where does this feeling turn to pain?
When does the passion become shame?

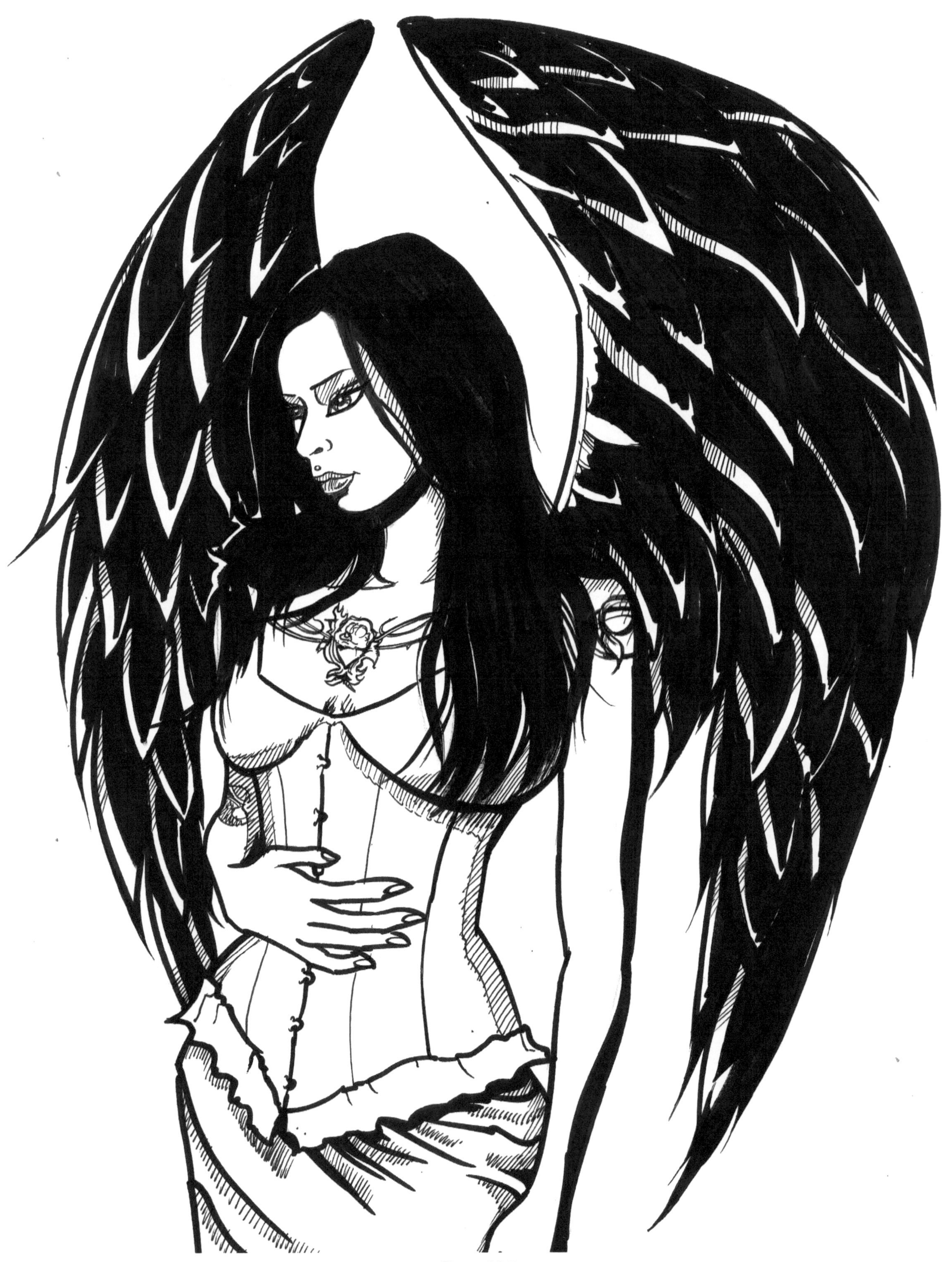

From Scratch

I'm not asking you
To do what you don't want to do,
Just to understand me.
To see what I can see.
I don't need a stool,
I can see quite well from this height,
You can see it all from here.

When this dizzy cloud fills in on itself,
Is I when I brush this old shit from my shelf,
And begin it all from scratch.
All the fresh ideas can hatch,
And ease on in to the whirlpool.
And when the lines begin to swirl,
You can be that special girl ,
And soon everybody's singing love songs
About my love for you.

And if you leave me with a broken heart,
And you take all your things and depart,
I will still love you,
Cause I never fall out of love.
There's a thousand things I want to say,
Maybe I'll find the courage today,
Or turn them into lyrics,
And sing them just for you.

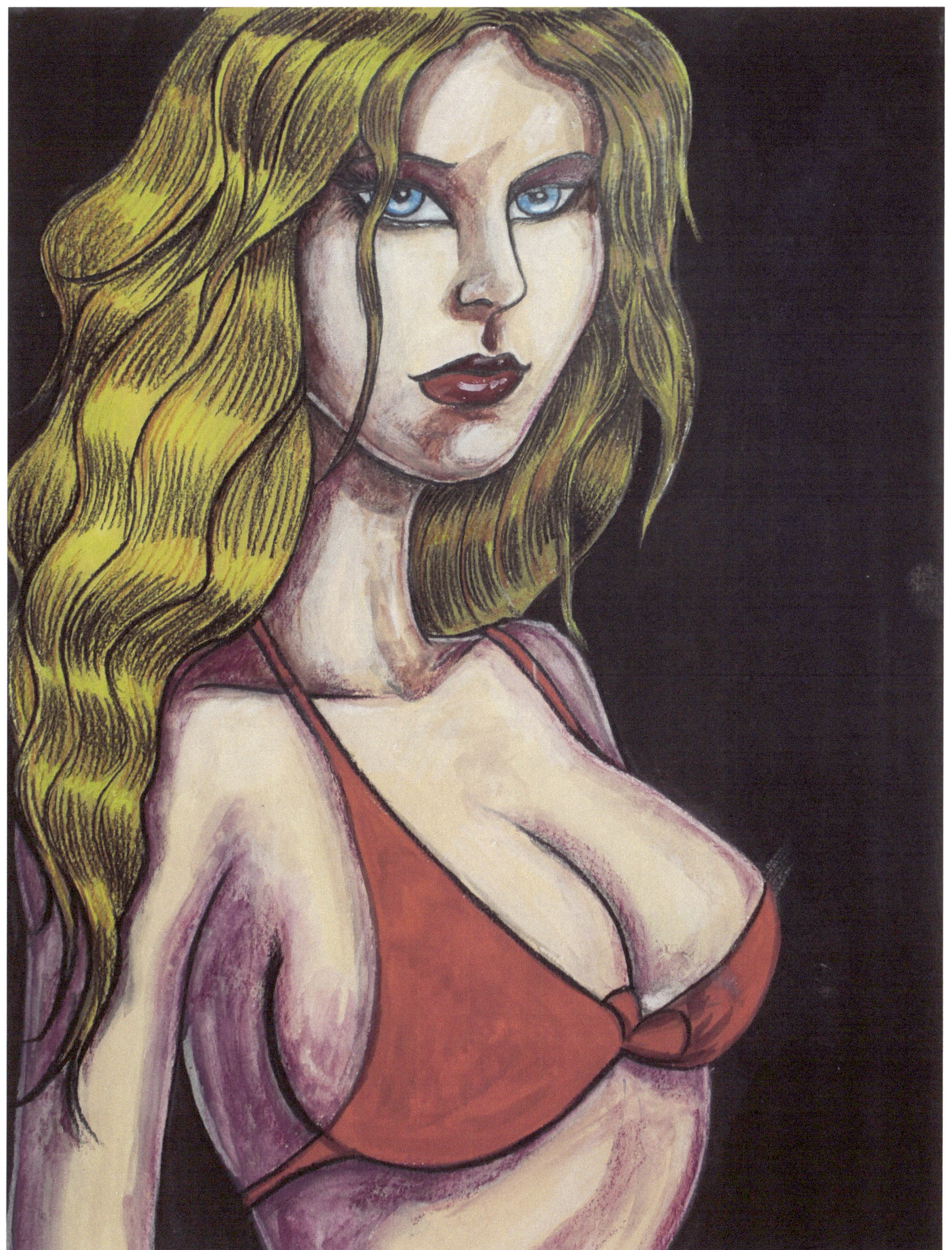

To Be Real

Can't help feeling alienated,
In this esoteric place.
Trying to say that I'm a freak,
Cause I don't wear that face.

Everybody get real,
Gotta move how you feel,
Till you break these shackles.

Funny how the masks mean something,
When you all wear the same.
And when you're outside the crowd,
Facades can seem so lame.

Hate to burst your bubble baby,
But soon these masks will fall.
Will the answers show you something?
...Or are you nothing at all?

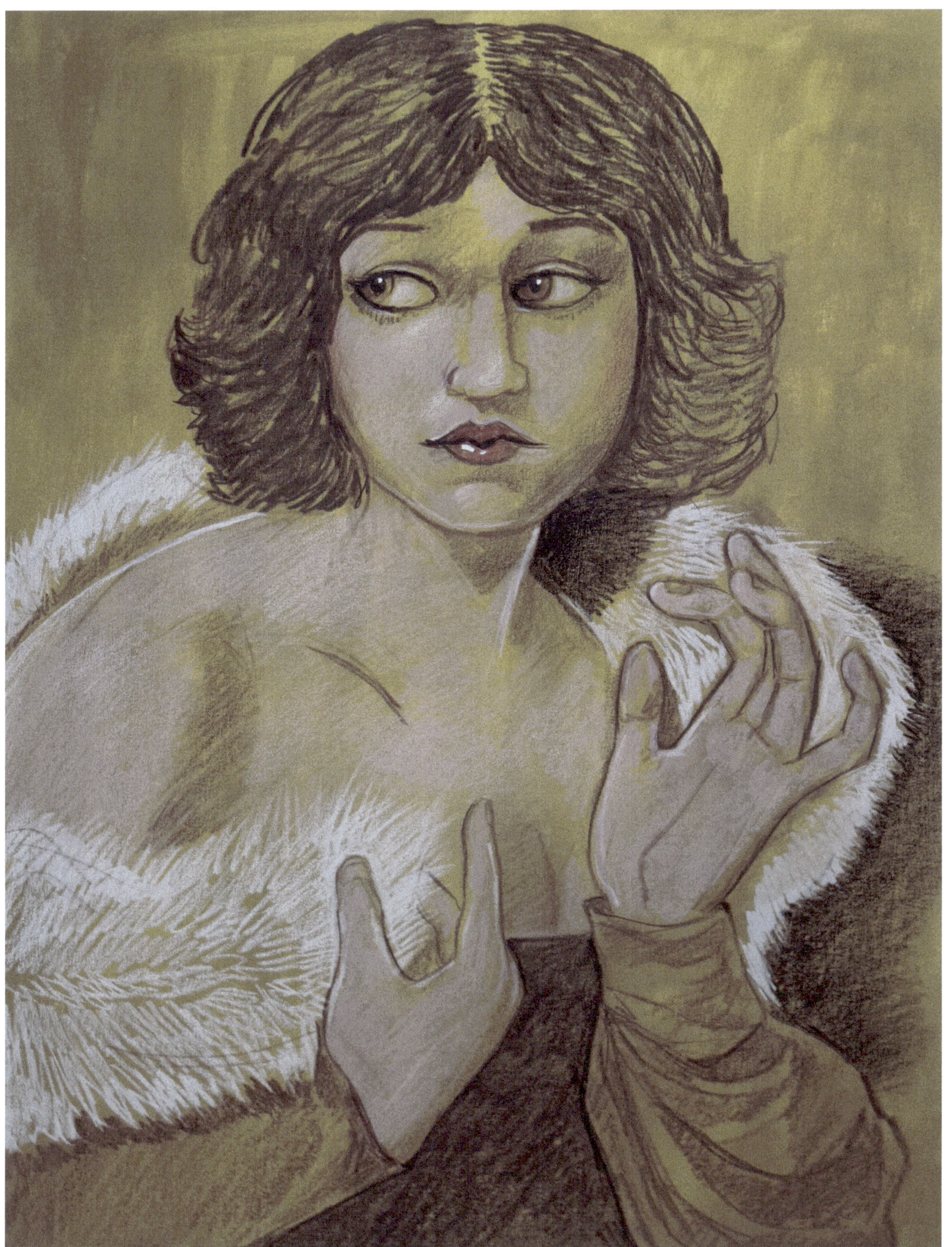

Damaged Waters

Been this way for years,
Hiding all my fears,
And I want to go.
Then you walk on in,
My world begins to spin,
And I want to go.
See it all go dark,
Watch as I am lost,
Don't want to go.

Falling over me,
This cold and open sea.

Oh and where's my heart?
Lost it from the start,
Why can't we go?
So now that I forgot,
Seems I lost a lot,
Now I've got to go.

Falling over me,
This cold and open sea.

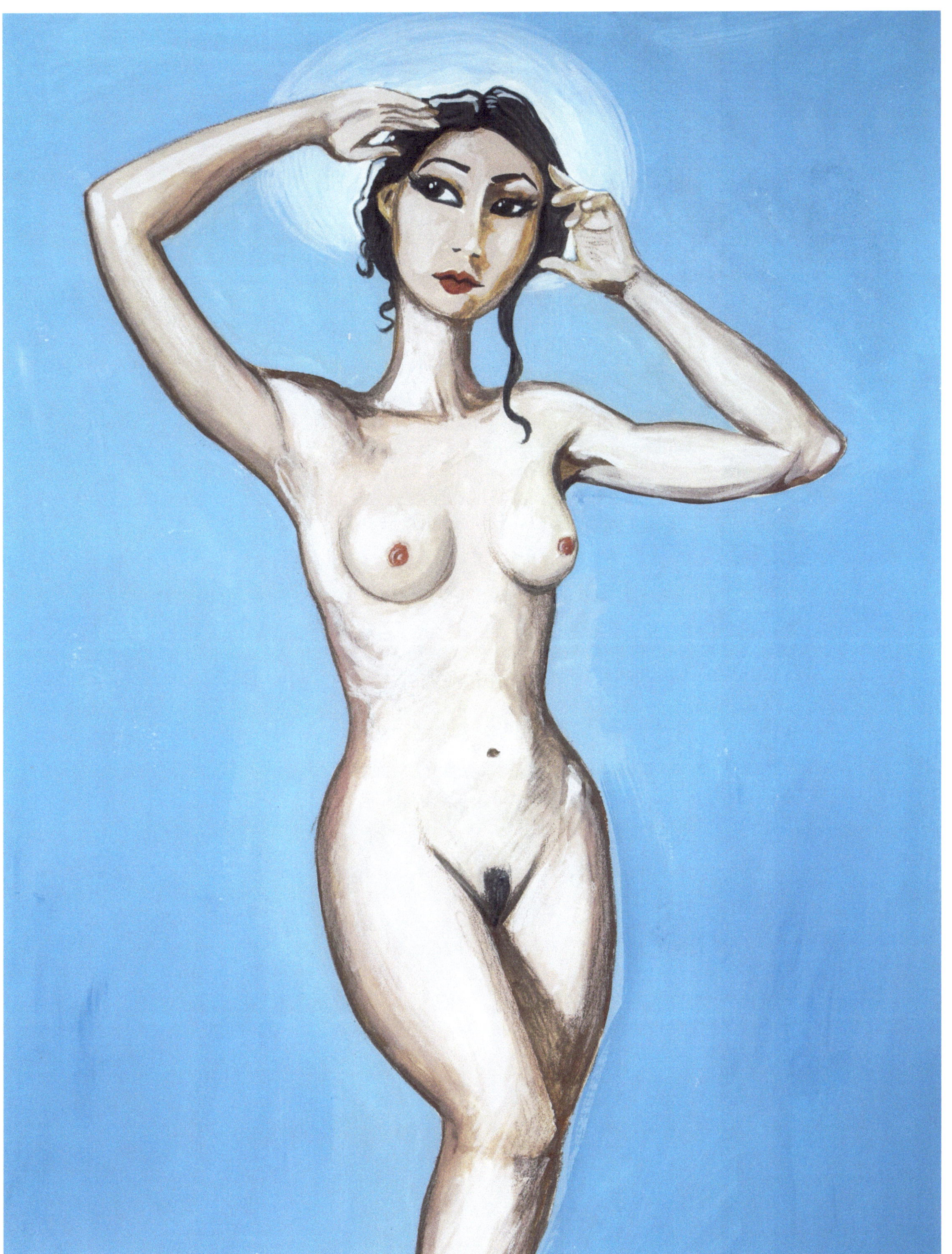

All The Animals

Dogs don't go to Heaven,
so who 'll see to all the animals?

Switched off the television,
It's not helping my condition.

This rose of inhibition,
Will bloom within its mission.

This white heat it moves between my hands,
Doesn't mean that I'm part of their plans.

I want to be the beasts messiah,
I want to be the one who finds them homes.

Saint Francis seems to have moved on,
Saint Francis has passed over.

We died and walked down that road,
Huckle on my shoulder,
Bandit and Bella by my side.
Came to a sign that said no trespass,
So we keep on walking.

Saint Francis seems to have moved on,
Saint Francis has passed over.

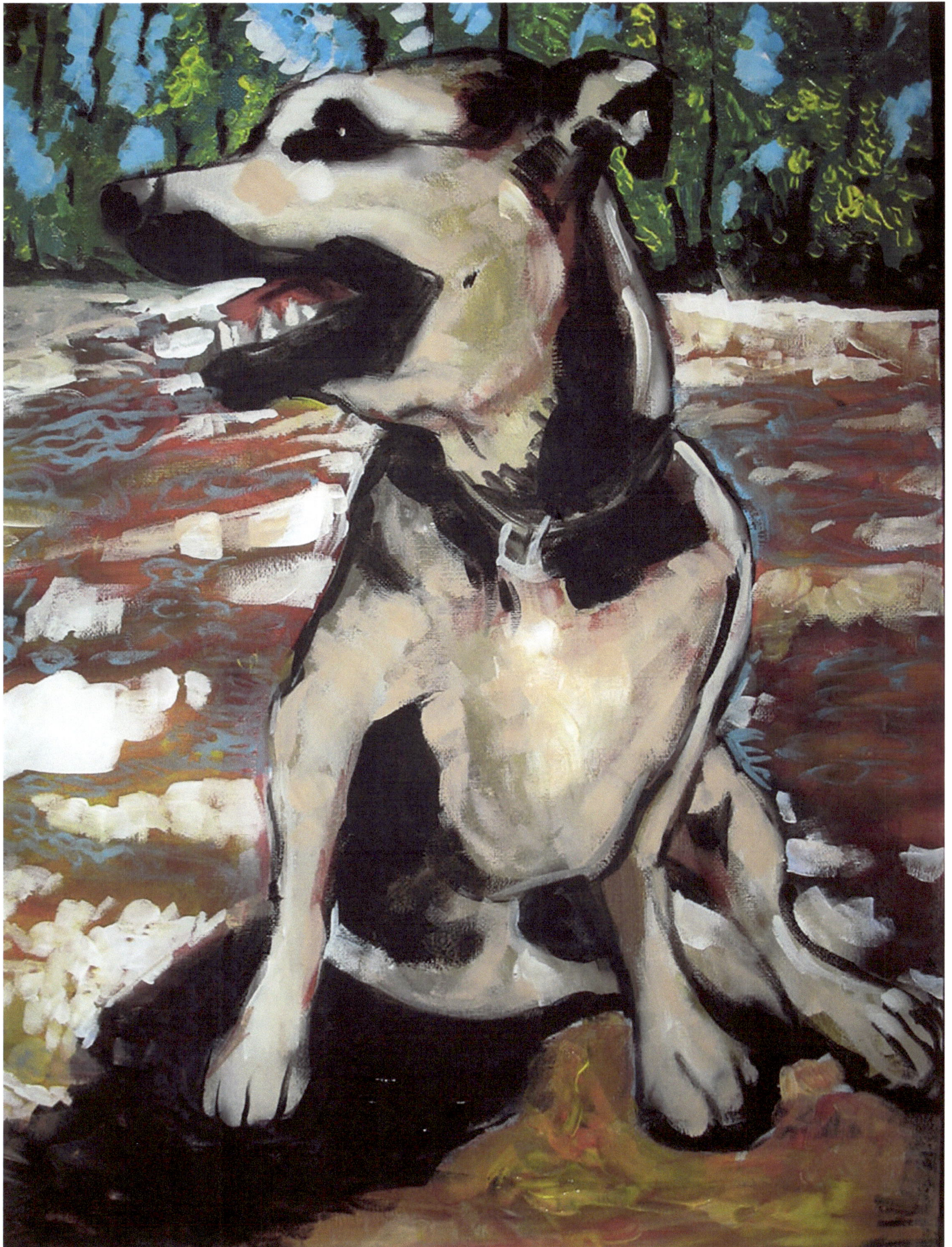

R.S.I. (Repetitive Strain Injury)

I move this way for a long time,
Tongue tied around your lip-less words baby.

You shave a layer of skin for me,
I gratefully accept, I gratefully accept.

You move between the worlds for me,
I graciously accept, I graciously accept.
All that I have left is denial of my lead.

Wild thoughts,
Tripping me up,
Making me crazy,
Making it up.
Gone the ghost,
Gone reproach.
Wild thoughts tripping me up,
Making me do dumb things,
Thought I'd never do,
Making me make you cry.
Never want to make you cry.

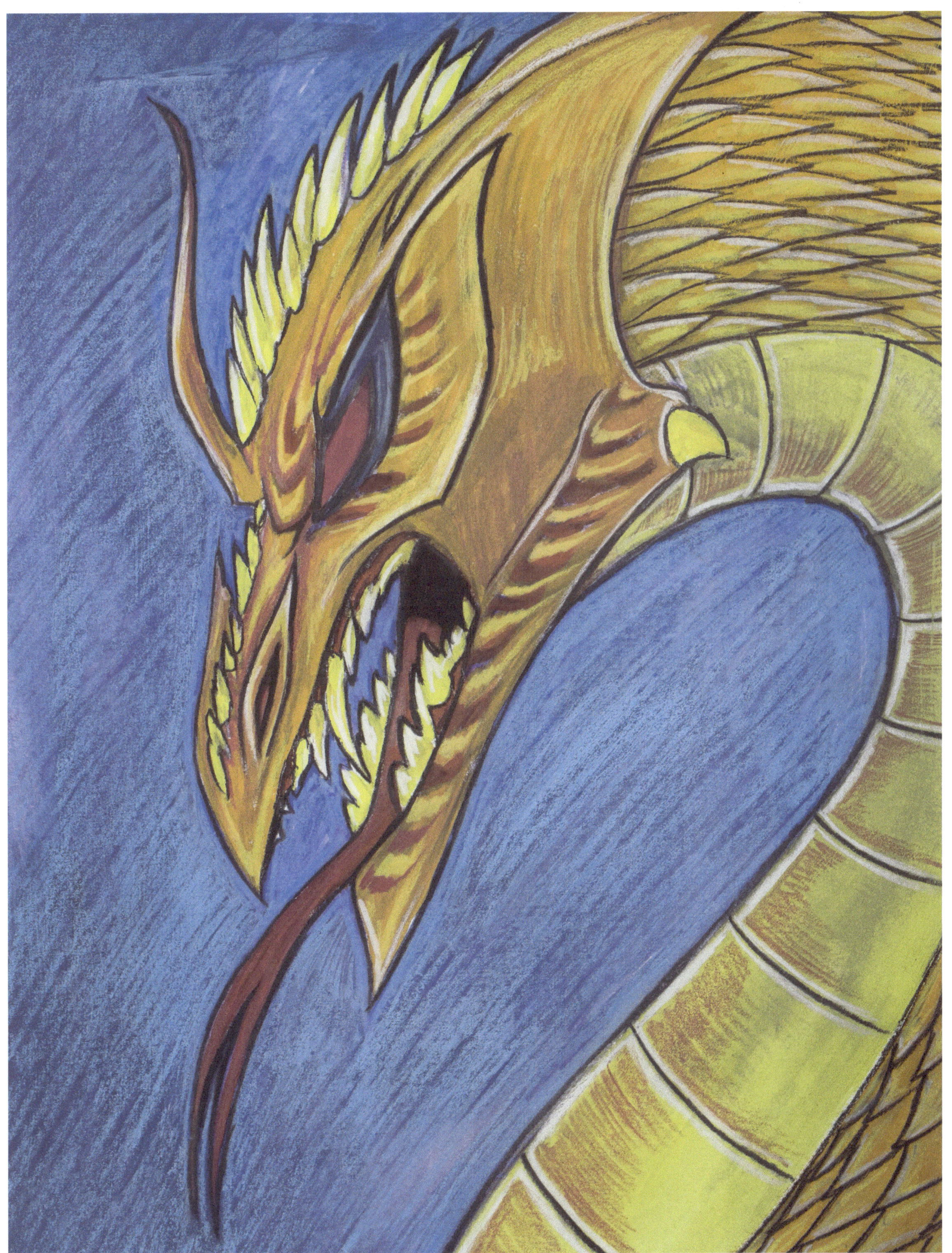

Home

Been gone so long.
Traveling between worlds.
Through other dimensions,
Dating alien girls.
Shooting overlords right between the eyes,
Dodging laser beams and blasting through the skies.

But now I'm home,
Feel so good being home.
Now I'm home,
Ain't nothing like being home.

Went to get some coffee in the middle of the day,
Officer 734 tried to put me away.
Trying to mess with me and getting in my head,
Words so loaded they'd fill you full of lead.

Now I can build my robot army,
And reign death upon the reptilian villainy.
Cause now that I have idle hands,
I can complete my master evil plans.

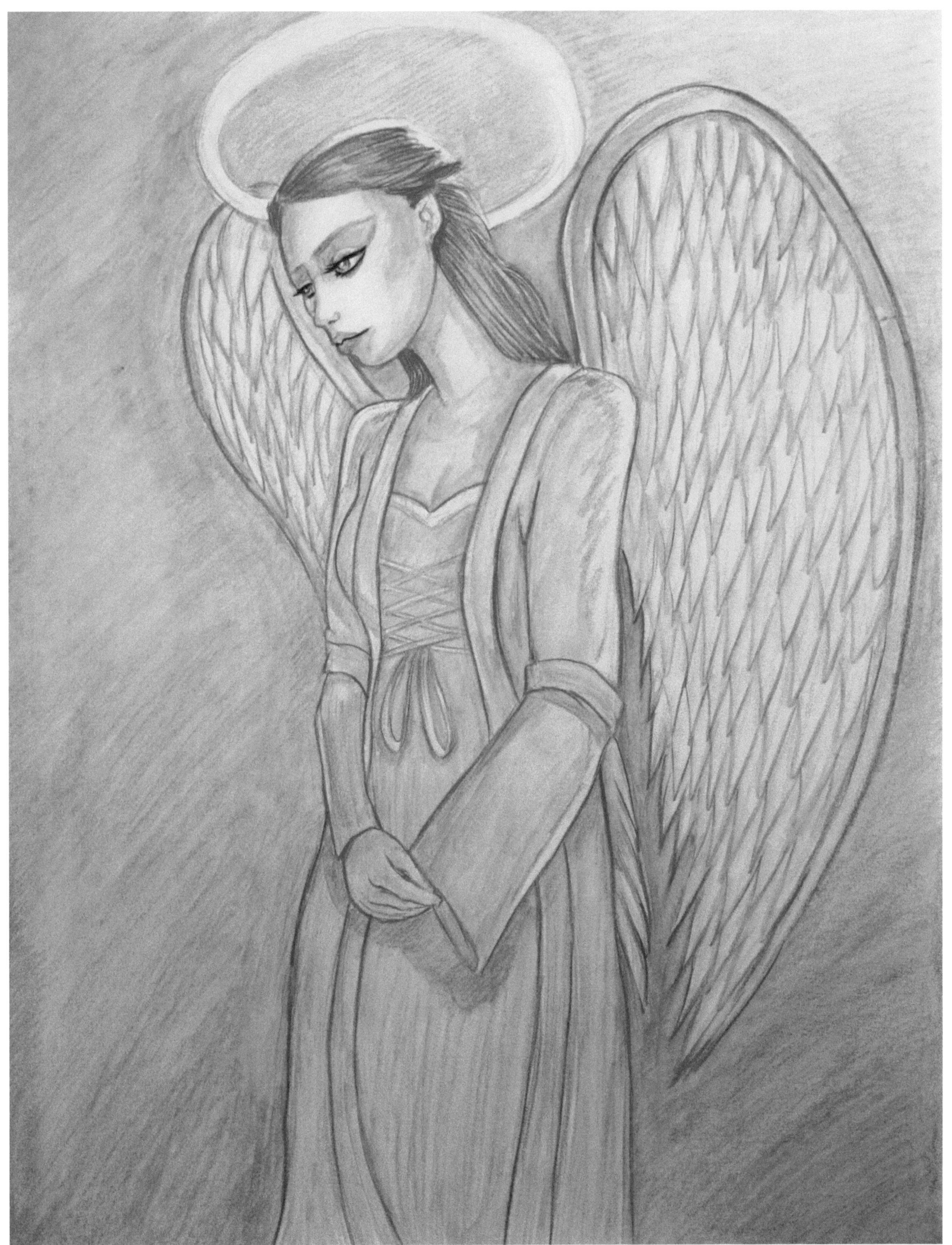

Index

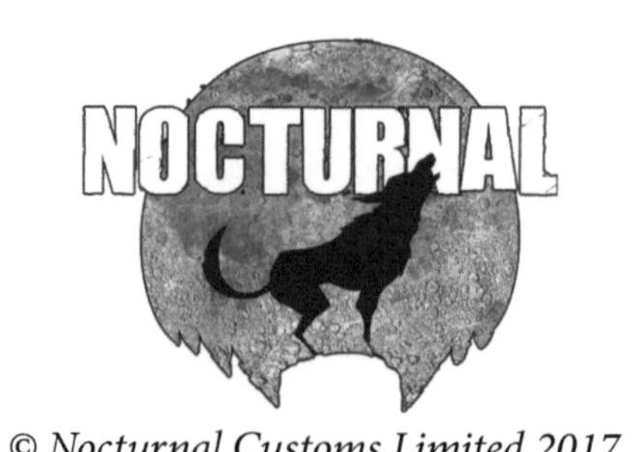

ISBN 9780473406585

www.ingramcontent.com/pod-product-compliance
Lightning Source LLC
LaVergne TN
LVHW070119110826
845147LV00002B/154

* 9 7 8 0 4 7 3 4 0 6 5 8 5 *